PRAISE FOR *THE ETHICAL EDUCATOR: POINTERS AND PITFALLS FOR SCHOOL ADMINISTRATORS*

Given the dilemmas that education leaders face, easy answers are a rarity and decisions are often subject to intense public scrutiny. Over the years, I and many of my colleagues have turned to AASA's Ethical Educator column for practical insights and useful approaches to the challenges we face. In a time when every decision is questioned, this book is a much-needed resource to help us reflect on the how and the why of our decisions and to remind us that ethically grounded solutions will best serve our students and all our constituents. —**Aaron C. Spence**, superintendent, Virginia Beach City Public Schools

Every superintendent and school administrator should keep a copy of *The Ethical Educator* handy. By compiling and augmenting a decade's worth of AASA Ethical Educator columns, the authors have created a resource for K–12 leaders that is filled with thoughtful analyses of real-world ethical dilemmas involving conflicts of interest, grading practices, taking stands on community issues, and many other topics. When ethical questions arise, this guidebook will assist superintendents and school administrators in arriving at sound and well-reasoned answers. —**Craig Hawkins**, executive director, Coalition of Oregon School Administrators

The superintendency can be a lonely position. Since dilemmas are often politically charged or confidential in nature, the superintendent can't readily confer with others in the school district. This book delivers a much-needed network of experienced colleagues who offer thoughtful and practical guidance on many of the toughest issues faced by school leaders. I predict that copies of *The Ethical Educator* will soon be marked-up with margin notes, dog-eared, and residing on the desks of superintendents everywhere. —**Colt Gill**, director, Oregon Department of Education; adjunct professor, University of Oregon; former district superintendent

The authors have constructed a remarkable illustration of ethics as a leadership function, not a management task. While circumstances often are nuanced, doing the right thing requires transparency and the courage to meet issues head-on. For current superintendents and other education administrators, it is a reminder that who you are and what you do define the organization. This is a must-read for those aspiring to lead a school district. The examples are authentic, trustworthy, and easily digested. In summary, this work reinforces

Einstein's observation that relativity applies to physics, not ethics. —**Joseph J. Scherer**, chief executive, National Education Exchange; past executive director, Superintendents' National Dialogue

The Ethical Educator provides practical insights on the real dilemmas faced by school administrators in the day-to-day operation of our schools. The book's hypotheticals are easily understood because they arise regularly in schools all over the country. The book is well-grounded in law and policy and is anchored in overriding principles designed to serve the common good. It would be an excellent resource for small-group discussions among school administrators and board members. —**Jim Walsh**, Esq., partner, Walsh Gallegos Treviño Kyle & Robinson P.C., Austin, TX; former member of board of directors, NSBA Council of School Attorneys; author, education law blog: www.edlawdawg.com

Superintendents deal with complex issues daily. Today's problem for a neighboring superintendent may well be yours tomorrow. Sharing varying perspectives on these problems tends to produce better decisions. *The Ethical Educator* is a terrific tool to do just that. —**Thomas A. Scott**, executive director, Massachusetts Association of School Superintendents; former school superintendent

When it comes to curriculum, instruction, and so many other topics, district leaders know that they must adhere to a strong set of ethics and values. These authors bring depth and breadth of experience to issues in education, law, and the complexities of running schools. You will appreciate their thoughtful and pragmatic approach. I highly encourage you to keep this book as a resource for many years to come. —**Sandy Husk**, interim CEO, ASCD; past CEO, AVID Center; former district superintendent

I am so excited to share *The Ethical Educator* with my graduate students. As a retired P–12 administrator who now teaches aspiring principals and superintendents, this book is just what I've been looking for. There has never been a more challenging time to be a school or district leader. Complex decisions have to be made in real time every day—often without precedent or clear foundation. The cases in *The Ethical Educator* are thought-provoking and authentically reflective of the kinds of difficult situations administrators will almost surely face. —**Lu Young**, executive director, UK Center for Next Generation Leadership; associate professor, educational leadership studies, University of Kentucky; chair, Kentucky Board of Education; former district superintendent

The Ethical Educator

The Ethical Educator

Pointers and Pitfalls for School Administrators

Sheldon H. Berman, David B. Rubin,
and Joyce A. Barnes

Published in partnership with the
American Association of School Administrators

ROWMAN & LITTLEFIELD
Lanham • Boulder • New York • London

Published in partnership with the American Association of School Administrators

Published by Rowman & Littlefield
An imprint of The Rowman & Littlefield Publishing Group, Inc.
4501 Forbes Boulevard, Suite 200, Lanham, Maryland 20706
www.rowman.com

86-90 Paul Street, London EC2A 4NE

Copyright © 2022 by Sheldon H. Berman, David B. Rubin, and Joyce A. Barnes

All rights reserved. No part of this book may be reproduced in any form or by any electronic or mechanical means, including information storage and retrieval systems, without written permission from the publisher, except by a reviewer who may quote passages in a review.

British Library Cataloguing in Publication Information Available

Library of Congress Cataloging-in-Publication Data

Names: Berman, Sheldon, 1949- author. | Rubin, David B., 1953- author. | Barnes, Joyce A., 1946- author. | American Association of School Administrators, co-publisher.
Title: The ethical educator : pointers and pitfalls for school administrators / Sheldon H. Berman, David B. Rubin, and Joyce A. Barnes.
Description: Lanham, Maryland : Rowman & Littlefield Publishers, 2022. | "Published in partnership with the American Association of School Administrators."
Identifiers: LCCN 2022027639 (print) | LCCN 2022027640 (ebook) | ISBN 9781475865530 (cloth) | ISBN 9781475865547 (paperback) | ISBN 9781475865554 (ebook)
Subjects: LCSH: School administrators--Professional ethics--United States. | School management and organization--Moral and ethical aspects--United States. | Educational ethics--United States.
Classification: LCC LB1779 .B47 2022 (print) | LCC LB1779 (ebook) | DDC 371.2/011--dc23/eng/20220718
LC record available at https://lccn.loc.gov/2022027639
LC ebook record available at https://lccn.loc.gov/2022027640

To school administrators everywhere who strive each day to find and follow an ethical path.

Contents

Foreword, *Jay P. Goldman*		xi
Introduction: The Why and the How of Making Ethical Judgments		1
1	Conflict of Interest	9
2	First Amendment Rights	23
3	Unequal Treatment	35
4	Religious Liberty	55
5	Duty to Report or Maintain Confidentiality	71
6	Grading Practices	87
7	Student Discipline	105
8	Hiring, Résumés, and References	121
9	Employee Discipline	135
10	Relationship Boundaries	157
11	Funding	173
12	Taking a Stand on Community Issues	195
13	Board Relations	209
Conclusion: Ethical Choices Are Not an Afterthought		237

Appendix: The Code of Ethics of AASA, 241
The School Superintendents Association

About the Authors 243

About the Contributors 245

Foreword

As someone who has considered himself a journalist since his teenage years, I've had occasion to wrestle with in-the-moment ethical decisions for quite some time. The first came in junior year of high school when, as sports editor of the school newspaper, I found myself reporting on an outbreak of spinal meningitis among members of the championship-caliber varsity football team. How to sensitively cover a subject of intense public interest involving young students' personal lives gave me a first taste of professional challenges lying ahead.

Now, as long-time editor of *School Administrator,* the monthly magazine of AASA, The School Superintendents Association, I am able to give the subject of ethical decision making ongoing attention in the school leadership arena. In January 2012, as part of a magazine upgrade, we launched a monthly column that we called "Ethical Educator" to provide a constant presence to address the real-world dilemmas that superintendents and other school system leaders confront regularly in many facets of their responsibilities.

The premise behind the column was this: Each month we would cull from the actual experiences of education leaders and others in public life a succinctly framed scenario that posed a dilemma of some nature. Four experienced school system leaders would serve as a standing panel to provide independent analyses of each difficult set of circumstances involving fellow educators, board of education members, parents, and students.

The panelists' analyses and recommendations for what they considered the most appropriate action or decision in each case often were at odds with one another. That was not unexpected. Nor was it unwelcome. Publishing those differing views has considerable value. Dilemmas, by their definition, are predicaments in which a difficult choice has to be made between two or more alternatives, often equally undesirable ones. Superintendents face an array of such situations with no easy answers.

That's certainly been true during the two-plus years of the politically divisive COVID-19 pandemic, when hard-wrought decisions have had to be made over public health practices and mitigation measures in schools. Dilemmas have confronted school leaders at every turn during this time, and the Ethical Educator column has focused on situations connected to the pandemic in multiple issues.

When we commenced planning for the Ethical Educator column, the first individual I consulted was Shelley Berman, a veteran school superintendent who is well regarded among his peers as an organizational leader of great sensitivity and sharp thought. Shelley had served as president of Educators for Social Responsibility for many years and had written for *School Administrator* on a couple of occasions, so he was a logical starting point.

For a small magazine with a minimal staff, it was an ambitious undertaking that we honestly weren't sure we could sustain over the long term. But Shelley's enthusiastic endorsement of a proposed monthly column on ethics in school leadership pushed us forward. He agreed to serve on the first panel foursome, and he continues to this day as one of the column's analysts. His unyielding support has been very much appreciated.

Over time, the column has been well received, repeatedly garnering the highest readership count among *School Administrator* articles and other content in surveys conducted by outside firms. The column also was recognized with a Gold Editorial Tabbie Award in 2021 by the Trade, Association and Business Publications International for best monthly department in association publications.

As Ethical Educator reached the ten-year mark, having published more than one hundred real-world dilemmas, Shelley approached me with the idea of repurposing the cases and responses of the sixteen individuals who've served as panel members over that time for use in a book project. The idea had much merit, and I was pleased that Thomas Koerner and his colleagues at Rowman & Littlefield thought so too, resulting in the publication of *The Ethical Educator: Pointers and Pitfalls for School Administrators.*

The book received an additional boost when David Rubin, a longtime school attorney in New Jersey and past chair of the Council of School Attorneys, accepted the invitation to sign on as co-author. David's incisive writing for the legal brief column in *School Administrator* over many years has yielded practical guidance on matters commonly reaching the superintendent's desk. A third co-author, Joyce Barnes, a retired school district special education administrator, contributed other insights about the content as well as important editorial skills.

The timing of this work is fitting. AASA, founded in 1865, did not adopt its first code of ethics until 1966, calling it a "Statement of Ethics for School Administrators." The latest revision to AASA's code of ethics took place in 2007. The most recent AASA publication on the subject, beyond a few articles in *School Administrator* over the years, is a 1985 book *Ethics: A Course of Study for Educational Leaders* by Ralph Kimbrough, a professor at University of Florida. Given the implications of ethical decision making in the complex environment of today's school systems, we are long overdue for a fresh look at this vital aspect of educational leadership.

My hope is that *The Ethical Educator: Pointers and Pitfalls for School Administrators* will be seen as an important contribution to the field, by practicing administrators as well as students and faculty in universities' graduate programs in educational leadership. The need for attending to appropriate behavior and thoughtful decision making by leaders in public education has never been greater.

Jay P. Goldman
Editor, *School Administrator*
April 2022

Introduction

The Why and the How of Making Ethical Judgments

Education administrators make numerous decisions on a daily basis. Some are pragmatic decisions about how best to make progress on a particular goal. Others call on us to apply law, regulation, or policy to a situation.

Although all decisions involve ethics to a lesser or greater extent, the most difficult and trying decisions are those that summon us to make a clear, ethical judgment or take an ethical stand on an issue where there may be multiple alternative solutions as well as divergent perspectives as to which solution is the correct one. These are the decisions that test us as administrators, for what we decide sets a precedent both for how others perceive our ethical judgment and for the ethical identity of the school or district administration.

Decisions involving ethical dilemmas, however, take more than reasoning from a set of ethical principles. They require a deep understanding of the dimensions of the issue, an appreciation of the different perspectives on the rationale behind particular solutions, and the courage to take a stand, knowing that it will be received with acclaim by some and with significant dissent by others.

Those who teach and write about administrative ethics point out that ethical reasoning is a skill that requires modeling, rehearsal, and practice. Explaining why a particular curriculum will serve the district well based on the district's curriculum review process is far different from giving voice to our values when we challenge a course of action that we see as unethical or propose a policy or strategic direction that takes a stand on an issue of justice or care for others.

These decisions become even more controversial in politically divisive environments, where accepted practice is seen through a political lens and where teaching about race and racism or social-emotional learning or even critical thinking is politically contentious. Because administrators have power and influence over the lives of staff and students in defining what is right, fair, just, or good, our decisions matter both practically and ethically.

How we as administrators handle these issues defines us as individuals and often plays a role in shaping our career paths. In fact, as we make decisions, be they major or minor, we create for ourselves an ethical identity or ethical character. This ethical identity influences how we see ourselves, as well as how others see us—and, by extension, how they see the organizations we represent.

Ethical dilemmas often require that we make hard choices in situations that are both complex and ambiguous—situations characterized by conflict, tension, uncertainty, and risk (Strike, Haller, and Soltis 2005). For example, at what point does participation in a professional activity become a conflict of interest? When is an action on the part of an administrator a misuse or abuse of that person's position? When does non-school behavior or business conflict with school employment? What are the boundaries around memberships and affiliations with professional, nonprofit, or for-profit organizations?

Also, what are the appropriate responses to incivility or interpersonal conflict? Under what circumstances can we use personal discretion to stretch or show flexibility in the application of policy? And what is the administrator's role when a board member or an entire board proposes an action that the administrator views as unethical?

In some cases, we can turn to laws, regulations, policies, and court decisions for guidance. However, oftentimes these formal tools fail to provide the specificity sufficient to the case at hand. The administrator is faced with discerning the ethically right path and providing the rationale for that choice to superiors, staff, or even the public at large, knowing that some will disagree, even vehemently, with that choice.

In some cases that vehemence will prompt a legal or policy challenge. In the absence of a statute or regulation directly addressing an issue, in many jurisdictions the courts or governing bodies will judge an administrator's conduct by a "rule of reasonableness" under the general principles of negligence law—that is, how would a reasonable school administrator be expected to react in this situation given all the attendant circumstances?

When the answer is not clear as a matter of common knowledge, courts may require expert testimony from respected authorities in the field of school administration to establish the expected duty of care in that community. That expected duty of care is often defined on the basis of both pragmatic and ethical principles.

ETHICAL PRINCIPLES

Ethicists point to some general ethical principles that we as administrators can use to guide our decision making. Mackenzie and Mackenzie (2010) pose four of these principles:

1. The Golden Rule: Act toward others as you want them to act toward you.
2. Rule of benevolence: One should act in ways that conduce to the greatest good for the greatest number or the least harm to the greatest number.
3. Rule of universality: Would it be acceptable if everyone else did it?
4. Rule of publicity: Would it be acceptable behavior if everyone knew about it?

Cooper (2012) adds a fifth principle of justice—treat equals equally and unequals unequally. In other words, when inequality is present, it is ethical to provide preference to those who are less advantaged so they can participate on an equal basis.

In the arena of moral development theory, Kohlberg, Levine, and Hewer (1983) also focus on justice. Kohlberg's stage theory of moral development culminates in the principle of justice involving equality and mutual respect. Gilligan (1982), a colleague of Kohlberg's, argues that justice is only one moral dimension. The other dimension involves an ethic of care, that is, an ethic of responsiveness: Is everyone included and cared for in a situation? Echoing the Golden Rule in terms of fairness and the rule of benevolence in terms of care for others, these dimensions represent important perspectives to bring to our assessment of alternatives for taking ethical action.

There are additional reference points to help sort out our thinking about ethical issues. As Cooper (2012) indicates, codes of ethics and ethics legislation represent well-accepted sources of guidance. (AASA's code of ethics for administrators appears in the appendix as an example.) These codes arise from the collective wisdom of the professional community. However, they tend to deal with only the most routine situations common to the life of a public administrator.

In reality, ethical dilemmas are seldom that simple. Education administrators often find themselves confronting myriad paths out of a quandary—each with its own consequences. Thus, one problem with professional codes of ethics, and even with ethics legislation, is that they provide only general guidance; meanwhile, many of the dilemmas that we face are complex and nuanced, limiting the applicability of these codes.

Applying educators' typically pragmatic approach to issues, administrators facing a dilemma may default to either expedience—that is, finding a stopgap solution that allays immediate concern without solving the root problem—or political acceptability—that is, selecting an alternative that those with the greatest influence prefer—as a guidepost for making decisions. However, these measures tend to provide only short-term fixes, rather than long-term, ethically grounded solutions. Unfortunately, some administrators continue to be tempted to use these two criteria to justify questionable practices or to rationalize taking advantage of a situation.

Another vulnerability in our decision making around ethical issues is believing that the just ends we are pursuing justify compromised or unjust means to achieving those results. In ethically challenging situations, the means we pursue to address an issue have to be consistent with the ethical ends we want to achieve. Otherwise, we undermine the very goals we are attempting to reach. In the responses to the ethical dilemmas posed throughout this book, therefore, the contributors not only focus on what is the ethically right thing to do, but also what is the right process for achieving that end.

As Cooper (2012, 21) points out, "Most of the time we are ad hoc problem solvers, not comprehensive moral philosophers" (266). Yet ethical dilemmas require reflecting not only on our own values but also on our obligations, the immediate and long-term consequences of possible decisions, and the ultimate ends we seek to achieve.

SERVING THE COMMON GOOD

In the final analysis, administrators are accountable to serve—and to make decisions that are in the interest of—the greater public and the common good. By accepting an administrative position, we also accept that responsibility. We are not acting simply in the capacity of our employment role, but as a moral actor who has to set one's job-related responsibilities in the context of our values, foundational ethical principles, and the common good in a democratic society. At some point, this commitment may even mean putting our own job at risk if the board, the organization, or the community is not aligned with our values and ethical orientation.

Mary Gentile (2010), a leader in ethics education, suggests that the problem we have in adequately addressing ethical dilemmas is our lack of practice and experience. Ethics is not a static judgment, but an action-oriented process. It's not just knowing what is the right thing to do but "how we can get the right thing done" (51). She suggests three strategies for being effective in taking ethical action.

First, normalize ethical conflicts as an expected part of administrative leadership and reframe them as choices. Viewing conflicts as normal choices within our roles reduces the emotion and surprise and unleashes the freedom, creativity, and confidence to find ethical solutions (Gentile 2010).

Second, think broadly about our personal and professional purpose. What are our larger, long-term goals and what are the organization's long-term goals? What is the impact we personally want to have and be known for? What is most ethically consistent with these larger goals?

> By stepping back and reflecting on both our broader personal purpose—why we work—and our broader professional purpose—what impact we want our organization to have—we find a wellspring of new arguments to use in voicing our values, and perhaps even more important, of energy to draw from when we do so. (Gentile 2010, 107)

Third, we need to understand ourselves, our values, and our self-image and pursue alignment between them and our organizational decisions. According to Gentile, most administrators will encounter troubling situations in their careers when deep personal values appear to be in conflict with the expectations of one or more levels of the organization that employs them (Gentile 2010).

Recognizing when there isn't alignment, and nevertheless acting in ways that have integrity with our beliefs and values and the values society holds dear, requires courage and practice—but can foster a sense of responsibility, meaning, and empowerment. It can also be in the best long-term interest of the organization as well as ourselves—as education administrators and as role models for the community.

> The attitude required of administrators in serving the public interest . . . is an attitude that attempts to eschew short-run personal gains and resists immediate pressures. It is a frame of mind that struggles to maintain a commitment to an evolving social system, a vision of the distant future, and a sense of equity that excludes none. It assumes that public servants can realize that they are primarily members of the public, whose fortunes will rise or fall with the concern and fairness exercised in the conduct of the public's business. (Cooper 2012, 82)

THE DAY-TO-DAY PRACTICE
OF ETHICAL DECISION MAKING

This book is meant to serve as a resource for the day-to-day practice of education administrators in dealing with difficult ethical situations. Beginning in January 2012, superintendents and other school administrators regularly described ethical dilemmas that they or their colleagues experienced and then submitted those situations to *School Administrator* magazine for its monthly Ethical Educator column. That these are real-life cases provides a lens into the range and breadth of practical situations administrators face that require ethical judgments.

School Administrator publishes eleven scenarios each year, with responses to each dilemma provided by a changing panel of four education administrators from a variety of roles. Sheldon Berman, a co-author of this book and the lead author of this introduction, has been a contributor to the monthly column since its inception. (Brief bios of the contributors and the co-authors can be found after the appendix.)

Most of the column's cases across the past decade have been collected in this book. The book is divided into chapters based on major areas of ethical decision making for district leaders. We begin each chapter with an insightful and down-to-earth introduction by co-author David Rubin, a nationally recognized school district attorney, who touches on some of the important legal parameters, precedents, and case law we should consider.

The dilemmas stretch across every aspect of administration from First Amendment and religious liberty issues to personnel and board relations. Although the scenarios are stated briefly to get at the core dilemma as well as protect the anonymity of the individuals involved, each case provides an opportunity to think through how we might handle that issue or a similar one and to consider the guidance of several experienced administrators who were contributors to the column.

Given the limited space in a book of this nature, we have not included all the dilemmas published over the years and generally have presented two of the four responses to each scenario. We selected from among the many cases those that provide the reader with the broadest range of issues, and from the responses those with the greatest diversity in approach. Some responses were edited slightly for length and clarity.

Consistent with the complexity of the cases, the contributors approach them from differing perspectives and offer a variety of resolutions. In an effort to provide practical and pragmatic guidance, they not only discuss what might be appropriate solutions, but also suggest paths for realizing those solutions.

School Administrator publishes two versions of the responses—abbreviated ones in the print magazine itself and longer ones online. Wherever possible, we have used the longer, online versions of the responses, which reveal greater depth in the contributors' reasoning. All the dilemmas and responses can be found on the AASA website archives at these three sites:

www.aasa.org/content.aspx?id=28274
www.aasa.org/SAethics.aspx
https://web.archive.org/web/20140912164551/http:/www.aasaconnect.com/The-Ethical-Educator

It is said that to get to the right answers, you must start with the right questions. In this book you will find more probing questions than direct answers, but our experienced contributors' perspectives on the scenarios should help guide your thinking in reaching the answers that are most appropriate for you and your school district. We close the book with a thoughtful conclusion, written by former special education administrator and co-author Joyce Barnes, that offers a few ideas for honing your own powers of ethical thinking.

We hope that in the spirit of Mary Gentile you are better able to give voice to your values as a result of reading this book. We trust that reflecting on these problematic situations will help you become a more effective education administrator, a more courageous leader of your organization, and simply a human being with a greater sense of ethical alignment and purpose.

REFERENCES

Cooper, Terry L. 2012. *The Responsible Administrator: An Approach to Ethics for the Administrative Role*, 6th ed. San Francisco: Jossey-Bass.

Gentile, Mary C. 2010. *Giving Voice to Values: How to Speak Your Mind When You Know What's Right*. New Haven, CT: Yale University Press.

Gilligan, Carol. 1982. *In a Different Voice: Psychological Theory and Women's Development*. Cambridge: Harvard University Press.

Kohlberg, Lawrence, Charles Levine, and Alexandra Hewer. 1983. *Moral Stages: A Current Formulation and a Response to Critics*. Basel, NY: Karger.

Mackenzie, Sarah V., and G. Calvin Mackenzie. 2010. *Now What? Confronting and Resolving Ethical Questions*. Thousand Oaks, CA: Corwin Press.

Strike, Kenneth A., Emil J. Haller, and Jonas F. Soltis. 2005. *The Ethics of School Administration*, 3rd ed. New York: Teachers College Press.

Chapter One

Conflict of Interest

This chapter addresses conflicts of interest. All school administrators know the phrase "conflict of interest" and understand it's something to be avoided. But where did the doctrine come from and what are its implications for modern-day school administration?

In the context of public service, conflicts of interest typically arise when government officials are tempted to use the power of their positions in some unwarranted manner to advance their own personal or economic interests. For that reason, legislatures and agencies at all levels of government have adopted ethics codes defining and prohibiting relationships and activities that pose an intolerable risk of such temptations. As noted in the introduction, professional associations such as AASA have adopted their own ethical codes that do not have the force of law but reflect the profession's expectations for itself.

The conflict of interest doctrine is intended to protect government officials from falling victim to the frailties of basic human nature. As Chief Justice Earl Warren once wrote, "The moral principle upon which [these prohibitions are based] has its foundation in the Biblical admonition that no man may serve two masters, Matt. 6:24, a maxim which is especially pertinent if one of the masters happens to be economic self-interest." *U.S. v. Mississippi Valley Generating Co.*, 364 U.S. 520, 549 (1961).

Warren's pithy observation incorporates two distinct but related themes: the emotional challenge of divided loyalty to competing interests generally, and that, as between those competing interests, the public good always must take precedence over one's own. There's yet another theme that surely applies when school administrators are involved. In many jurisdictions, the conflict of interest doctrine forbids not just unethical conduct but other behavior that would appear unethical to a reasonable observer (even if it isn't).

This so-called appearance-of-impropriety rule poses significant challenges to public officials looking for clear guidance on what's permissible. Give us rules and we'll follow them. If more rules are necessary to prevent harms that weren't anticipated earlier, adopt them and we'll follow them, too. But for professional reputations to be sullied not because of what school administrators actually did but because of what a hypothetical "reasonable person" might have thought they'd done, where's the fairness in that? The answer, from those jurisdictions imposing that standard, is that government cannot function without the trust of the public it serves.

If public officials conduct themselves in a manner that breeds suspicion in the mind of a reasonable citizen, that trust is lost even if the officials actually did nothing wrong. For that reason, school administrators must be mindful that appearances count and, as the saying goes, if something looks like a duck and walks like a duck, you can't blame the public for concluding it's a duck. The take-away is that if we sense we're anywhere within striking distance of a prohibited conflict of interest, we need to step back ten paces.

We also must be mindful that the ban on conflicts of interest is aimed not so much at unscrupulous government employees likely to ignore ethical constraints anyway, but at honest employees who might, without realizing it, enter into relationships fraught with such temptation to advance their own interests that the public interest may be compromised as a result.

When given a chance to feather one's own nest with a privileged government position providing the means to do so, there's a natural human tendency for tunnel vision to kick in, to the point where we may not even see the ethical corner we've backed ourselves into until we're already there. By defining the situations where that's most likely to occur, the conflict of interest doctrine serves as a guidepost to protect us from ourselves.

In law school, future lawyers are not so much taught the law per se, as how to think like a lawyer and, more than anything, how to spot issues requiring legal advice early on before they blossom into full-blown crises. Conflict of interest statutes, regulations, and codes are often drafted so generally that public officials cannot rely on the literal text alone but must depend on their own issue-spotting radar to sense when they may be drifting into dangerous waters. As we were taught when learning to drive, we need a constant awareness of what is going on around us so we don't get surprised by something dangerous in our blind spot.

What are the most common real-life scenarios where school administrators may be faced with a conflict of interest? The answers should come as no surprise given the multitude of opportunities for self-aggrandizement available to public school officials. Vendors looking to retain lucrative contracts may offer financial incentives to curry favor with those responsible for district procurement decisions. It need not be an outright bribe, perhaps nothing more than an innocent "token of appreciation" around holiday time. But, as we'll see in this chapter, that modest gesture may be an ethical Trojan horse for the unsuspecting administrator.

Then there are the opportunities available to school employees from the superintendent to rank-and-file teachers to profit from students vying for favorable treatment. Consider, for example, the teacher who moonlights as a tutor for district students, or the baseball coach who operates a private batting clinic on the side. There may be no nefarious intent, but the prospect of perceived favoritism toward students who avail themselves of these outside ventures raises serious ethical concerns.

Naturally, avoiding conflicts of interest in the first place is the goal, but what are your obligations if you find yourself already mired in a conflict you didn't realize existed until you were neck-deep in it, or when you find that staff under your supervision have already crossed that ethical line? You may not be able to undo what's done, but you do have an ethical obligation to neutralize any unwarranted advantages conferred by that misconduct, and to remediate any harm that the conflict may have caused.

The thought-provoking cases presented in this chapter, all based on school administrators' real-life experiences, will bring these concepts sharply into focus. They may also serve as helpful reference points in thinking through potential conflicts of interest you may confront in the day-to-day administration of the schools under your control.

A CLUB ADVISOR'S PERK

Scenario: The faculty advisor for her high school's Diversity/Cultural Exchange Club has organized student trips to Europe through an educational travel company and recruited students, parents, and chaperones for the annual overseas trips. The tour company enrolled the advisor in its rewards program as a group leader, giving her travel points and stipends based on the number of travelers she recruited.

Over five years, the teacher received $5,530 in stipends and 4,516 travel points from the tour company, redeeming the latter for airline tickets and a European vacation. The school district's business administrator is raising questions whether the club advisor's actions represent a conflict of interest.

Responses

Sheldon Berman

This is clearly a conflict of interest and an ethics violation that could result in an adverse decision before the state's ethics commission, requiring the faculty advisor to pay substantial fines and face potential employee discipline. Although the awarding of stipends and points is common among tour companies, ethics commission decisions have identified the practice as a conflict of interest (Massachusetts Ethics Commission, Disposition Agreement in the Matter of Stephanie Viens, Docket No. 19-0009, September 25, 2019). For more information, visit www.mass.gov/settlement/disposition-agreement-in-the-matter-of-stephanie-viens.

A conflict of interest occurs when a person receives personal benefit from actions taken in their professional capacity. As a public employee, the faculty advisor is subject to the state's conflict of interest laws that prohibit individuals from gaining personal advantage through actions within their official areas of responsibility. The provision of stipends and travel points to the person arranging the trips creates an opportunity to bias the selection of a tour company based on personal advantage rather than effective provision of services to students, thereby creating a conflict of interest.

The business administrator is correct in raising the issue, and the superintendent should immediately inform all faculty advisors who organize student trips that they are not allowed to accept any rewards from a tour company for their efforts. Although this action is the right step to take, it may decrease faculty interest in organizing and facilitating student trips since the excursions require an enormous amount of preparatory work and supervisory responsibility.

The stipends and travel points were offered by the tour company as a significant incentive to encourage faculty to take on these roles. Without these incentives, the district may need to seek other ways to compensate faculty advisors for their leadership in facilitating student travel opportunities. One alternative would be district-funded stipends, which would incentivize faculty while avoiding any potential conflict of interest.

Louis N. Wool

The circumstances in this dilemma pose multiple troubling ethical problems. The first and most apparent is that a teacher should not be garnering outside rewards by rendering service to her students, especially recruiting students and parents to attend field trips. The business official is correct; the teacher has a conflict of interest in her relationship with the travel agency.

While unstated, she is likely receiving a stipend from the district as an advisor to the Diversity/Cultural Exchange Club. Any reward earned from these trips should accrue to the district and defray the cost of these trips or other field trips for students. Many families would struggle to pay for overseas trips. The business administrator should immediately stop this practice and determine if the teacher must reimburse the district for the rewards.

The critical information unaddressed here is: Is the club fostering diversity and cultural awareness by ensuring students have equal access to this experience? The irony is this is the advisor of the Diversity/Cultural Exchange Club. If participating in the trip is based on the ability to pay, the advisor and the district work at cross purposes in fostering diversity and cultural awareness.

In many states, the education law requires that the district pay for field trips; this is often not the practice. Clubs and booster clubs regularly engage in fundraising to defer the cost of trips for students and the school district. Extracurricular trips and activities are an enriching high school experience and should be equally available to every student. It seems unlikely that access is the center of the teacher's considerations; any personal reward based on the number of participants is likely to influence her behavior.

HOLIDAY GIFTS

Scenario: The head of the instructional technology department receives at her school district office a beautiful gift basket just before Christmas. It's a thank-you present from a software publisher, a longtime vendor whose contract recently was renewed by the school district. The department head shares many of the basket's contents with central-office colleagues. The school board has no policy about employees accepting such gifts. Did the department head act appropriately?

Responses

Sarah Mackenzie

Because no school board policy governs this situation, the department head did nothing wrong by accepting the gift. However, whenever a district employee is unsure of the rules or expectations, it would be a good idea for the gift recipient to check with a supervisor. The safest response is to decline the gift, which may mean returning it somehow, although that may not be easy if perishable contents are included.

It is a good idea to have a gift policy. This doesn't mean there can be no gifts accepted by employees, but a policy clarifies the parameters regarding gifts. Then school employees are clear about what they can and cannot receive. Likewise, parents and businesspeople know what they are allowed to offer as gifts.

Mario Ventura

School personnel can easily get caught up in the spirit of the holiday season. Student performances, decorations, and celebrations promote thoughts of holiday cheer and joy. This time of year can interfere with an employee's responsibility to fully consider the implications of accepting gifts from vendors.

Although a school district policy for receiving gifts does not exist in this scenario, an educator must consider not only if the act of receiving a gift is ethical but also how the acceptance of a gift may appear to others. Could the vendor's gift be perceived as unethical?

One may conclude that the department head did not act inappropriately by receiving the gift because there was no personal gain for the department head. However, what about appearance? Could school district staff or vendors presume that special consideration was given to the awarded vendor? Could it appear that a relationship with the awarded vendor affected the objectivity of the decision-making process for awarding the bid? In this situation, the acceptance of a gift could give the perception of impropriety.

SALES IN THE CLASSROOM

> Scenario: A couple with two children in the school district donate time and money to computerize a successful remedial math program started by one of their children's middle school teachers. Several educators, including a private-school administrator, have come to observe the program in action and are interested in using it in their classrooms. The teacher would be pleased to sell the program to them and other math teachers. May the public-school classroom be a showroom for interested visitors and should the teacher be allowed to profit off her idea?

Responses

Sheldon Berman

The teacher deserves credit and acknowledgment for creating a successful remedial math program, as do the donors for supporting its development. However, marketing one's own materials during one's employment as a teacher has the potential to undermine public trust in the independence of teacher/administrator judgment in the selection of programs and materials.

Given that the teacher developed and tested the math program as an outgrowth of her employment, the product is not legitimately a private product that she can market or sell. If the program was developed in the scope of her teaching duties or during school time, even though it was funded by donations, she does not "own" the program unless there is a district policy specifically allowing it. This precludes using her classroom as a showroom to advertise a program from which she—or relatives or friends—may profit, since she would be using her position and district facilities for personal gain.

In most states, statutes and guidelines for public employees make it unlawful and/or unethical for this teacher to use her position to obtain financial benefit for herself or for a private business to which she has a connection. A teacher may operate a private business while employed by a district, but should not use public time or facilities to promote or profit from that business.

Karl Hertz

Individually, the parts of this scenario do not present an ethical problem. Parents helping financially is laudable. The teacher having intellectual property is creative. Showing people what we are doing in public schools is commonplace. Profit is a good outcome. Each of these variables standing by itself is fine.

When the ingredients are interwoven, this mingling brings on the potential unethical pitfalls. Should the parents share in the profits of the teacher's intellectual property? Should the public-school classroom become a showcase for promoting a profit-making scheme? Should the school system share in the profits? Are school policies being violated? Who would realize any profits from this?

This is a complicated ethical question when we join the four major variables. The parties to this case might be wise to put aside the profit feature of this dilemma.

PROFITING OFF EXCESS

Scenario: To make way for new PCs to be installed over the summer, the school district's facilities director asks teachers and school staff to place existing computers in the hallway for trash pickup. A teacher gathers several of the old computers in his classroom and uses them for backup over several more years.

Now the teacher is retiring and wants to sell the PCs with the proceeds being donated to charity. Would you allow this?

Responses

Maggie Lopez

The PCs don't belong to the teacher. They are owned by the school district. Whether or not they were going to be thrown out, they still are considered district property. These computers were paid for with taxpayer dollars, so they don't belong to any individual. Accountability is expected for all district purchases.

The teacher should not be selling these to garner funds, even with good intentions to support a charity. District policy ought to address how to dispose of school assets, including hard drives that may contain student data.

The district's facilities director should have applied existing policies or worked with the superintendent to develop a policy regarding disposal of district property before putting computers in the trash. These computers probably contained confidential student data. Disposing of computers or selling them puts students' data at risk. Typically, the protocol for computer disposal can involve hard-drive shredding, which would render the computers useless.

Sheldon Berman

The teacher's intentions are positive. However, the computers remain the property of the district. Many people don't understand the legal requirements around the disposal of district equipment. Most states have specific requirements for designating equipment as surplus and then disposing of it in an appropriate way. Often, a district must provide the public with an opportunity to purchase surplus equipment at a public sale before it is donated or designated as trash. Computers must undergo a process to ensure that all district-related information (such as licensed software, names, and test results) is permanently removed.

Although the district was collecting the equipment for disposal, it cannot be claimed by a teacher as a personal possession. Such a move would give staff an unfair advantage over other members of the public to benefit from the district's disposal of surplus equipment that had been purchased with public tax dollars or through a grant or donation to the district. In addition, the teacher's choice of a charitable organization could become a source of controversy.

Had the teacher purchased this equipment at a district auction or sale, he could have sold it and used the proceeds in any way he chose. However, in this case, the equipment remains district property and must be disposed of according to state regulations and district procedures.

PAY YOUR WAY TO PLAY

Scenario: After varsity basketball tryouts, a parent complains that her son didn't make the team because he hadn't participated in the assistant coach's private off-season basketball club. The coaches contend they make selections based on performance criteria during tryouts and not on off-season play. The new athletic director discovers the majority of the varsity team participated in the assistant coach's off-season club. He asks the superintendent how he should handle the parent's complaint.

Responses

Meira Levinson

This case highlights how hard it can be to distinguish between appearance and reality in conflict of interest cases—and how the former can morph into the latter even if no one intends that to happen.

It is quite possible the assistant and head coaches are acting ethically, as are the other parents who sign up their children for the off-season club. One way to get better at basketball, after all, is to practice hard in the off-season. By honing their skills and working out with potential teammates—thereby potentially building their team communication skills—the students who take part in the off-season club may well perform better during tryouts than other aspiring varsity players do.

Nonetheless, the parent's complaint is legitimate. It certainly appears that families who spend money to join this off-season club give their children a leg up in the varsity tryouts, and there's no way under the current tryout system to prove otherwise. Furthermore, even if there is no intentional corruption on the coaches' part, families who want their children to make the varsity team are incentivized to sign up for the club. The assistant coach thus benefits financially, whether or not he intends to do so.

This form of pay-to-play should not be allowed. The new athletic director should direct the coaching team that the assistant coach should neither participate in tryouts nor select the varsity basketball team. Nor should the assistant coach communicate with the head coach before tryouts about potential players. Families and players should be informed about this policy, so then they can make independent decisions about whether to sign up for the off-season club, and all athletes can feel confident that team assignments are based on demonstrated performance during tryouts.

Sheldon Berman

If playing with the off-season club gives students an advantage in securing a spot on the varsity team, it is both a conflict of interest for the assistant coach and an unfair and biased tryout process. If athletes aspiring to make the varsity team perceive that their chances are improved by membership in the assistant coach's off-season club, they are more likely to join his club rather than another individual's or organization's club.

Because it is likely the assistant coach derives revenue from the off-season club, he has a financial interest in having athletes he coaches in the off-season secure a place on the varsity team. Even if he doesn't derive revenue, it creates the appearance of a biased tryout process.

Although the coaches may contend that their judgments are based on specific performance criteria, these judgments and the resulting consequential decisions are, in part, subjective assessments of particular abilities and skills. While the coaches may strive to make fair and unbiased judgments, the situation presents, at a minimum, the appearance of a conflict of interest.

However, making a decision about this situation is more complicated than simply viewing it as a conflict of interest or an appearance of one. The complexity results from what may be considered mitigating factors. Many coaches are devoted to their sport and participate in off-season clubs or camps, viewing them as a way to grow the sport and strengthen the skills of those who choose to participate. In fact, a coach could argue that participation in the club results in significant improvement in an athlete's abilities, and this improvement is the primary reason so many from the club make the varsity team.

In some cases, particularly in small communities, the individual coach may be one of only a few persons with significant expertise in coaching that sport. Although some individuals are full-time employees or summer employees of athletic clubs for the sport for which they are also a high school coach, for most the income derived from off-season activities, or even from a high school coaching position, is a marginal supplement to a full-time salary elsewhere.

In terms of looking for guidance from the state's athletic association, in many states there is no rule against this kind of activity in the state association's handbook for coaches or in school board policy. The superintendent should suggest that the athletic director (AD) review school board policy, as well as the rules and guidelines of the state's athletic association, regarding conflicts of interest.

The AD should then meet with the coaches to better understand the overall tryout process as well as their perspectives on this particular student-athlete. Because the head coach of a sport is responsible for the final decision as to who makes the team and who doesn't, the AD needs to determine the degree of influence the assistant coach has on the final decisions of the head coach.

The AD should review current and historical data on the tryout process and the degree to which athletes who participated in clubs other than the assistant coach's, or who didn't participate in a club at all, were selected for the varsity team. He should also review the evaluation used by the coaches during the tryout process to discern its thoroughness, the specificity of skills included, and the degree to which it relied upon subjective assessments. As part of that review, he should compare the coaches' evaluation of the student who did not make the team against those who did and then meet with the parent to hear the parent's perspective.

To pursue a long-term solution, the AD needs to meet with all coaches and discuss the issue of conflict of interest. He needs to work with them to set up tryout processes that are as free from bias as possible, even if that means some coaches must give up their off-season activities, restructure the off-season programs to exclude prospective members of their own teams, or abstain from participation in the tryout process.

The solution may also involve a review of tryout evaluation forms and processes to ensure objectivity. Finally, the pursuit of fairness may mean that those who have significant conflicts of interest are no longer able to coach a high school team. The tryout process is an emotionally difficult one for coaches and athletes alike and needs to be viewed as thorough and unbiased by athletes and their parents.

A CONFIDENTIALITY CONFLICT

Scenario: Anxious to boost the school district's image, a superintendent hires as a part-time communication consultant the education reporter for a small weekly newspaper that covers the schools. The newspaper's publisher warns her about the ethical perception but sanctions the relationship.

The district pays her $75 an hour for 150 hours of work over six months. She publicly discloses her consulting arrangement only after being called by a rival news outlet. In her defense, the consultant says she signed a confidentiality agreement with the school district at the beginning of the contract, agreeing not to use information obtained in the performance of her duties for any other purpose. Was the district wrong to hire a reporter to concurrently work as a consultant?

Responses

Sarah Mackenzie

This whole situation is ethically repugnant. No self-respecting news organization should allow a reporter to take a job with an institution whose activities he or she covers. And a school system that hires such a person is essentially involved in bribery. Harsh words, but that is what it looks like to an onlooker and, obviously, to rival news outlets. Furthermore, even though the amount is not large, taxpayers might have concerns about money allotted to "boost the school system's image" as opposed to addressing student learning.

The system could hire someone who is retired or a freelancer who is not a local beat reporter. The journalist could change her beat—preferably not covering education, but at least not covering this particular school system. This situation does not pass the "smell" test, and both parties to this arrangement have much to lose if this set of circumstances continues.

Mark Hyatt

This uncomfortable and unnecessary situation is better avoided altogether by hiring an experienced public relations coordinator without this type of conflict. To guard against even the appearance of impropriety, the school district must have a clear conflict of interest policy and be committed to applying it consistently. Also, the district should know that a reporter is never truly "off the record," so the idea of putting them on the district payroll clearly crosses an ethical line that appears to be buying favorable coverage from the newspaper.

For this reason, it is surprising that the newspaper has endorsed this situation. After all, the newspaper's reputation suffers even more than the school district's if and when the relationship is exposed. As leaders, we always must think twice about putting people (including ourselves) into situations that might tempt good people to do the wrong thing. Setting ourselves up—and the people under our authority who depend on us—for success every day in every way is what good leaders do.

A HEFTY GIFT OF APPRECIATION

Scenario: In appreciation of an elementary school principal's care and personal attention to their eight-year-old autistic daughter during the pandemic, a couple present him with a pair of front row Elton John concert tickets. The principal thinks he must refuse them as a conflict of interest, but colleagues in other schools feel he should accept the gift as it was the parents' decision. How should he proceed?

Responses

Louis N. Wool

At its core, this is an issue grounded in the principles of equity and access. Accepting this gift, a heartfelt gesture from these parents, would be unethical and likely illegal, but most importantly would adversely impact other parents. Parents of lesser means could feel diminished and disenfranchised, and its acceptance could even change parent perceptions of the principal.

For a good reason, most districts have policies limiting the value of gifts a teacher or principal can accept. Whether intended or not, parents who gift extravagantly may expect, even unconsciously, preferential treatment for their child. Gifts would not influence most educators, but acceptance complicates an already complex partnership between principals and parents.

Sheldon Berman

The principal should thank the parents for their generous gesture and let them know he can't accept their gift. The state ethics laws that apply to public employees generally identify it as a conflict of interest to accept gifts valued over a particular dollar amount. It may be permissible in some states to accept an item such as a gift basket valued at less than $25 or $50.

Because no one person is solely responsible for a student's success, it would be appropriate to share any item such as a gift basket with other staff members. In lieu of a personal gift, the principal might suggest that the parents make a gift or donation to the school in their name to benefit the school's curricular or instructional program.

Whenever a public employee receives something of value, even if it is not substantial, the specter of a conflict of interest may arise. Though it is unlikely that such a gesture would improperly influence an individual's future decision making, it could still give the appearance of impropriety by advantaging those who can provide such gifts over those who can't.

If, as an alternative, the parents presented the principal with a small gift, it would be wise for him to formally disclose the gift to the superintendent or school board to ensure that he is meeting the standards of the conflict of interest law. Disclosure is considered an acceptable way to address a potential conflict of interest. In the long run, it is best to let the parents know that a thank-you note would be an ample gesture of appreciation.

Chapter Two

First Amendment Rights

The First Amendment to the U.S. Constitution protects us from a wide range of government abuses, including unwarranted infringements on freedom of expression. But so-called "free speech" isn't unlimited. Government officials and agencies may impose reasonable restrictions on the time, place, and manner of citizens' speech when necessary for government to function. Restrictions on the *content* of speech, however, are rightly circumscribed by a long line of decisions from our federal courts.

What rights does the First Amendment give members of the school community? What are school administrators' ethical responsibilities when faced with offensive, disruptive, or otherwise troublesome speech on campus and off? The answers to these questions are to be found in separate lines of federal court decisions addressing the rights of students, staff, and members of the public.

For students, the U.S. Supreme Court's 1969 landmark decision in *Tinker v. Des Moines Independent Community School District*, 393 U.S. 503 (1969), established the "substantial disruption" test, which remains good law today at least for expressional activity occurring on school grounds or at school-sponsored functions. Students generally have the right to express themselves at school on matters that may be controversial, or even offensive, as long as it doesn't substantially disrupt the orderly operations of the school or violate the legal rights of others.

Unfortunately, there is no consensus among the lower federal courts on precisely what's required to show substantial disruption. Over the years, the Supreme Court has carved out a few exceptions to the test—for profanity, speech in official school-sponsored publications, and advocacy of illegal drug use—but as of this writing the Court has not provided any meaningful clarification on what constitutes substantial disruption. So, it's important to seek guidance on the formulation of this test adopted by the courts in your jurisdiction.

The hard cases are where a particular school activity gives students some discretion to offer their opinions or viewpoints, but school officials find a student's input troublesome. A student in a school play has no First Amendment right to deviate from the script. But if a school sponsors a student talent show, or invites students to speak at graduation, the First Amendment limits the school's ability to suppress students' speech based on their viewpoint alone once that door is opened.

Until recently, many federal courts applied some version of the *Tinker* substantial disruption test to students' speech occurring off campus or online, but a 2021 Supreme Court decision in *Mahanoy Area School District v. B.L.*, 141 S. Ct. 2038 (2021), significantly limited schools' ability to impose discipline in those cases. In *Mahanoy*, the Court held that when students are away from school and not participating in any school-related activities, any offensive statements they make, or post online, are for their parents—or if necessary, the police—to deal with and are not subject to discipline at school.

The Court carved out an exception for targeted bullying or threats directed at school staff or fellow students, and a few other scenarios where parents might expect school officials to stand *in loco parentis*, but left it to the lower courts to determine the outer limits of a school district's disciplinary power on a case-by-case basis. The *Mahanoy d*ecision dealt only with *expression* protected by the First Amendment and not *conduct,* such as drinking or fighting. Still, many states by law or local district policy limit a school district's disciplinary authority over off-campus conduct as well, unless there's a direct impact on the school community.

Since the *Mahanoy* decision overturned the student's removal from a cheerleading team, not a suspension from school, the Court also cast doubt on the long-held notion that school officials have greater discretion to deny students participation in extracurricular activities because these activities are a privilege, not a right. Previous court rulings in your jurisdiction on the right/privilege distinction must be reevaluated in light of *Mahanoy* to determine if they remain good law.

The free speech rights of school staff are governed by a different line of Supreme Court decisions, starting with *Pickering v. Board of Education*, 391 U.S. 563 (1968), and *Connick v. Myers,* 461 U.S. 138 (1983). The *Pickering-Connick* balancing test recognizes the right of public employees, in their capacity as private citizens, to speak on matters of general public concern as long as it doesn't undermine working relationships necessary for the proper functioning of the agency where they work. In other words, the right to criticize the superintendent in public may depend on whether you're a rank-and-file teacher or the superintendent's personal secretary.

In *Garcetti v. Ceballos,* 547 U.S. 410 (2006), the Court later clarified that First Amendment protection is not available for public employees' speech in the performance of their officially prescribed duties, such as preparation of reports that are an inherent part of the employee's job. State-level whistle-blower statutes may provide some protection to fill that gap, but employees cannot look to the First Amendment for protection when acting in their official capacity.

What about teachers' "academic freedom" to teach what they think is beneficial for their students, or school employees' right to express their political or religious views on the job? Most courts have held that teachers at the K–12 level are expected to teach the curriculum prescribed by their employers. While creativity is to be encouraged within the four corners of that curriculum, teachers have no First Amendment "academic freedom" to teach what they please.

Similarly, they may not turn their classrooms into soapboxes for their personal viewpoints on politics, religion, labor relations, or other controversial subjects irrelevant to the lessons they've been hired to teach. There are two main reasons for this restriction: first, unlike the general public who can choose to ignore a pamphleteer on the street, students are a captive audience; and second, whatever school staff say while on the job could be perceived as reflecting the position of the school district itself.

What about the rights of the public to express themselves at school board meetings or other school-sponsored functions? That depends on what sort of meeting or other gathering is involved. If it's structured as an opportunity for the public to speak on matters of concern to them, such as the "public comment" portion of a board meeting, the district can impose limitations on the length of a speaker's comment or how long the session will last overall.

Generally speaking, however, you may not stifle speakers' comments based on the viewpoints they are expressing. If it's a meeting held for a specific purpose, on the other hand, such as a curriculum committee meeting to review a new math textbook series, discussion can properly be limited to the topic at hand.

A cautionary note: This brief overview of the state of First Amendment law is just that. The body of decisions from our federal courts addressing the First Amendment is nuanced, fact-sensitive and constantly evolving. Interpretations also vary from one federal court to another since the Supreme Court paints with a broad brush and usually will not step in to address a constitutional issue until the lower federal courts are in disagreement.

The scenarios discussed in this chapter reflect the views of experienced school administrators on how certain situations might be handled, but you should consult with your district's attorney on whether your local federal courts have yet ruled on a similar fact pattern.

BRING DOWN THE CURTAIN

Scenario: The high school graduation includes performances and presentations by students. A week prior, several students inform the principal that a student who expects to do a musical performance has been posting racist and anti-Semitic comments on his Facebook page. The students are upset about him representing their class. The principal considers withdrawing this presentation and reprinting the program. She worries about student protests and disruption of the ceremony. She seeks the superintendent's advice.

Responses

Sarah Mackenzie

In lieu of a district policy, the principal is correct in consulting with the superintendent. The latter needs to consult the district's lawyer.

The principal should investigate the student group's claims by looking at the Facebook page and talking to the poster of the material. Ultimately, parents may need to be involved as discussions continue. The principal might discover that the situation turns into a teachable moment for the Facebook poster regarding the impact of his actions on others and on himself if his performance is barred at graduation.

If the student resists removing the comments on his Facebook page and apologizing to his classmates, additional action must be taken. The high school principal will have to anticipate some reaction if she removes the performance from commencement, but doing so will be an important statement about what is acceptable behavior of students.

Sheldon Berman

The posting of racist and anti-Semitic comments by students is deeply disturbing and shouldn't be ignored. By providing an opportunity to perform at the graduation ceremony, the graduates acknowledge the talents of classmates, memorialize the spirit of their experience together, and present their legacy to the school. Presenting at the ceremony is a privilege rather than a right.

However, there are significant limitations to pursuing discipline for off-campus speech. To warrant administrative action, that speech must create a foreseeable risk of substantial and material disruption to the school. In this case, given that the Facebook postings are known among the student body, the threat of disruption to the graduation ceremony may meet the legal standard to justify the administration's taking action.

Before doing that, however, it would be appropriate for the principal to meet with the Facebook-posting student and his parents to discuss her concerns about the content of the postings, the damage that the student's musical performance could inflict on the meaning of the graduation ceremony, and the potential disruption that could occur at the ceremony.

She should encourage the student to remove the offensive comments from his Facebook page and replace them with an apology. She should also counsel the student to withdraw the musical performance as a way of acknowledging the inappropriateness of the statements and his desire to ensure a positive graduation experience for all.

If the student does not choose to withdraw, the principal should inform the students and parents that she is withdrawing the presentation and reprinting the program. She also may offer to fill that program slot with a commentary on racial/ethnic tolerance and acceptance presented by another member of the graduating class.

THE DESPERATE OUTBURST

> Scenario: In the days after a presidential election, a high school teacher considered well-respected and highly effective feels desperate about the outcome. He sees increasing reports of students harassing others and making racial slurs. He posts a lengthy letter for his students to read that says in part: "If you backed the president-elect, you aligned yourself with someone who is racist, misogynistic, homophobic, and egocentric. That choice says something about you." Several parents complain to the principal and aim bitter attacks at the teacher. How should the administration respond?

Responses

Sheldon Berman

In this kind of environment, teachers must remain respectful of differing viewpoints, create a climate of thoughtful dialogue, and engage students in an examination of factual evidence. One thing they should not do is enlist students in their own political perspective or attack students for their political opinions. We are not here to teach students what to think, but how to think critically. Therefore, it is essential that we are aware of and careful about imposing our own biases.

Although this teacher has a First Amendment right to his opinion of the president-elect, he is accountable to his students and to the school community for maintaining both the integrity of his position and his composure. Above all, he has a professional obligation to create an emotionally safe environment for his students. He clearly violated that expectation by attacking his students for their opinions and labeling them as prejudiced toward others.

However, this teacher's concern about harassment and racial slurs is a worthy issue to address. There is no place in our schools for racism, anti-Semitism, prejudice against Muslims, bigotry, bullying, discrimination against LGBTQ individuals, hatred or violence. It is not the responsibility of only the administrators to make it unequivocally clear to students and the community that expressions of these sentiments by word or deed are not acceptable; it is the collective responsibility of the faculty.

Educators should take a stand for the values of justice, respect, tolerance, and acceptance of difference. One of the essential ways to communicate those values is to model them. In this case, despite his concern about harassment and racial slurs, the teacher undermined his stature and his instructional leadership by criticizing and labeling his students for their political preference.

The administration needs to respond immediately by meeting with the teacher. Given the teacher's positive reputation, he may be able to address the situation by writing a letter of apology to students and their families and by demonstrating his understanding of how he had violated their trust. Still, he has compromised the confidence and respect that students and families have in his instructional abilities, and it may take time to rebuild that confidence.

In addition, a letter of reprimand to his file would provide documentation to deter any future occurrence. However, if the teacher remains adamant in his position, the administration needs to consider more significant disciplinary consequences.

Sarah Jerome

The teacher has an opinion shared by many, but obviously not all. Whether the teacher is right or wrong in his opinion does not matter. The teacher must create and insist on an environment in his classroom where each student has the opportunity for informed debate on issues and civil discourse.

The teacher may not be able to control all environments where racist, misogynistic, Islamophobic, homophobic, egocentric behaviors are evident, but in his classroom he can insist that all people are treated with respect and that racial slurs and harassment of others are not tolerated.

The teacher can set the example for how thoughtful, reasonable, informed, mature adults conduct themselves in a diverse society. And the teacher must respect diverse opinion and allow—and even encourage—civil discourse of differing views.

The administration needs to support the teacher by guiding him to remember that his students are a "captive audience." The teacher is in the classroom to educate, enlighten and encourage reflective citizens who respect each other's right to make informed choices.

Modeling this behavior for students is a critically important role for the teacher. The administration can bring the teacher's focus back to the real impact he can have with his students—not by forcing his opinion on his students, but by modeling good citizenship for his students and giving these students the opportunity to practice these citizenship skills in the classroom and in their lives outside the classroom.

HALLWAY PROPAGANDA

> Scenario: A long-term substitute at your high school notices a lot of partisan propaganda taped to the outside of a colleague's classroom door. The colleague teaches wood shop and world history, and this material is unrelated to both. It includes a Jokeresque image of the U.S. president with the word "socialist" underneath. With students a captive audience, has the teacher crossed the line of appropriate behavior by sharing his political or religious views in the classroom? The long-term sub thinks so and has brought the issue to you. How will you handle it?

Responses

Joan McRobbie

School and school district grounds are politically neutral. It should be clear to all employees that they cannot conduct political activities during on-the-job hours. Those activities include use of email or copy machines for political advocacy, circulating political petitions, wearing a campaign button during the school day, and posting materials that advocate political positions or intend to influence support or opposition among students or others. So, yes, this teacher has crossed the line of appropriate behavior.

It is, of course, appropriate for a teacher of world history to engage students instructionally on issues related to political systems and parties, including discussion or assignments related to political campaigns. But as teachers promote knowledge of democracy and critical thinking, they need to avoid partisanship or advocacy. Teachers often find themselves walking a difficult line when the class addresses controversial issues. But a derogatory image of the president on a classroom door is a straightforward violation. It not only violates a school district's ethics code but sets a poor example for students in terms of civic dialogue.

One response would be to send this teacher an email with a friendly reminder of the school district's policy, including a link to the policy, which should be available to all employees online. Then follow up (without involving the sub) to ensure that the image is removed. If it appears that similar activities are occurring elsewhere in the school, issue a reminder in the regular staff bulletin as well as review and discuss this aspect of the ethics code at a faculty meeting.

Sheldon Berman

Faculty members are representatives of the school district. They have freedom of speech within certain limits of the district's curriculum, but clearly not the discretion to propagandize their own viewpoints and positions. Education involves teaching students how to critically think about important social and political issues, not what to think about those issues.

It may be appropriate and beneficial for a teacher to use highly propagandized materials in a lesson about propaganda or to engage students in critically thinking about the divergent positions and arguments around an issue. However, the goal of all teachers should be to create a safe environment for students to hold and discuss multiple perspectives on issues.

Instruction that is politically positional, or the posting of materials that are propagandistic, shuts down that dialogue, inhibits respectful interaction, and silences dissenting voices. It undermines the educational goals to which we aspire.

In this case, the teacher appears to have stepped well beyond what is germane to quality instruction or the district's curriculum. In posting the derisive image of the president, disparagingly labeled, the teacher might possibly have intended to engage students in a profound discussion of the strategies implicit in propaganda. However, given the materials' hallway placement and the subject area assignment of the teacher, the action more likely reflects the teacher's political beliefs and is an effort to enlist students in those beliefs.

Such behavior is not an ethical or legally authorized practice within the schoolhouse doors. Recent court decisions affirm the authority of a school district to restrict teachers from stating viewpoints or covering topics that do not mirror the district's curriculum, particularly when the teacher's statements or actions present information that is self-serving, deliberately false or intentionally defamatory.

However, this situation is not simply a legal issue but an ethical one—and one that goes to the very core of an educator's responsibility. The administrator should request that the teacher remove the poster—or the administrator could personally remove the poster. The substitute teacher specifically should not be asked to take any action, by word or deed.

The administrator would then meet with the teacher to discuss the rationale for posting the materials and determine if they were being used in an appropriate instructional manner in the context of the district's curriculum. If they were not and instead were simply a way for the teacher to express a private political viewpoint, the administrator would issue a directive to the teacher to refrain from such actions and, depending on the teacher's response, potentially take other disciplinary action.

THE "MORALLY OFFENSIVE" MAGAZINE COVER

> Scenario: The chair of the social studies department, who also teaches journalism, at a small suburban high school started having his seniors pay for a six-month subscription to *Time* magazine for use in writing summaries and discussions of current affairs. The principal of the school informs the teacher he is canceling the subscriptions because he objects to the magazine's cover that depicts a breast-feeding mother, claiming it is "morally offensive." The teacher sees it as a great opportunity to discuss freedom of the press. The dispute reaches the superintendent for resolution.

Responses

Maggie Lopez

The superintendent needs to help the principal reconsider his stance on this issue. Calling out a picture of a breast-feeding mother as morally offensive and wanting to cancel the subscription to the magazine is an overreaction. Does he also plan to ban *National Geographic*? Photos in that magazine also could be viewed as offensive if this is the perception of the principal.

Though perhaps well-intended, the principal's attempts to prevent exposing students to a potentially controversial topic could create a controversy of its own. The students are seniors and undoubtedly already have been exposed to books, news articles, and reports of a controversial nature (just turn on the TV). Students need to be able to process such topics, and the journalism class provides an opportunity to do this in a manner that can be responsibly and thoughtfully led by the teacher, particularly if the discussion is structured from an instructional perspective that aligns with journalism study.

These students are young adults. Some probably know teen moms. Some have probably already been exposed to this topic. The principal and teacher working together must find common ground and a positive alternative to simply canceling the subscription and censoring/banning the lesson. These same students will see the same magazine cover when they are checking out at the grocery store.

We cannot protect our students or schools from all controversy or freedom of the press in our world today. At times, like it or not, we must find ways to address it in appropriate ways, defuse the often divisive rhetoric around such issues, and ask parents to help us do so.

Sheldon Berman

This situation reflects a classic escalation of conflict in which one person reacts to another's action without attempting to understand the other or to undertake a process by which the conflict might be resolved. There are a number of steps that should have been taken along the way to avoid the conflict in the first place.

The teacher should have consulted with the principal about students purchasing the subscription as a supplement to the curriculum. The principal should have discussed with the teacher his concerns about that issue of the magazine rather than unilaterally cancelling the subscription. Before reacting, the principal should also have discussed with the superintendent or others whether censorship was appropriate based on a picture of a breastfeeding mother in a magazine that is so widely read and has no connection to pornography.

Finally, the department chair should have appealed to the superintendent or another central office administrator to seek an opinion on how to best address this difference. It is critical that the issue be resolved before students become aware of the conflict, which could undermine the authority and credibility of both individuals.

The superintendent needs to meet with both individuals to discuss how this conflict could have been better addressed at multiple points along the way. In particular, the superintendent needs to counsel the principal about the inappropriateness of injecting his values before consulting with others about whether the picture could be considered morally offensive in a legal proceeding. The principal's unilateral actions and failure to manage a conflict situation in a way that prevents, rather than furthers, escalation demonstrate serious inadequacies in his leadership and may need to be addressed directly through the evaluation process.

Although the teacher may want to make a case that he has the right to use the material and even to discuss with students how this issue represents freedom of the press, he should acknowledge that he could have attained his original instructional goals by asking for advice and assistance from another administrator. As a department chair, he, too, is a leader and needs to demonstrate the ability to manage differences and conflict in a respectful and considered manner.

Both individuals have a responsibility to acknowledge to each other the errors in judgment that were made along the way. They may have their differences but need to work on ways of communicating that will reduce the likelihood of a similar conflict in the future. To resolve the current situation, the principal needs to restore the subscriptions, and the teacher needs to proceed with his original instructional plan rather than repurposing the magazine cover to review the principal's reactive decision.

Chapter Three

Unequal Treatment

This chapter addresses discrimination. The word itself means recognizing differences from one thing to another, which isn't necessarily bad. After all, if a friend called you a discriminating shopper, you'd probably take it as a compliment. It's only when you discriminate based on factors society has determined to be irrational or unfair that it becomes unethical and perhaps even illegal.

We live in a racially, ethnically, culturally, politically, and religiously diverse society, and school administrators have an ethical obligation to be "equal opportunity" educators. That means fostering a school climate where students and staff feel they are welcome, included, and judged on their merit. But ethics aside, what are our *legal* obligations? And in cases where the law doesn't provide the answer, what's the right thing to do?

The ethical duty of fairness incorporates the precept that similarly situated individuals are entitled to similar treatment unless there's a good reason why not. The "equal protection" clause of the Fourteenth Amendment to the U.S. Constitution imposes this obligation on government officials and agencies as a matter of law. The federal courts, over the years, have developed several different standards to test the legality of differential treatment under the equal protection clause, some more rigorous than others depending on the criteria in question.

To pass constitutional muster, most governmental action requires nothing more than some rational basis—a very low bar. For example, requiring some students to take their lunch at noon and others at mid-morning based on their class schedules likely would pass the rational basis test, even if reasonable people might differ on the point. Discrimination based on sex must overcome a higher burden of justification, and differential treatment based on race must pass so-called "strict scrutiny"—the highest standard of review, requiring a compelling governmental interest that can't be served through other means.

The First Amendment provides additional protection for the free exercise of religion. Unlike most anti-discrimination laws that prohibit worse treatment based on membership in a protected class, the First Amendment entitles citizens to preferential treatment in the form of reasonable accommodation of their religious beliefs and practices.

Congress has also adopted legislation prohibiting discrimination by public and private actors. The statutes most relevant to school administrators are: Title VI, prohibiting discrimination based on race, color or national origin in federally funded programs; Title VII, prohibiting discrimination in employment based on race, color, religion, sex or national origin; Title IX, prohibiting discrimination on the basis of sex in any aspect of federally-funded programs; and the Americans with Disabilities Act ("the ADA") and Section 504 of the Rehabilitation Act, prohibiting discrimination on the basis of disability.

Like the First Amendment duty of reasonable accommodation to religion, the ADA and Section 504 also entitle disabled individuals to reasonable accommodation, not just freedom from worse treatment than the non-disabled.

State anti-discrimination laws often provide broader protection than federal law, sometimes far broader. The most high-profile case in point is transgender rights. In recent years, there has been much litigation in the federal courts over whether the word "sex" in Title IX is limited to biological sex assigned at birth or includes protection for transgender individuals. That's a non-issue in New Jersey, for example, whose Law Against Discrimination has explicitly included "gender identity or expression" as a protected classification since 2007. It's vital to get up-to-date guidance on the full measure of the legal obligations applicable to your district.

Unlawful discrimination doesn't necessarily require direct evidence of a discriminatory mindset—a "smoking gun"—to prove intent. Statistics alone can sometimes make the case. Say the percentage of African Americans in a particular job category in your district is drastically less than their availability in the relevant labor market. Under the "disparate treatment" theory of liability, absent a persuasive explanation the courts may allow an inference of unlawful discrimination from those numbers alone, on the grounds that this disparity most likely wasn't just coincidental. The scenario in this chapter addressing evaluations delves into that issue.

It's important to be mindful that good intentions aren't enough to overcome a claim of unlawful discrimination, especially when race is a deciding factor in your decision making. Many well-intentioned decisions made in the name of "affirmative action," including some for which your district may have received accolades in the 1970s, may now be blatantly illegal under our courts' current interpretation of the anti-discrimination laws; be sure your actions align with the latest rulings applicable in your jurisdiction.

Over the course of your career you also will be faced with opportunities for differential treatment that aren't illegal but still raise ethical concerns. Here's where you must harmonize your ethical duty of fairness with your equally important duty to pursue the greater good for the school community as a whole.

Is a student from an economically disadvantaged home with no access to Wi-Fi similarly situated to a student from an affluent family, and thus entitled to no special accommodations? Maybe so, if they're competing for a spot on the basketball team. Maybe not, if you're offering a free Wi-Fi hotspot to students who don't otherwise have access so they can keep up with their schoolwork.

Is it acceptable to give a financial benefactor reserved 50-yardline seats at the new football stadium in return for donating the concession stand? Maybe so, but moving the benefactor's daughter to the front of the line for enrollment in a highly competitive honors course would raise obvious ethical concerns.

How you answer questions like these will necessarily reflect your district's approach to social justice, access, and equity. Under our system of public school governance, the elected or appointed school board's role is to set the tone on these issues, presumably reflecting the standards of the community with input from administration on best practices educationally.

The cases in this chapter encompass teacher evaluation rubrics, discriminatory hiring practices, preferential treatment for prominent members of the school community, and other real-life situations that school administrators may confront. Whether it's compliance with federal and state laws, or just the prudent exercise of discretion, these scenarios bring the principles outlined above sharply into focus and should provide helpful guidance when confronting issues of discrimination and preferential treatment in your district. The first several cases examine the issue of when a discretionary act crosses the line and becomes discriminatory.

A RUBRIC TESTING COLOR

Scenario: A school district has collaborated with the local teachers' union to adopt new teacher observation/evaluation protocols. Although the rubrics seem quite clear and unbiased, male teachers of color are disproportionately receiving "unsatisfactory" evaluations. The system has been in place for three years. Should the superintendent advocate for staff to revise the rubric and push for the district to change how it uses the evaluation to retain, promote or dismiss teachers?

Responses

Chris Lee Nicastro

All evaluation systems can benefit from ongoing and regular review. Conducting such reviews every three to five years is appropriate and necessary. Changing staff, changing leadership, and current social realities suggest that how supervisors approach evaluation and how employees receive it change all the time. Ongoing review and training ensure that communication is clear and that the system works to improve employee performance and foster growth. The process must be open and collaborative.

While the leadership of the district, with all good intentions, believed that these conditions were in place when the current system was developed, there's nothing to say that male teachers of color were consulted nor that special attention was given to issues of discrimination and equity. Were supervisors given targeted training to avoid inherent biases? Was there a significant effort to recognize and confront internalized oppression on the part of supervisors of color or internalized racism in white supervisors? If it is apparent that the system over-identifies males of color for poor evaluations, there is a problem.

Board policy needs to be reviewed in terms of the current reality of issues related to race. School boards and superintendents committed to equity would be well advised to do a thorough review of board policy and administrative procedures through the equity lens. Districts that assume a proactive and aggressive stance in such action will benefit greatly in terms of employee relations and satisfaction, community relations, and—most importantly—in modeling for and serving the children of the district.

Sheldon Berman

Disproportionality could clearly be an indication of bias within the evaluation rubrics and protocols and should be examined more closely. Three years of experience with the new evaluation system provides an ample basis for determining whether it is achieving the goals that prompted its revision, as well as whether the new version contains any unintended biases.

Although any review of the system should engage a broad audience of both those performing the evaluations and those being evaluated, the examination should specifically focus on the perspectives of teachers of color, particularly those who have received unsatisfactory evaluations. Hearing their feedback firsthand could provide insight into differing interpretations of the rubrics and protocols relative to expectations for instructional delivery and student-teacher relationships.

However, the district must also be prepared to examine whether the disproportionality may reflect not a problem with the rubrics, but rather hidden bias among those performing the observations. The analysis will need to review data on who performed the evaluations and whether or how the perceptions of these individuals differed. The district would be well served to ensure that those performing the observations receive training that includes issues related to cultural diversity, hidden bias, and other subtle forms of racism.

The superintendent should open a dialogue with the teachers' union and urge its leaders to join in the review, thereby continuing the collaborative process that led to the adoption of the revised evaluation system. Any teacher evaluation process should set high standards and expectations for teacher performance, but also be unbiased in both its rubrics and its administration. It's in everyone's best interest to ensure a culturally inclusive evaluation process that supports the retention of a diverse teaching staff, reflecting the races, ethnicities, and cultures of the students they teach.

A GAY WOULD-BE PRINCIPAL'S ASPIRATIONS

Scenario: A candidate for a middle school principalship—someone who has taught in a neighboring school system—is passed over for the opening. He contends he has been rejected because he is openly gay. Some parents at the school with the vacancy have voiced concerns about having their children under the daily direction of gay employees. How should the superintendent deal with these complaints—from the parents as well as the gay teacher?

Responses

Sheldon Berman

Sexual orientation cannot be a factor in the hiring process. Federal law (Title VII) prohibits employment decisions based on gender stereotyping, and about half of the states have laws expressly prohibiting sexual orientation discrimination in employment decisions.

Apart from legal considerations, best practices in hiring exclude discussion of any personal issues unrelated to job responsibilities, including a candidate's racial or familial background, sexual orientation or political beliefs.

Whether or not the applicant files a complaint with the district, the superintendent has an obligation to investigate and determine if the process was biased. If it is found there were comments or discussion about the candidate's sexual orientation that influenced members of the hiring committee, the superintendent should void the decision of the committee and restart the entire process.

If a complaint is filed with the EEOC or the state counterpart of the EEOC, that agency will initiate a formal investigation and the process will assuredly become a lengthier one. This fact underscores the need for the district to conduct its own investigation promptly and—if it uncovers evidence that the hiring decision was based on unlawful considerations—to immediately correct its process.

Although societal values have changed dramatically in the last decades around the issue of openly gay individuals, some parents are still concerned when gay teachers and administrators are in a position of authority relative to their children. The superintendent should see this situation as an opportunity to engage with these parents and listen carefully to their concerns. It is only through school leaders' listening and responding appropriately that parents can become more at ease with the inclusion of all types of diversity.

After spending time listening, the superintendent can respond to parents' concerns by emphasizing it is inappropriate for any staff member to advocate for a particular sexual orientation and that sexual orientation has no bearing on one's professional abilities. Any staff member hired by the district is expected to hold high moral standards, and it is anticipated that someone who is openly gay will hold those same standards.

If, in the judgment of the hiring committee, an individual is found to have professional assets that will serve the district better than those of other candidates, the district should take advantage of the opportunity to have that person join the district. Sexual orientation has no role in the decision.

Some parents may still find this stance personally difficult. The superintendent needs to grasp this situation as a teachable moment that may broaden the perspective and understanding of these parents and enable them to become more open and appreciative of the opportunity to be inclusive. At the same time, the superintendent must take a firm and positive position on professional, moral, and legal grounds.

Paula Mirk

Documentation, as the data for decision making, is so important for cases such as this one. The superintendent should have a clear picture of the process for choice of principal and, even if the details are confidential, the factors or criteria for selection shouldn't be. The process should reaffirm the laws of the land by being "blind" to gender, race, and sexual orientation.

Meanwhile, the superintendent also needs a process to help parents understand these inalienable rights. The process should underscore the district's commitment to fairness and respect and should perhaps include an element about parental responsibility in a public school environment.

All of us should be committed to schools that do not discriminate, particularly in a public school context. If parents are raising "gay employees" as an issue, they're undermining the district's and their own children's ability to operate according to a basic philosophy of our nation, which public schools represent.

A WITNESS TO DISCRIMINATION

Scenario: In the midst of a hiring process for a principal, the superintendent learns that a candidate who is not being recommended for appointment experienced what the candidate viewed as discrimination during the job pursuit. The superintendent expected her to file a lawsuit if she didn't get the job—and that happened. The superintendent has been called as a witness and must decide whether to support the district or admit the district made a mistake.

Responses

Sheldon Berman

The superintendent must speak the truth when testifying. However, the truth may be more complex than simply agreeing that the district made a mistake. Hiring is a complex, multi-tiered process. Although a candidate may construe a question, comment, or action to be discriminatory, there could be differing perspectives on its meaning and intent. In this case, the plaintiff must prove that there was a discriminatory motive to the question, comment, or action or a pattern of discrimination within the school or district.

During the hiring process, the superintendent had a responsibility to investigate whether the search had been compromised and whether discriminatory action had occurred. Based on that investigation, the superintendent had a choice to move forward or to stop the search and then restart it in a way that ensured a clean process.

In this case, the superintendent moved forward despite knowing that the candidate might view the process to be discriminatory. Therefore, the superintendent likely noted other factors that made the candidate's perspective incomplete or flawed.

The comment or action in question could have reflected a motivation other than the intent to discriminate. Or a review of the applicants' qualifications could have indicated that other candidates were stronger and better qualified, providing a legitimate and non-discriminatory reason for hiring another individual. In addition, there may be no pattern or history of discrimination toward the candidate's protected class at that school or in the district.

Upon learning of the candidate's concerns during the hiring process, the superintendent should have sought immediate guidance from the district's attorney. If the decision in this case was to move forward, the superintendent can testify to factors other than discrimination toward an individual of a legally protected class that were critical to making the determination of whom to hire.

Maggie Lopez

The superintendent and school district were in error by not following up once they were made aware of the allegation of perceived discrimination by the interviewee who didn't get the job. The concern should have been investigated. Had this occurred prior to the completion of the hiring process, there may not have been a lawsuit filed against the district.

At the very least, there would have been the opportunity either to restart the process if inappropriate protocols for interviewing and hiring were used or to clarify with the candidate that the protocols used were appropriate and legal. When leaders become aware of allegations of inappropriate behaviors on the part of our staff or students, it is our responsibility to address them immediately.

The superintendent is a steward of the community and a role model, as well as the school district leader. We ask students to tell school staff when they see or experience something they believe to be wrong; when we as leaders become aware of a potential misstep, we too must address it. As the organization's chief who answers to the school board, students and community, the superintendent, once aware of the serious allegation, carries the responsibility to intervene. The superintendent should not have waited until the issue became a legal challenge or a lawsuit.

A HAIRY BACKTRACK

Scenario: An experienced preschool teacher applies for a job teaching in the primary grades at a local public school. The principal is impressed by his résumé, recommendations, and interview responses but tells the candidate his beard might upset parents in the community. The principal asks him if he'd shave it. The teacher declines, prompting the principal to withdraw the job offer. Was the principal's action ethical?

Responses

Meira Levinson

The principal's action was not ethical for three reasons. First, as a public school administrator, the principal is a representative of the state. By withdrawing the teacher's job offer, the principal has used the power of the government to deny employment to a qualified individual on prima facie irrelevant grounds. Of all employers, the state must be held to the highest standards of inclusion and non-discrimination, given its obligation to represent and serve the public.

Second, even if this were a private school, employers may not use their customers' (in this case, parents') prejudices as grounds to deny employment to an otherwise qualified candidate. Civil rights-era case law makes this clear. Even if a store can show it is likely to lose customers because they do not want to be served by a black salesclerk or a hospital can show it will lose patients who mistrust female doctors, these employers may not discriminate in hiring on the basis of race or gender. The same principle holds here.

Finally, schools are, by definition, places of education. Their purpose is to help people develop into better and more informed individuals, learners, and citizens. At the very least, by hiring this teacher, the school could teach its students to value and respect bearded men and thus avoid their parents' misbegotten fears. Furthermore, by modeling an inclusive and diverse community, the school might teach parents to overcome their prejudices and thus promote learning among adults as well as children.

Sheldon Berman

Although beards are not covered in the list of legal protections against discrimination, unless they are worn for religious or health-related reasons, it is unethical and perhaps illegal in some states and cities to discriminate against this teacher based on his beard. Employment decisions should be based on the ability to perform the tasks of the position, not solely on physical appearance. The assumption that parents might be upset may be inaccurate. In fact, some parents also may have beards.

Employers may establish reasonable dress codes related to a position that could include cleanliness and neatness, such as a beard that is appropriately groomed. However, beyond personal hygiene, physical appearance has no relationship to teaching. Would the principal hold all male staff members—including custodians, bus drivers and instructional assistants—to the same beard-free standard? Would the principal allow parents with beards to volunteer in classrooms?

Discriminating against this individual because of his beard is a slippery slope that could be used to justify discrimination against people with tattoos, piercings, unusual hair styles, different body types, etc., none of which are related to performance on the job. Such a decision by the principal also could become a proxy for other, more traditional forms of discrimination, such as race, religion, or sexual orientation. This inappropriate bias could create a hostile environment for those who differ with the principal's biases.

The larger ethical issue is our responsibility as educators to introduce students to the concepts of diversity and inclusivity. Faculty diversity in appearance, as well as in race, ethnicity, gender, sexual orientation, religion, or physical disability, supports students in learning how these concepts are demonstrated in everyday life. Creating uniformity through the trivial rejection of a person with a beard represents the antithesis of a basic tenet of our democratic society.

A DUBIOUS JOB POSTING

Scenario: The personnel coordinator of a school district with a strong music program receives job postings from a community program seeking "female piano teachers." The program head says he is replacing a retiring female teacher whose students have requested a female replacement. Knowing the gender references are illegal, the district's personnel coordinator distributes the postings without mention of gender as many teachers rely on outside work. However, he feels ethically implicated in the program head's problematic hiring practice. Has he acted appropriately?

Responses

Chris Nicastro

The personnel coordinator should contact the community program to let them know he distributed the posting and explain why he did not specify gender. It's possible a community group, especially one run by volunteers, might not be aware of the legal implications of advertising a gender-specific job.

This assumes the district has no policy prohibiting the posting of external positions. Most districts limit the kind of information that can be distributed. Opening this up to community groups has some inherent risk, offset at least in part by positive community relationships. The superintendent and school board need to ensure their policies are clear and that staff are compliant with these policies.

Sheldon Berman

It's time for the personnel coordinator to have a discussion with the program head about the problematic nature of the posting. The personnel coordinator may have avoided a direct legal challenge by not mentioning gender himself. However, if the program head intends to consider only female applicants, the school district coordinator has been ethically and legally complicit with this practice by knowingly redistributing the posting.

Although he has already acted on the request, the personnel coordinator should initiate a frank discussion with the program head. He should encourage the program head to withdraw the posting and repost the position without specifying gender and with the addition that the program is an equal opportunity employer. He should also encourage the program head to meet with the retiring teacher's students and their parents and explain that gender cannot play a role in choosing a replacement. The best qualified person should be hired.

Given that teachers in the school district are a prime source of candidates, the program head is likely to heed the personnel coordinator's counsel. If the position is reposted, and for any future program posting, the personnel coordinator needs to feel confident that the position will be open to any qualified individual and that the hiring will not be gender-related.

A LESSON IN FIRST-PERSON REALITY

Scenario: For a course in a doctoral program in educational administration, students (most of whom are superintendents or assistant superintendents) have been studying underserved and marginalized groups that compose a large part of the area's student population. For one project, the professor requires each student to spend an afternoon walking in the shoes of a member of such a group—for instance, a homeless person requesting money, an overweight person shopping for clothes, a same-sex couple visiting a wedding store.

Jeremy, an EdD student working as an assistant superintendent, tells you he's unsettled by this assignment, wondering about using deception as a learning tool and whether he should raise a question of integrity? What might you advise?

Responses

Sheldon Berman

It is reasonable for a professor to require that students more deeply understand the lives of underserved and marginalized groups. John Howard Griffin's experience, recounted in the 1961 classic *Black Like Me*, revealed both the overt and subtle ways black people were disparaged and how the majority culture accepted this treatment as the norm. Although society is now more aware—and hopefully more compassionate—regarding the everyday challenges faced by marginalized groups, a simulated experience is clearly a way to deepen our understanding.

However, Jeremy's concern about using deception as a learning tool is a valid one. The TV series *Candid Camera* justified its decades-long premise of deception as a harmless way to make us more thoughtful about our behavior patterns. Similarly, the Milgram experiment, involving the supposed infliction of pain on another person, yielded startling insights into human responses to authoritarian direction. However, such experiments now are considered unethical because of the psychological harm they caused to unwitting participants.

Today's megadoses of "reality" TV have further blurred the lines between fact and fiction, perhaps contributing to our confusion about ethical propriety. With the possible exception of carefully designed and controlled scientific experiments, to intentionally misrepresent oneself or a situation is ethically problematic and dishonest and has no place in a program for developing educational leaders.

Jeremy should be encouraged to suggest to the professor some alternative, non-deceptive strategies for increasing empathy with members of underserved and minority groups. One approach could be to accompany a gay friend or colleague to a wedding store to discuss plans for an engagement ceremony. Another tactic could involve spending time with an individual from one of these groups, shadowing him or her through the daily routine.

Volunteering in a homeless shelter, mental hospital or nursing home for the indigent or attending meetings of Alcoholics Anonymous or Overeaters Anonymous would provide alternative opportunities to listen to and interact with marginalized individuals and to develop understanding without resorting to a ruse.

Joan McRobbie

This professor, apparently aiming to teach empathy, perhaps is an admirer of journalistic classics like John Howard Griffin's *Black Like Me* (1961) or Barbara Ehrenreich's *Nickel and Dimed* (2001). But those writers chose their assignments and immersed themselves in long-term efforts to live another's life, then share the experience broadly through their books. Empathy was the driver, not the goal.

It's harder to see the value of an afternoon's random act of pretense. This "requirement" also feels insulting to mid-career adults in a doctoral program who should have a say in shaping their own assignments in keeping with the goals of the course. And it would seem the professor could anticipate responses like Jeremy's. Many individuals would object to misrepresenting themselves and deceiving others. Minimally, the class should have the chance to discuss the assignment, express their qualms and suggest other options, such as interviews, that would be experiential without violating anyone's integrity.

Perhaps Jeremy saw the Fox News segment where John Stossel scruffed himself up and sat outside a New York subway station one afternoon, panhandling. He didn't try to make ends meet for a year on $7 an hour, as Barbara Ehrenreich did, to experience the reality of the working poor. Instead, he let people give him money for a couple of hours as part of an effort to demonstrate his contention that we're becoming a nation of freeloaders. He later gave the money back. But it was enough to make any viewer queasy about the idea there may be a trend toward briefly masquerading as someone from a marginalized group.

I would advise Jeremy to show his leadership by gathering his like-minded classmates and jointly taking this up with the professor. The professor may not have thought this through from all perspectives and may well appreciate the insights and be open to change.

The six preceding cases examined the issue of when a judgment or action moves from being discretionary to being discriminatory. The remainder of this chapter will explore the question of whether it is ever appropriate to provide preferential treatment for individual employees or students. Is favoritism the flip side of discrimination?

THE FLEXING OF A BENEFACTOR'S STRONG ARM

Scenario: A prominent community member who contributes significantly to the local education foundation is dropping broad hints to the superintendent that she wants her daughter admitted next year to the school district's selective high school, which has entrance criteria. Occasionally, parents have requested similar meetings, and the superintendent has obliged, but these did not involve apparent attempts to strong arm. Should you give additional consideration to the daughter's application?

Responses

Sheldon Berman

Admission to the district's selective high school must be based on consistent application of the entrance criteria and a fair process for selecting entrants. Allowing individuals to use their influence to "purchase" seats at the school through donations to the district would undermine the integrity of the school and the confidence of the public. It would set in motion a cascade of requests based on political influence and financial means.

If the superintendent makes it a practice to meet with parents interested in having their child attend the school, those meetings should simply be a discussion of the entrance criteria, the school's curricular program, and the academic expectations of students. The superintendent should make it clear to anyone with whom he meets that he has no influence on or participation in the selection process. In general, it would be best for the superintendent to remain at a distance from the admissions process and to refer all interested parents to the principal or guidance counselors at the school for these conversations.

Selective high schools often have a built-in bias toward students possessing the cultural capital that accompanies higher socioeconomic status, including the educational advantages of growing up with parents who have degrees from higher education and the means to provide enriching experiences. To ensure that these schools are equally accessible to students of all economic means, the criteria for entrance should be broader than test scores, which can reflect cultural biases.

In addition, the district should provide enrichment experiences for younger talented and gifted students from economically disadvantaged homes to prepare them for the challenges of meeting the school's entrance requirements. On an ongoing basis, the district needs to track the demographics of the selective high school's student population, determine whether it reflects the racial and socioeconomic diversity of the district as a whole, and make adjustments as needed to its programs and policies to ensure such diversity.

Paula Mirk

You should not give additional consideration to the daughter's application if the only reasons for doing so are the parent's prominence and significant contributions. With any "apparent attempt to strong arm," a red flag is in order and further steps should be examined very carefully, perhaps using the "Front Page Test." If the superintendent agrees to discuss the daughter's admission and this is reported on the newspaper's front page tomorrow, how will the superintendent defend the action? The daughter's application should be subjected to the same process as everybody else's and let the chips fall where they may.

RESERVED FOR HEAVY HITTERS

Scenario: The inner-city headquarters of the school district has a limited number of adjacent parking spaces for staff members. An administrative support staffer who arrives early many days finds that the only spots available are reserved for the later-arriving administrators and department heads, forcing her to park her car much further away. Is it ethical for the others to receive preferred parking spaces based on their professional standing in the school system?

Responses

Joan McRobbie

Parking turns into a difficult problem in school districts where the central office has many more employees than convenient parking spaces. It doesn't seem fair that a hard-working employee who must arrive early has to park far away when high-ranking officials later slip into convenient spaces.

On the other hand, many people with high-level roles are required to dash in and out throughout the day to attend meetings and events in far reaches of the school district and community. Given their jobs' intense demands and tight scheduling, it can be imperative that people with these responsibilities have parking that makes it logistically possible to meet the demands.

Parking dissatisfaction is widespread, not just at urban school district headquarters but at many other workplaces as well. At a minimum, policies for assignment of spaces should be clear and consistently applied. They should also be periodically reviewed by a committee convened for this purpose, with recommendations sought from the range of stakeholders. Solutions should include incentives that lower the parking need (e.g., spaces reserved for carpool vehicles, covered and secure bicycle parking, and/or pre-tax commuter accounts to pay for public transit).

Paula Mirk

At first, this might seem like a trivial issue, but it means a lot to anyone facing a parking shortage day after day. And if the ethics of this parking tradition never have been explained, the preferential structure could easily build resentment among the ranks.

It could seem unfair to the staffer who needs a place to park as much as administrators and department heads do. These small things matter, especially if they're disrupting your schedule day after day. If respect and fairness are core ethical values, who gets to park where becomes a way to demonstrate them. It can come down to an educational philosophy about inclusiveness and the goal of our moral parameters.

Are we teaching extension and application of core ethical values as widely as possible? Then re-examining the basis and traditions of parking might be in order. Was there an ethical basis for it in the first place? Perhaps the superintendent is out visiting schools and therefore arrives late but needs to be able to use time efficiently since taxpayers are paying that high salary. This could be a valid reason for maintaining the status quo, and understanding this could help to calm the person left searching for a spot each day. Usually, explaining the ethics behind a tradition goes a long way in defusing resentment or preventing it from building.

THE QUEUE FOR VACCINATIONS

Scenario: The governor asks the state superintendents' association for its position on prioritizing school districts to receive COVID vaccine doses for staff. A group of urban superintendents contend that high-needs districts deserve priority due to the pandemic's inequitable impact on the education of historically disadvantaged children and the urgent need to return them to classrooms full-time. Other superintendents, feeling community pressure, argue that no district should receive special consideration over any other district. What position should the association take?

Responses

Chris Nicastro

The association has an obligation to represent all members and, indirectly, all the children and communities they serve. The leadership should explain to the governor that they strongly approve of giving school district personnel priority in receiving the vaccine—starting with those most at risk according to CDC guidelines. That might mean giving older staff and those with underlying conditions throughout the state—in all school districts—the first opportunity to get vaccinated.

After that, priority should be given to those districts serving populations of historically disadvantaged children. This should include staff serving children in urban areas but also residential facilities, reservations, and other locations with high-density populations.

Education often apportions resources based on need. In this case, it might mean that some districts are prioritized over others due to COVID-related factors such as race, poverty, and population density. While some more advantaged communities might object, most would understand the rationale for the decision. In the case of a pandemic, most communities have come to accept and support relying on the science to guide actions. Such a rationale would give the association firm ground on which to stand.

Sheldon Berman

The urban superintendents make a compelling case. While many smaller districts have been able to provide more consistent instruction through hybrid models, the urban and economically disadvantaged districts have often had to rely on remote learning throughout the pandemic. In urban environments, even locating some students to provide equipment and access to remote learning has been challenging, causing significant learning time losses. Prioritizing urban and economically disadvantaged district staff could help balance some of the inequity that has emerged.

Nationally, vaccine administration has acknowledged those in greatest need by giving priority to health care and essential workers and senior citizens. It isn't a stretch to apply similar reasoning to high-needs districts.

However, a decision to prioritize some districts would require the agreement of the association's board or at least its officers or executive committee. This proposal may be divisive for association members depending on their prior discussions around issues of equity. Given that other districts, such as rural ones, may be able to make an equally valid case for deserving priority, the association would do well to allow input from all districts before a decision is made.

In previous years, many associations have addressed the issue of equity and have made recommendations on proposals such as more equitable funding of districts based on need. If the association has had these conversations and taken positions that differentiate among districts, providing a recommendation to prioritize vaccine for high-needs districts, whether urban or rural, would be appropriate. If the association has not had these conversations, now would be an apt time for district representatives on the association's board to take up the issue.

A PASS TO THE BASEPATHS

Scenario: During player tryouts for the freshman baseball team at the district's high school, the coach is asked to give special consideration to a boy whose father recently died of cancer. The boy is not very good at baseball, unlikely to be among the fifteen who earn roster spots. The community is pressuring the coach to "do the right thing" for the boy and a family coping with tragedy. They say some things transcend baseball skill. But what about the better player whose spot he would be taking? What is the right action? The coach comes to you for advice.

Responses

Joan McRobbie

This is a very tough dilemma for a coach. Fairness to other players seems to dictate sticking strictly to merit, choosing only those players who earn selection during tryouts. Yet cutting this boy seems heartless under the circumstances. And despite pressures from community members sympathetic to this boy, there will be pushback from others if they feel better qualified players were denied.

Rather than box himself into just these two choices, the coach may want to consider alternative courses of action. One is to expand the number of players on the roster. The size of the roster was likely based on multiple factors, including resources. But the number is also arbitrary. Expanding to 16 may look too obviously like an accommodation for this boy, but is that a bad thing? Players this young are still growing and developing and can improve in all sorts of ways over the coming months and years. This boy may practice intensively, improve markedly, and have a very good season.

Moreover, it is the case that school sports are about more than winning—or should be. A good coach takes many factors other than baseball talent into account when deciding who will make the team. Among those are human concerns, such as how much the chance to play can mean for a boy trying to cope with the loss of his dad. Coaches are important teachers of caring and citizenship. This is a chance to demonstrate for the players and community that being a team means more than going for trophies, that competitiveness without compassion is hollow.

Sheldon Berman

The community's concern and desire to support the student is an important expression of compassion. It should be acted upon in a meaningful way.

However, given the cut policy for making the team, placing him on the roster of fifteen would not be beneficial or equitable for that student or for other students. It could even lead to some resentment from non-selected players and their families and friends.

An unearned selection is not the kind of expression of care and support that would help him recover from this loss. If the student is interested, the coach might consider involving him in another capacity, such as equipment manager, scheduling assistant or data recorder during practices.

There is a larger ethical issue related to roster-cut policies. Athletics in high school and below should be about learning, development, and teamwork, particularly at levels lower than varsity. A no-cut policy provides opportunity for all students, even those with physical disabilities, to participate. Schools can support expanded rosters or multiple teams at various levels and schedule appropriately competitive games that provide all students with the opportunity to develop and enjoy being part of an athletic team.

If the school had a no-cut policy in place, the student's participation would be a question of choice, not exception.

Chapter Four

Religious Liberty

We're all familiar with Thomas Jefferson's famous reference to a "wall of separation" between church and state. In this chapter, we focus on how that wall functions in the setting of our nation's public schools.

The First Amendment to the U.S. Constitution protects the freedom *from* state-sponsored religion (the "establishment clause") and the freedom *to* practice the religion of one's choice or none at all (the "free exercise clause").

The establishment clause isn't limited to formal designation of a government-sanctioned denomination but has been extended by the federal courts to a wide range of government activities reasonably perceived as endorsement of one religion over another—or of religion over atheism.

Some of us may remember when public schools began the day with a recitation of the Lord's Prayer. Since the 1960s, however, the federal courts have prohibited school-sponsored prayer. Since then, the Supreme Court has provided some broadly worded guidelines on invoking religious themes at holiday concerts and graduation ceremonies, but the Court's tests for what's permissible are highly nuanced, fact-specific, and difficult for school officials to apply with assurance they're in a safe harbor.

One of the inherent problems in developing a coherent legal theory on this topic is that, as a matter of historical fact, religion has played such a prominent role in the development of western civilization. Religious themes are unavoidably present in our history, art, music, and culture—to the point where the federal courts have struggled to distinguish between religious-themed symbols that cross the line and those that have acquired enough secular significance to pass constitutional muster.

The changing composition of the U.S. Supreme Court over the past few decades has had no greater impact than in cases involving religious freedom. Whether you believe the Court has gone too far, or not far enough, there's no denying its decisions in recent years have reflected an ever-broadening acceptance of religion in public life to the point where school officials are understandably uncertain about how much reliance they can place on earlier precedents. Adding to the confusion, lower federal courts across the country have adopted different interpretations of the High Court's rulings.

To be clear, nothing in the law prohibits school districts from teaching about religion in a comparative religion lesson or as a factor in American or world history. It is only when schools promote a particular religion, or religion in general, that they cross the line.

The rules also are different when schools permit outside organizations to use their facilities for after-hours activities. Once that door is opened to community groups, you've created what the courts call a "limited public forum," and the First Amendment's free speech clause imposes strict limitations on school districts' ability to bar the door to groups based on their religious affiliation or viewpoint.

The "limited public forum" problem can catch you off guard if you don't realize you're creating one. For example, if you generally allow local community groups to set up tables at Back-to-School Night to publicize their activities, you may be on thin ice barring local religious congregations from taking part. One federal court found that a district violated a student's First Amendment rights by barring her from singing a religious-themed song, "Awesome God," at an after-hours talent show that was not part of the school curriculum. Once you allow these community activities, you have limited control over the particular viewpoints expressed.

Many districts used to prohibit student Bible Clubs for fear of running afoul of the establishment clause. In 1984, Congress attempted to strike a constitutionally acceptable balance with The Equal Access Act, 20 U.S.C. § 4071, prohibiting districts that allow any non-curricular clubs at the secondary school level from barring other clubs on the basis of "the religious, political, philosophical, or other content of the speech" at their meetings, as long as the club is student-initiated with strict limitations on staff involvement in club activities. Now, if a high school allows even one non-curricular club, say the Key Club, it must allow religious clubs, too.

The free exercise clause requires school districts to afford reasonable accommodation for students' and staff's religious beliefs and practices. The Supreme Court spoke to the issue in *Wisconsin v. Yoder*, 406 U.S. 205 (1972), holding that compulsory attendance laws had to give way to Amish families' religious interest in terminating their children's public education before high school. A more familiar example for most districts would be a Muslim student's right to wear a hijab, or an Orthodox Jewish teacher's right to wear a yarmulke, in the face of a district policy generally barring head coverings while in school.

Reasonable accommodation also comes into play when families request exemptions from numerous other school requirements that conflict with their religious beliefs. The operative term here is "reasonable." For example, over forty states recognize religious exemptions from vaccinations, but some deny that exemption when an epidemic is raging in the school community. Districts often permit parents to opt their children out of the more intimate aspects of sex education, but not the more general instruction on human sexuality deemed necessary to foster understanding of others' sexual orientation or gender identity.

The sheer number of religious holidays poses additional challenges in developing the school calendar. There's no legal requirement to close the schools on all holidays of every religion, so the dilemma is more one of community relations and local school district politics. But since you may need to allow religiously observant students and employees to be absent on certain holidays, you'll want to factor that into your decision-making just from an operational standpoint.

A threshold problem in evaluating accommodation requests is the difficulty in determining whether they are based on sincerely held religious beliefs or are just a pretext for some other non-religious objections. The courts have generally deferred to families in these situations because of the difficulties in gauging sincerity, and the fluid definition of religion to begin with. Some state regulations mandate a hands-off approach once the word "religion" appears in an exemption request. Be sure to familiarize yourself with the standards applicable to your district.

Even when there's no question that a request is based on sincerely held religious belief, distinguishing between strict religious obligations and religiously inspired preferences can be challenging, and the law is unsettled on how much of a difference it even makes.

Does a Jewish teacher have a constitutional right to the day off to prepare for the first night of Passover? Probably not; that's what personal days are for. But does a Muslim student who prefers to worship at his local mosque instead of praying in a private place at school have the right to leave the building during the school day? That's a closer call, and good reason to develop ongoing lines of communication with local clergy to secure authoritative guidance on such matters.

Access to reliable information about religious beliefs and practices is especially important in diverse communities that may practice dozens of religions, and denominations within them, that may be unfamiliar to you. Recognizing that there may be differences of opinion even among clergy from the same religion, it's helpful to have a baseline understanding of what's actually required so you can fairly and credibly weigh these requests.

The duty of reasonable accommodation has also been codified in "religious freedom restoration acts," adopted in many states, imposing a heavy burden on government agencies to justify rules that are facially neutral but in practice unduly burden the exercise of religious freedom. For example, a Texas student from the Lipan Apache Tribe successfully challenged a district's hair policy based on a sincerely held religious belief that wearing long hair symbolized his family's ancestry and length of life. Sikh ceremonial knives (kirpans) have also been allowed in schools despite "no weapons" policies.

Be careful not to allow a reasonable accommodation to morph into an establishment clause violation. Students who want to take a few minutes during recess to pray together in a nondisruptive manner have a right to do so, but if the teacher on duty takes charge to lead the activity and encourages other students to join in, you risk the perception of school district endorsement. In that same vein, staff have a right to their religious beliefs but may not use their district position as a soapbox to proselytize their beliefs to a captive audience.

Another example would be allowing employees paid time off for religious observances. You may be obligated under the free exercise clause to honor their request to meet their religious obligations, but that doesn't necessarily mean you're obligated to finance it. In fact, recognizing an entitlement to paid time off specifically for religious observance—time that isn't available to nonbelievers—likely would create an establishment clause problem. The religiously observant may need to take a contractual personal day, if available, or risk getting no pay at all.

The Supreme Court has recently held that a purely private expression of religious sentiment or prayer by district staff, at times and places when they are otherwise free to attend to personal matters, is protected by the First Amendment. In *Kennedy v. Bremerton School District*, decided in June 2022 shortly before this book was published, the Court applied this principle to uphold the right of a high school football coach to recite a private prayer at the fifty-yard line at the conclusion of football games.

Although players and others would sometimes join in, the Court, in *Kennedy*, still found this behavior to be private expression by the coach, distinguishing it from organized rituals where coaches lead their players in prayer while performing their official coaching duties. The broad view of what's "private," embraced by the Court's current majority, will undoubtedly create challenges for school administrators trying to determine when staff's conduct crosses the constitutional line, so consultation with legal counsel is critical before imposing any consequences on staff for religious-oriented expression.

Note: This chapter's scenario about a prayer vigil for a colleague appeared in *School Administrator* magazine well before *Kennedy* was decided. The situation addressed by our contributors was presumed to be a school-sponsored event sanctioned by the superintendent and unaffected by the *Kennedy* decision. Had the administrator who suggested the idea staged it on his own, it remains to be seen whether the federal courts would apply *Kennedy* to recognize a constitutional right to do so.

Another area that often gives rise to local school district controversy is that of speeches at graduation exercises and other ceremonial events, which can pose both establishment and free exercise clause issues if not structured thoughtfully in advance. A January 2020 guidance memo from the U.S. Department of Education summarizes the federal government's position as of that time:

> School officials may not mandate or organize prayer at graduation or select speakers for such events in a manner that favors religious speech such as prayer. Where students or other private graduation speakers are selected on the basis of genuinely content-neutral, evenhanded criteria and retain primary control over the content of their expression, however, that expression is not attributable to the school and therefore may not be restricted because of its religious (or anti-religious) content and may include prayer. To avoid any mistaken perception that a school endorses student or other private speech that is not in fact attributable to the school, school officials may make appropriate, neutral disclaimers to clarify that such speech (whether religious or nonreligious) is the speaker's and not the school's speech. (U.S. Department of Education 2020)

Such guidance documents from federal agencies don't have the force of law but do reflect their enforcement position at that point in time. Since those positions often change from one presidential administration to another, you should check for any subsequent developments.

Social media have complicated matters because so much of what goes on in our personal lives is no longer private. In a highly publicized case in New Jersey, a high school teacher with a sincerely held religious belief that homosexuality was a sin lost her job for posting a homophobic rant on her personal Facebook page protesting a Gay Pride display at her school. No one disputed her right to her opinion, but in this case the *expression* of that opinion, and the school community's awareness of it, so gravely impacted her ability to do her job effectively that the school board felt it had to terminate her.

In this chapter, our contributors offer their perspectives on handling holiday celebrations, prayer at school, and even what qualifies as a religion, and then offer food for thought to help you avoid running aground in these choppy legal and ethical waters.

CELEBRATING FAITHS OR STUDYING THEM?

Scenario: A group of parents have come to the school board to complain that the school district allows celebrations of Halloween and Día de los Muertos (Day of the Dead) but doesn't allow the schools to host any religious celebrations in connection with Christmas. The school board has a policy that schools can teach about religion but must refrain from hosting religious celebrations. The board asks the superintendent for advice on responding to the claims of religious bias.

Responses

Sheldon Berman

> The history of nations makes this truth manifest: When religion controls government, political freedom dies; and when government controls religion, religious freedom perishes.
>
> —Sam J. Ervin Jr., U.S. senator from North Carolina,
> in *The Journal of Church and State*, February 1985

As public institutions, schools can teach about religions but need to refrain from promoting or celebrating any particular religion. The separation of church and state is one of the core principles that guide our democracy and our public institutions. That principle supports the free expression of religious beliefs within our society and promotes tolerance of belief and freedom from persecution within our political system.

The concept of separation of church and state has deep roots that stretch from Roger Williams to Thomas Jefferson to modern Supreme Court decisions. In this case, the school board policy is appropriate. However, despite the simplicity of the principle of the separation of church and state, it is sometimes challenging to distinguish between religious and cultural celebrations.

Many people draw a distinction between such religious holidays as Christmas, Good Friday, Rosh Hashanah, and Eid Al-Fitr and what have come to be viewed as cultural celebrations such as Halloween, Día de los Muertos, and Valentine's Day. Others, however, view all these days as having religious connections. In fact, although Halloween and Día de los Muertos have historical roots in Celtic and Aztec traditions, they also were Christian traditions before becoming more secular in their modern celebration. Therefore, the objections of this group of people need to be heard and respected.

As a first step, it is critical to understand what the group is requesting. If the group is arguing that because schools celebrate these days, they should also celebrate Christmas, it would be important to help them understand that Christmas is clearly considered a religious, not a secular, holiday and that there is a good deal of guidance in law and policy that surrounds how schools can and should approach religious holidays. Because it may seem to this group that there is a fine line between what is considered religious and what is considered cultural, clarifying the difference between religious and cultural holidays will be important for everyone.

More important, it would be helpful to discuss why the separation of church and state is so essential to freedom of belief and religious liberty within our political structures. Some useful resources would be "Finding Common Ground" from the First Amendment Center (www.freedomforum institute.org/wp-content/uploads/2016/10/FCGcomplete.pdf) and Americans United for Separation of Church and State (www.au.org).

Alternatively, the group may be arguing that none of these days be celebrated in school because of their historical connection to religion. It will be necessary to acknowledge that while these days have some historical religious connection, as currently celebrated in schools they represent opportunities for cultural awareness or simply enjoyable traditional activities and don't involve prayer or any religious instruction.

The superintendent should advise the school board that schools may continue to celebrate these days provided they celebrate them as cultural traditions and refrain from religious instruction or religious practices. However, individuals who object to these celebrations have the right to have their child excused from discussions and activities related to these holidays or from attendance on those days. These requests should be granted.

Although the concept of separation of church and state is familiar to most people, we rarely spend time delving deeply into the roots of this concept to see the vitality it brings to freedom of religion within our society and tolerance for diversity within our political system. This group's presentation to the school board presents an opportunity to refresh parents' and staff's understanding of the reasons this concept is so vital.

At least two Supreme Court justices, Felix Frankfurter and Hugo Black, made profound statements that reveal the importance of this Constitutional principle. Their words may be useful in communicating both the essential reasons for the principle and the longstanding tradition it has throughout our nation's history.

> The nonsectarian or secular public school was the means of reconciling freedom in general with religious freedom. The sharp confinement of the public schools to secular education was a recognition of the need of a democratic society to educate its children, insofar as the state undertook to do so, in an atmosphere free from pressures in a realm in which pressures are most resisted and where conflicts are most easily and most bitterly engendered. Designed to serve as perhaps the most powerful agency for promoting cohesion among a heterogeneous

democratic people, the public school must keep scrupulously free from entanglement in the strife of sects. (Justice Felix Frankfurter, U.S. Supreme Court, in *McCollum v. Board of Education*, 1948)

By the time of the adoption of the Constitution, our history shows that there was widespread awareness among many Americans of the dangers of a union of Church and State. These people knew, some of them from bitter personal experience, that one of the greatest dangers to the freedom of the individual to worship in his own way lay in the Government's placing its official stamp of approval upon one particular kind of prayer or one particular form of religious service.... The First Amendment was added to the Constitution to stand as a guarantee that neither the power nor the prestige of the Federal Government would be used to control, support or influence the kinds of prayer the American people can say— that the people's religions must not be subjected to the pressures of government for change each time a new political administration is elected to office. (Justice Hugo Black, U.S. Supreme Court, in *Engel v. Vitale*, 1962)

Sarah Mackenzie

No matter what the school population, it is important to consider the distinction made by the First Amendment Center (www.firstamendmentcenter .org). There is a "legal bright line between teaching about religious holidays, which is permissible under the First Amendment, and celebrating a religious holiday, which isn't." And in policy, this is what this school system is doing. Teachers or school leaders, though, may not be clear about the difference between studying about a religion or religious practice and celebrating it.

Learning about Día de los Muertos could involve making and displaying face masks, sampling specific foods, or hearing music associated with the holiday. However, role-playing the day's traditional religious procession would not be acceptable.

The board's role in this situation is to make sure the school system follows its policies, so it behooves the superintendent to examine related curriculum and remind all teachers of the guidelines provided by the First Amendment Center about studying religion in public schools. Furthermore, the superintendent can emphasize that it can be acceptable and appropriate for students to learn about the holidays and traditions of various religions as part of music, art, or social studies classes, for example. The point is to make certain that such study is in keeping with the curriculum and provides accurate information.

A FAITH-FUELED OPT-OUT

Scenario: With the first round of Common Core testing approaching, some parents in the school district are opting out their children. The state's regulations allow parents to do so based on disability and religion. However, these parents contend any set of beliefs can be construed as religious and have dared the district to reject their application, threatening to litigate. The state defers these decisions to the school district. The board asks the superintendent to articulate the basis on which the district should decide a religious-based objection.

Responses

Sarah Mackenzie

In spite of initial widespread support for the Common Core, the testing programs associated with it have generated controversy. The tension between federal government expectations and states' implementation of the Common Core and assessments associated with it has produced a variety of responses—in this case, parents' ability to have their children released from taking the tests. Some states have not dealt with the question; others have allowed parents to opt out for any reason, while a few have imposed parameters on parents' ability to opt out.

By deferring the decision to individual school districts, this state is indicating its unwillingness to take a stand even if the state itself established parameters for decision making. It would seem that individual school systems and their boards have been given carte blanche to decide for themselves how to approach policymaking on this issue.

Considering the difficulty of deciding what is truly a religious belief, it would behoove the superintendent to suggest a decision rule that is very liberal. Any parent who articulates an objection on religious grounds has no obligation to explain the objection any further, and the voicing of an objection provides sufficient grounds to grant the opt out.

Sheldon Berman

A religious exemption should be founded on a sincerely held religious belief, as opposed to a personal, political or sociological belief. However, if parents cite religious reasons for their decision to opt their student out of state testing, it is not appropriate or feasible for a district to make a judgment about whether their beliefs meet that standard.

Across the country, resistance to state testing has been growing based on sincere concerns about the assessments' value in terms of the information they provide, their impact on the overall structure and nature of the curriculum, and the time required for preparation and administration. Opting out of state testing is a way to express that opposition.

A far more appropriate avenue for dissent would be to take these concerns to the state board of education and to state legislators with a proposal for a better or more balanced system of assessment. However, parents and students with serious concerns not based on religion may believe that the religious exemption is their only viable means of calling attention to their views.

Required participation in statewide assessments has several purposes. It enables schools to consistently track individual students' learning progress across time. It allows comparisons of learning progress between groups of students, helping us to identify and work to address achievement gaps. Finally, it facilitates comparisons of student performance between schools and districts and between different states.

Schools, districts, and states can use the resulting data to improve educational programs and design interventions to ensure students make steady progress toward being college and career ready. Statewide assessment systems are not perfect. Yet, to serve their intended purposes, they must be administered fairly, thoroughly, consistently, and equitably.

By opting out in significant numbers, parents undermine the credibility of the student achievement and school accountability data gathered, reduce the value of information gained from these assessments, and limit educators' and the public's ability to know how students' learning compares with that of other districts and states. Of particular concern are the inequities that opting out could introduce or exacerbate.

If assessments are not administered consistently to all students, the real and persistent achievement and opportunity gaps our students experience could be artificially masked, thus reducing the impetus and the ability to address these gaps. Even worse, schools desiring to enhance their achievement scores could counsel students who are performing at less than proficient levels to opt out of testing, suggesting that the stress of the test and the potential damage to students' self-concept make opting out a beneficial choice.

These threats to equity prompted, in part, the federal standard for participation in assessments and the sanctions against schools and districts violating that standard.

In this case, the state has abrogated its responsibility to clearly delineate criteria for opting out. Although a determination of disability may be unambiguous, districts lack the expertise to make a decision about whether someone's religious beliefs are sufficient to justify a religious exemption.

To seek expertise from the clergy would be difficult given the diversity of religious beliefs present in our society, as well as what may be considered acceptable as religious belief in a court of law. While articulating the positive reasons for participating in the state assessment and defining as best it can the boundaries of a religious exemption, the district needs to leave the final decision to the integrity of parents.

To help parents make a fair determination, the district could develop a document that informs parents of the nature and purposes of the assessment; the benefits of the assessment for the student, parent, school, and district; the justifiable reasons for opting out; and the potential negative consequences to the school based on state and federal regulations.

Such a document would make clear that a disability exemption is allowable for students who have IDEA-identified disabilities that interfere with their ability to participate in standardized testing, even with accommodations. It would also clarify that the religious exemption is allowable for students whose parents' sincerely held religious beliefs cause them to be opposed to state testing. It should indicate that merely wishing to avoid testing does not justify exemption; nor does having a political, personal, or sociological objection to testing that is not based on a sincerely held religious belief.

The exemption form could even ask the parents to acknowledge that they understand the allowable reasons for the exemption and the consequences that opting out may have on the student, school, and district. However, while providing that guidance, the district will need to leave the final determination to the parents, knowing that some will make that decision based on reasons other than religion.

Many parents understand the value that statewide assessments offer. Depending on the numbers of individuals choosing to opt out, the superintendent could also recommend that the board ask its legislative delegation to spearhead a dialogue on the role, design, value, and impact of the current assessment system, and clarify definitive participation criteria that districts can implement.

PRAYING FOR A COLLEAGUE

> Scenario: The principal of a high school in South Carolina asked to hold a prayer vigil on the school's campus at 7 a.m. on the day after the death of a faculty member who was prominent throughout the community. The superintendent acknowledged the public prayers infringed on the Constitution's separation of church and state. "But in the Bible Belt," he says, "I felt like this is what was best for the staff, for that community, and it didn't involve students. In this case, you're on shaky ground but then you have to let your personal beliefs come into play." Should the administrators have acted differently?

As noted in the introduction to this chapter, the U.S. Supreme Court's *Kennedy* decision in June 2022 changed the legal ground rules for distinguishing religious expression that is purely private versus reasonably perceived as endorsed by the school district. The following discussion presumes that the prayer vigil was an official school-sponsored activity.

Responses

Sheldon Berman

The actions taken by the principal and superintendent were in direct conflict with what they should be modeling for the community. While a vigil or non-sectarian memorial service might have been appropriate to help the school staff and community mourn the faculty member, the introduction of prayer and religion was antithetical to the administrators' roles as school leaders.

Their actions constituted a state-sponsored exercise of religion on state property. Their recognition that the community's dominant culture is a religious one made it even more important that they protect the religious liberty of others and the non-sectarian role of public education by pursuing a non-sectarian approach to honoring this individual.

That the vigil was to occur prior to school and not involve students is irrelevant. As school leaders, the administrators hold the authority and responsibility to ensure and protect the rights of all individuals.

If they felt that a prayer vigil was the most appropriate way to honor this individual, it should have been scheduled at a religious or private institution and not sponsored by the school district. Their gut instinct that this activity was an infringement on the Constitution's separation of church and state should have overcome their personal beliefs and led them to find a different way of showing respect for someone who taught students of all creeds and faiths.

Opening the schoolhouse doors to a religious observance sets a precedent that schools are a public space for religious observations by any group, even one that may be offensive to the community. Unlike the rental of space to religious organizations, which may be allowable under school board policy, once the door is opened to administrator-sanctioned religious observance it is difficult to close.

As leaders for students, staff, and the community, the principal and superintendent are responsible for creating a safe space for individuals of all faiths as well as atheists. The separation of church and state is one of the core principles that guide our democracy and our public institutions. Approving this vigil undermined the school leaders' authority to uphold the Constitution.

Maggie Lopez

The administrators should have made a different choice. Though it is fully understood that there was a need to comfort the grieving faculty and community, there were other options. The prayer vigil could have been sponsored by a parent or community member as opposed to the administration and held at a church, park, or other non-school-affiliated facility close to the school.

This would have provided an opportunity to still honor the faculty member, without it being school-sponsored and "infringing on the Constitution" as the superintendent acknowledged.

The superintendent's assumption that students will not attend is of concern. If the vigil is held as stated here, what will happen to students who hear about the vigil and show up to honor their teacher? Will they be turned away? This is another good reason to have the vigil non-school sponsored so that if students do show up, they too can participate without the principal or superintendent having to worry about potential conflicts.

As district leaders, we must solve problems with our head and heart. Our students, community, and staff are watching to see how we solve life crises when they arise. We need to be good role models.

SERMONIZING FOR THE ASSEMBLED

Scenario: For years, a local church minister, who has been a strong supporter of the public schools, had a speaking role at student recognition assembly programs in the local school district. When the new superintendent attended one of these programs during her first year, she discovered the pastor clearly was crossing the line in his message from the podium involving separation between state and church. Though the pastor had good intentions, the superintendent was left wondering how to proceed.

Responses

Meira Levinson

The superintendent should build on the pastor's good intentions by helping him understand the constitutional barriers to publicly sponsored religious speech and the risk to which he is exposing the district by invoking religion in these assemblies.

She can begin by expressing gratitude for his long-standing support for the public schools and his ongoing participation in recognizing student achievement. Then she can inquire as to how he chooses what to speak about and whether he's aware both of local students' and families' religious diversity and of strictures against religious speech. Working together, they can craft a message that is more appropriate and within constitutional bounds.

To avoid backlash, the new superintendent would be well advised to line up allies early in the process. She might reach out to school board members first.

Sheldon Berman

Although the pastor had good intentions and is a strong supporter of the public schools, the superintendent has a responsibility to ensure his presentation doesn't introduce either prayer or religion in a way that violates the separation of church and state. The introduction of prayer or religion in the student recognition assembly can constitute a state-sponsored exercise of religion at a school event.

That the pastor's speech may represent the dominant religious culture of the community and appear acceptable to many makes it even more important that the superintendent protect the religious liberty of others and the non-sectarian role of public education by pursuing a non-sectarian approach to honoring student achievement.

It is the responsibility of the superintendent to ensure and protect the rights and religious liberty of all individuals. Her perception that the pastor's speech was an infringement on the Constitution's separation of church and state should be sufficient to open a conversation about this with the pastor and her school board and change the program for future assemblies so that other community leaders, including religious leaders representing different faiths, offer their remarks in a non-sectarian way.

As a leader for students, staff, and the community, the superintendent is responsible for creating a safe space for individuals of all faiths as well as atheists. The separation of church and state is one of the core principles that guide our democracy and our public institutions. Even though the minister's speech may seem innocuous to many, it undermines the authority vested in school leaders to uphold the Constitution.

A YEARBOOK REVELATION

Scenario: A teacher of a popular comparative religion elective at the high school asks the school yearbook staff to avoid referencing the distinctive final project, which requires students to create their own religion. Some creative faiths reflect students' obsessions with sunflower seeds, chewing gum and makeup. The teacher fears criticism by other staff for the project's supposed "heresy" and shutdown of the course. She asks the principal to prevent the course's inclusion. The principal asks the superintendent for advice.

Responses

Sarah Mackenzie

This teacher may be making too much of the possibility that other teachers' criticisms would lead to the course being shut down. The principal should quell her fears and let her know he will stand by her if there are criticisms.

Other teachers may react to the showcasing of this assignment less as heresy. Rather, they may fear highlighting the results of this assignment could incite some kind of reaction from parents or other stakeholders. An inquiry into this course and the assignment could lead to investigations of the curriculum and assignments in other areas.

The principal should discuss with the superintendent and other district-level staff the process for complaints regarding curriculum and assessment. Just as there are policies in place for complaints about readings being assigned by teachers or books and materials available in school libraries, there should be policies established for other kinds of complaints regarding curriculum and assignments generally.

Sheldon Berman

All public education is public. If we are uncomfortable with the public scrutiny of a classroom activity, that activity should be reviewed. It is highly appropriate and beneficial to teach about the diversity of religious beliefs in the world. However, in doing so, a teacher must expect parents, community members, and other faculty members to have a strong interest in ensuring that the course follows legal, policy, and ethical guidelines.

Teaching about religion is a particularly sensitive subject, leading districts to establish detailed policies to comply with state and federal laws and court decisions. These laws and policies have been hammered out through many years of dialogue and debate among individuals with conflicting positions. This extended dialogue has culminated in the development of a well-defined common ground that enables most members of the public to feel schools are acting in a responsible manner when it comes to religion.

The teacher in this case needs to understand the boundaries within which she is working and be ready and able to defend the learning targets, instructional activities, assigned work, and assessments involved in the course. This course should be held to the same expectations as any other course in the school. The principal also must be ready and able to stand behind any course he has approved for inclusion in the instructional program of the school, whether that approval is through his own discretion or through a school or district curriculum policy council.

Attempting to hide the course by not including it in the yearbook would signal that it has not met school and district standards. If the course standards, learning targets and rubrics are academically appropriate and enable students to demonstrate their understandings of religious belief systems, they should be defensible publicly and not require veiling from scrutiny.

While aspects of some students' projects may seem fanciful, those projects could indeed be designed to correspond to the recognized elements of a religion, including the ritual, emotional, narrative, legal/ethical, doctrinal/philosophical, and social/institutional components.

By incorporating what appears to be a far-fetched idea (such as sunflower seeds), a student encourages his peers to momentarily suspend their traditional belief systems and examine the project's elements in terms of what constitutes a religion. It is this ability to examine new and even different ideas thoughtfully and respectfully that fosters the tolerance of diversity.

Not only should there be no expectation that any student will change his or her own personal beliefs, but the course should also be openly geared toward helping all students recognize the commonalities and value inherent in the world's many religions.

On the other hand, if the teacher perceives that some projects have crossed accepted boundaries, she needs to determine whether her instructional goals and learning activities may have led students to trivialize or misrepresent religious principles. Accepting that responsibility and articulating course changes to prevent such misunderstandings in the future may be the only strategy to continue offering a valuable learning experience for students.

In terms of the yearbook, the course should be included in a similar manner to every other course. Just as there is a diversity of student work products for any course, there may be more appropriate pictures or final projects that could be highlighted in the yearbook that would demonstrate the value of the comparative religion course. The teacher has already spoken with the yearbook staff, which is responsible for accurate and informative reporting. This situation presents an opportunity for the students on the staff to consider how best to represent the quality of learning offered by the course.

The principal might raise this ethical issue with the student editorial board and ask that they consider it in their deliberation, but should not seek to censor what they produce. Most significant, the principal needs to work with the teacher to ensure the instructional targets, activities, and assessments reflect the academic outcomes she desires and to prepare materials—including a course syllabus—for parents, community members, and other faculty that assist people in understanding these academic learning targets and the instructional design of the course.

REFERENCE

U.S. Department of Education. 2020, January 16. "Guidance on Constitutionally Protected Prayer and Religious Expression in Public Elementary and Secondary Schools." www2.ed.gov/policy/gen/guid/religionandschools/prayer_guidance.html.

Chapter Five

Duty to Report or Maintain Confidentiality

A fifteen-year-old girl confides to a school psychologist that she's pregnant but doesn't want anyone to know. A male student tells the principal he identifies as female but is afraid he'll be unsafe at home if his parents find out. The superintendent is sent an unsolicited video clip of a chemistry teacher bragging to friends about snorting cocaine on a family vacation over winter recess. This chapter will examine the ethical quandary faced by school administrators torn between their duty to report, their duty of confidentiality, and their duty not to get involved in matters that are none of the school district's concern.

Often, balancing these competing duties is the ethical equivalent of a high-wire act without a net. That's because you may, in the eyes of the law, be either required or forbidden to disclose information, with no room for discretion and no time to seek guidance from others. At other times, there may be no specific legal mandate either way, but also no consensus in the field of school administration on how to exercise your discretion most appropriately.

We consider these issues against the backdrop of our society's ongoing debate over the appropriate boundary between transparency and confidentiality in taxpayer-funded government operations. The most well-known law staking out that boundary in public education is the Family Educational Rights and Privacy Act of 1974, 20 U.S.C. §1232g, (FERPA), stipulating that education records are confidential as a general rule, while guaranteeing free access to parents and others with a legitimate need to know. That statute makes information available to those entitled to it but imposes no obligation to share information that hasn't been requested.

So, when are school administrators under an affirmative duty to share facts or evidence necessary to protect others' legitimate interests? Federal and state laws provide some guidance. For example, on the federal level the Child

Abuse Prevention and Treatment Act, 42 U.S.C. §§5101-5106a, requires states and U.S. territories to implement reporting procedures for suspected child abuse and neglect. These procedures typically identify the individuals and institutions required to make those reports, the information that must be shared, and the extent of confidentiality or even legal immunity for those who step forward.

Some states also have laws requiring cooperation and information-sharing between school districts and local law enforcement agencies. FERPA limits what school officials can share with the police about students absent an emergency, but state laws often mandate reporting of certain criminal activity by students or staff.

Reporting obligations also can arise from court decisions or ethical codes adopted by professional governing bodies. Mental health clinicians are familiar with the so-called *"Tarasoff* rule," based on the landmark California Supreme Court case of *Tarasoff v. Regents of the University of California*, 17 Cal.3d 425 (1976), where the court held that a psychotherapist had a duty to warn of a patient's intention to commit murder.

The premise of the *Tarasoff* rule is that professionals who normally owe a duty of confidentiality may have a superseding obligation to warn others facing the risk of imminent harm. Courts and legislatures across the country have adopted some version of the *Tarasoff* rule, though the balance between confidentiality and disclosure may be drawn differently from one jurisdiction to another.

School nurses, counselors, psychologists, social workers, and others performing therapeutic functions in the school setting all have some "duty to warn," but the extent of those duties may vary from one position to another because the confidentiality expectations are different for each of those professions. These obligations extend in some fashion to other school staff as well, but you should consult with your district's legal counsel on the legal standards that apply locally.

Superintendents and other high-ranking school administrators don't perform counseling functions and usually aren't the ones who receive sensitive information about students or staff in the first instance. Most often it is passed up the chain of command or provided by others outside the school community. What are your ethical obligations when it lands on your desk?

As we discussed in the book's introduction, if there's no statute or regulation explicitly spelling out your obligations, the courts in many jurisdictions will apply the reasonableness test, judging your behavior against the standards to be expected of a reasonably prudent school administrator in the community you serve. Expert testimony may be required to explain what would have been expected of you under all the attendant circumstances.

You'll also need to consider how much information you can share with the community in high-profile situations without violating legal confidentiality restrictions. We will address this matter later, in the Student Discipline chapter, and the same ground rules apply here.

At a minimum, school administrators have an ethical responsibility to warn of the likelihood of imminent physical harm to staff or students, even to the point of reporting to law enforcement or child welfare agencies. That's so even if the potentially violent individual had a reasonable expectation of confidentiality.

Those are the easy cases. The thought-provoking scenarios addressed in this chapter aren't as clear-cut but should help you think your way through to the correct response when the law doesn't dictate it for you.

A TICKING CLOCK ON ATTIRE

Scenario: The assistant middle school principal is shown by a former student a TikTok video of a high school freshman doing a sexual dance in revealing attire, apparently a regular occurrence on her social media. He knew the student had an unstable home life during the previous several years but doesn't know the details. The assistant principal wrestles with showing the video to the student's high school counselor, thinking the student may need help.

Responses

Maggie Lopez

The assistant principal needs to share the information with his principal and let him or her know he will be informing the counselor/administration at the high school. This is the best way to help this student who is a minor engaging in sexually explicit behaviors on social media that have now become part of his/her digital footprint.

Does the student even realize this? Could this be connected to a background of potential child abuse or endangerment? Is this minor doing this of her own accord or is she being encouraged by others? These are just a few of the questions that arise in contemplating this scenario, which is further complicated by the fact that the student has been identified as at-risk in the past.

There should be district policy/protocol for the high school staff to access as to when they address the behavior first with the student. The fact there was speculation by the middle school for several years that the student has an unstable home life will need to be considered when deciding how to inform the family.

This behavior is akin to sexting as it is of a sexual nature acted out online, in this case by a minor. The fact this has been ongoing for several TikTok sessions makes one wonder whether the student is seeking attention or help. Boundaries have been crossed for appropriate use of social media, and the behavior exhibited indicates potentially deeper underlying issues that should be addressed. It is apparently not a one-time occurrence and for a minor, whether at risk or not, it is a red flag.

The school's administration and the counselor may have caught the student in time to redirect what appear to be self-destructive behaviors that could permanently impact the student in a negative way.

MaryEllen Elia

It's the responsibility of every education leader to concern themselves with the mental health and well-being of all students within the organization, not just within their building's four walls. For this reason, the assistant middle school principal cannot just let this go. Too often kids don't fully understand the indelible nature of what gets posted online and how this can ultimately follow (and haunt) them into adulthood.

The right thing would be to contact the high school guidance counselor and explain the situation and potential complicating factors. The high school counselor hopefully has an existing relationship or rapport with this student, but if not, this is an opportunity to begin one.

Because the student is a freshman, this could be a chance for the student to form a meaningful relationship with a trusted adult within the school that will offer stability and guidance for the next several years. The counselor also would be wise to reach out to the middle school guidance counselor to obtain any relevant information that might help him/her better understand the student. Because the objective is not judgment, shame, or punishment, the counselor must connect with the student out of genuine care and concern and approach the situation supportively.

POST-GAME HISTRIONICS

Scenario: A longtime teacher runs onto the playing field following a high school football game to confront the head coach about what he viewed as his aggressive conduct toward his son, a junior on the team. The principal and two assistant coaches witness the profanity-laced remarks that nearly result in fisticuffs between the parent and coach. The principal steps in and asks the parent to leave the field. The teacher works in another school district. Should his actions be reported to his district's administrators?

Responses

Mario Ventura

Actual or perceived aggression toward one's child could easily push a parent over the edge causing a parent to react with hostility. In this situation, the teacher is not representing his district in an official capacity, so should not be reported to the district that employs him.

The coach's supervisor should reach out to the parent to better understand what happened between the coach and the player. The supervisor should remind the parent about protocols and procedures for reporting the abuse. The parent also should be reminded of policy in place to protect district staff from abusive language, threats, and bodily harm. Continued behavior such as this could lead toward legal action.

Both the parent and the coach should consider how their behavior could be perceived as unprofessional. Although the parent was not in an official school capacity, the community still sees him in the role of a teacher. Their public display of inappropriate behavior could have a negative impact on their reputation as educators.

Sheldon Berman

Spectators, including parents and members of the community, have a responsibility to be respectful and appropriate. The explosive conduct on the part of this parent was unacceptable, and even more so because as a teacher he should have known how to demonstrate restraint. Teachers are held to a higher standard of public behavior because their actions are expected to model appropriate behavior for students. This conduct could be considered an assault on the coach and, had the principal not stepped in, it could have led to a charge of battery as well.

The parent may have a valid complaint about the conduct of the coach toward his son, but that doesn't excuse confronting the coach on the field after the game or the offensive way he attacked the coach. The principal should insist that the parent meet privately with him to discuss the parent's actions, hear the parent's complaint, and decide whether the parent will be admitted to future games. Given the public nature of the conduct, the principal should encourage the teacher to inform his principal of the incident so that his principal doesn't learn of it from a third party.

The coach's argumentative response may have aggravated rather than defused the situation. The principal should meet with the coach to learn of any prior history with this parent or any circumstances that have emerged with the parent's son. The principal should discuss with the coach how his response may have served to escalate the situation and suggest ways he might have responded to de-escalate the confrontation.

To determine whether there is any substance to the parent's complaint, the principal should investigate the coach's treatment of the student athlete. Based on the coach's professional history and the circumstances of this episode, the principal may need to document the incident and issue a warning or reprimand.

Whether the principal should contact the teacher's principal is a judgment call. For three reasons, it may be better to err on the side of not making the contact. First, although the confrontation was inappropriate, there is not a clear nexus between the teacher's behavior as a parent and his work as a teacher. Second, while the verbal attack was troubling, it was neither criminal nor sufficiently egregious in nature to warrant notifying his employer. Third, the coach's behavior may have fueled the conflict, thereby creating a shared responsibility for the escalation of the argument.

Incidents of this nature are deterred by providing clear guidance on parent behavior in handbooks that student athletes and parents must sign, by requiring meetings with all parents and athletes prior to the season to review the rules related to respectful behavior and the consequences for violations, and by training coaches in how to respond to parent issues and how to de-escalate potential conflicts.

Coaches and parents must remember that high school athletics should focus more on supporting the development of each athlete's skills and character than on simply winning. Respect and sportsmanship are among the primary lessons that participation in high school or youth sports should teach to all.

VACCINATION RUMORS

Scenario: A school district employee hears about several acquaintances who are refusing to vaccinate their school-age children, fearing supposedly harmful side effects. They mention getting faked doctors' forms to enroll their children in their public schools. Does the district employee have a duty to report what he has heard to the respective school districts?

Responses

Sheldon Berman

All states have enacted laws requiring specific vaccinations for school children. These laws are intended to achieve an immunity level that limits the outbreak and spread of serious, preventable diseases among community members. However, most states also allow exemptions for medical, religious, or even philosophical reasons. The implication of an exemption is that when there is an outbreak, the unvaccinated child is more likely to be excluded from school for a period of time to protect both that child and other children who may be susceptible.

Therefore, it is likely that these parents do not need to engage in fraud in order to have their children exempted from vaccination. The first step the district employee should take is to inform the acquaintances that they can secure an exemption. If they choose to submit a fraudulent doctor's certification instead, the individual has both an ethical and legal responsibility to let the respective districts know.

The knowledge that a fraud is potentially being perpetrated on these districts makes the individual complicit with an illegal action if he or she doesn't report it. The issue is not whether the legal requirement of vaccination is good or bad. Submitting a false certificate is a clear violation of the law.

However, there are also ethical implications. Not informing the district leaves children and staff in the district more vulnerable to the spread of contagious and preventable diseases. The district's awareness of children who have been identified as unvaccinated enables the district to respond in a way that best protects all students and employees if an outbreak occurs.

Although the district employee may feel that reporting this illegal activity to the respective school districts could compromise his relationship with the acquaintances, their willingness to engage in fraudulent actions that endanger other students should be an overriding ethical concern that moves him to act.

Maggie Lopez

The school district employee should talk to his supervisor and get guidance regarding what next steps to take. What are the applicable state policies, district policies or federal laws and reporting requirements? With whom does he share what he knows?

Although the information he heard was "off the clock," what the acquaintances told him has implications for student safety. A measles outbreak at the children's schools, while the schools are under the impression all students are safe from infection, would potentially put students at risk.

This is a moral dilemma for the employee who is being forced to choose between his friends and his obligations as a district employee who serves students. He is in possession of knowledge that could result in harm coming to students. Beyond his liability is his responsibility to kids in and out of school.

In wanting to solve one problem (by refusing to vaccinate their children), these parents have potentially created health problems for their own children and their schools.

TATTLING ON TRUANT PEERS

Scenario: A central-office administrator learns through her teenage son, confidentially, that his two closest friends, who attend school in a neighboring district, had skipped school three times in recent weeks to play video games while parents were working elsewhere. The administrator sits with the information but wonders whether to contact the two boys' parents or someone at their high school.

Responses

Sheldon Berman

Each district has a system for tracking attendance and class participation. Although tracking is harder in remote classes, it is still the responsibility of teachers and school administrators to be cognizant of absences and students cutting classes. The friends' school should be the one contacting the boys' parents about their absences. As this is not a health, safety or endangerment issue, the administrator should respect the confidentiality requested by her son and not contact the other district.

However, the administrator could thank her son for trusting her with the information and applaud him for recognizing how problematic his friends' behavior is. She also could engage him in a conversation about how he could talk with his friends about the risks they are taking and the impact those missed classes might have.

In casual conversation with the boys' parents, she might also mention that parents have had to develop new strategies and assume some responsibility for monitoring their adolescents' remote participation—without divulging that she is aware of their sons' reported behavior and without casting suspicion on her own son as a source of information.

Glenn "Max" McGee

Of the many lessons remote learning has taught us, one of the most important is the power of relationships and the need to preserve them. Teachers have learned their virtual lessons will be tuned out if they cannot connect with each individual student, and parents have learned the more isolated their kids are, the more their (the kids' and the parents') mental health is at risk.

The administrator is first a mother and second a district office leader, and she needs to respect the confidentiality of her son. In fact, parents of many, arguably most, teenage boys are envious that a son would confide in his mom at all! She should let her neighboring district police its own students. She should not contact the parents, and she should let her own son know how much she values that he is engaged in his remote learning classes and deeply appreciates his choice not to blow off classes to play video games.

A CONFIDENTIALITY PLEDGE

> Scenario: A recently retired superintendent now works on education research at the nearby state university. He is reviewing papers submitted by former graduate students, all of them now employed by his former district as teachers and professional staff. He has promised them confidentiality in using their work. He discovers one paper has been plagiarized. Should the retired superintendent report his discovery to the graduate studies chair without revealing the student's name to keep his promise?

Responses

Sarah Jerome

When students enter the university, they are expected to pledge they will not cheat or plagiarize the work of others. Based on that pledge, the professor has a responsibility to report plagiarism to the chair and to name the student involved. It does not matter what the professor's past role was nor does it matter that the plagiarizer is employed by the professor's previous school district nor does it matter that the professor promised confidentiality.

The essential issue is the errant student's stealing someone else's ideas without giving proper credit or recognition to the creator of those ideas. That student has broken a pledge to the university. The professor has an obligation to the university to reveal his discovery.

Sheldon Berman

Plagiarism is a fundamental violation of academic integrity. All educators, no matter their position, serve as role models for their students and are held to a high standard of academic integrity. When an educator plagiarizes another's work, the consequences can be severe, sometimes even costing the individual his or her job.

Universities also have severe punishments for plagiarism that can extend from disciplinary probation and a failing grade in a course to expulsion from the university. An incident of plagiarism is sometimes noted on a student's permanent transcript and has lifelong impact on that individual's future opportunities.

The retired superintendent's pledge of confidentiality pertained to the use of the individual's work, not to remaining silent in the face of a violation of academic ethics. The superintendent needs to review the university's official policy on plagiarism and determine how best to proceed. As part of this process, he needs to relay his concern to the individual and follow the university's prescribed reporting procedures. As a graduate student and an educator, the individual who plagiarized should have known the responsibility to meet the ethical standards and integrity of that role and the seriousness with which this violation would be treated.

PLAGIARIZER FROM HER PAST

Scenario: The district's deputy superintendent receives a call from a college student she knows from her principal days. The collegian says a friend lifted for her own use without credit part of a document the deputy superintendent wrote years ago that now resides on the deputy superintendent's personal web page. The college student believes her friend will be expelled if the professor discovers the original document and begs the deputy to remove the paper from her website to prevent her friend's academic career from being ruined. What should the deputy superintendent do?

Responses

Meira Levinson

The deputy superintendent should explain to the college student that her responsibility is to help her friend learn how to meet academic and ethical standards, including standards for academic integrity, not to help her friend avoid detection for plagiarism.

Saving the student from detection in this particular assignment is not called for, as it will likely simply embolden the student to appropriate others' work in the future. Better that she get caught now, early in her academic career, than later in college, graduate school, or professional life. Furthermore, automated plagiarism detection programs keep archived and current websites in their databases. If the professor uses such a program, it is highly likely that the student's malfeasance will be discovered whether or not the deputy superintendent has removed the original document from her website.

But the more important considerations are not about the likelihood and consequences of the student's getting caught. Rather, they are about both college students' understanding and development of academic integrity. The deputy superintendent's former student needs to learn that her own integrity is at stake if she tries to alter the published record to protect her friend.

A more responsible approach is to help her friend own up to her mistake and negotiate a consequence (ideally short of expulsion) with the professor or the college administration. The friend needs to learn that plagiarism is a form of intellectual theft; just as she would presumably not burgle a house or engage in identity theft to solve a problem that is stressing her out, nor should she plagiarize others' work to get a paper done in time.

Furthermore, both young women will likely learn that their college offers more support than they expected; many colleges take a developmental approach to a student's first academic violation, especially when they are honest about their mistake, as they recognize that students are still learning and growing.

Sheldon Berman

This presents a great opportunity for the deputy superintendent to provide advice on ethics to both the collegian and her friend. It is inappropriate to ask the deputy superintendent to remove a document from her web page in order protect the student's friend from the consequences of plagiarism. To comply with this request would make the deputy superintendent complicit with—and, in effect, endorse—the friend's plagiarism, compromising both parties. Given that material remains on the internet somewhere, it is possible that a search could reveal this plagiarism, even if the document is no longer on the original website.

Instead of agreeing to this request, the deputy superintendent should recommend that the student advise her friend to acknowledge to her professor that she mistakenly didn't provide credit for a section that was quoted from another document. Being proactive in admitting the mistake may reduce the consequences resulting from the plagiarism and would demonstrate both honesty and integrity.

Everyone makes mistakes; it is best to admit and address them rather than try to cover them up with distortions that may come to light later. Even if there are consequences for the student, doing the right thing results in feeling good about one's morals and one's sense of self. If the deputy superintendent can guide her previous student in understanding the ethical dimensions of this situation, she can potentially help both students learn a life lesson from this experience.

INTERCEPTED COMMUNICATION

Scenario: The superintendent/principal of a small rural district in the upper Midwest relies on his skilled and dedicated teachers to provide a top-flight education to students. One morning, he receives a voicemail message intended for one of the teachers from a staffing firm that suggests she may be seeking a new position. The superintendent wants to do everything possible to retain her and wonders if it's appropriate to broach the subject, having intercepted the call intended for the teacher.

Responses

MaryEllen Elia

We all know that the greatest asset a school district has are the teachers who work to provide success every day for their students. That is why this superintendent/principal would feel disheartened by the thought that one of the high-quality teachers might be leaving.

The administrator should approach the teacher in an upfront and truthful way—explaining how he got the message and how it disturbed him. This provides a great opportunity to find out what is precipitating the possible move, give feedback on the teacher's great performance and share his sincere feelings about the potential loss to the students.

The school leader might be able to suggest some changes or additional supports the teacher might want that could possibly influence her consideration to depart for a job elsewhere. Regardless of the reason for a possible move, everyone loves to feel valued.

Sheldon Berman:

Honesty is the best policy. Given that the superintendent received the voicemail in error, it's best that he let the teacher know the staffing firm left a message that implied she may be seeking another position.

His approach should focus on affirming and supporting her interests or concerns rather than attempting to convince her to stay. He should let her know that he appreciates her talents and skills and wants to support her professional growth. He also should convey that he respects any decision she may be making for personal or family reasons. He can offer to talk with her about directions that she is interested in pursuing and concerns she may have about her current situation to see if those interests or concerns can be accommodated within the district. He can also offer to provide her with a letter of reference if she wishes to pursue positions elsewhere.

Such a demonstration of positive support could mean a great deal to her, while signifying to others who know of her situation that the district is a caring community that is invested in the professional aspirations and interests of its employees. If the district can support her or address her concerns, such actions would represent the best way to encourage her to remain with the district rather than pursue a position elsewhere.

THE WAYWARD COMPLAINT

Scenario: The superintendent receives a lengthy e-mail accidentally sent from a clerk in the district. The message, intended for the clerk's sister with a similar name, complains about not getting a job transfer she had requested in the district. It complains about co-workers by name, their behaviors and perceptions of their poor work ethic and mentions possibly filing a grievance about the transfer process. In quick order, the superintendent receives a second e-mail from the disgruntled clerk apologizing and begging her to disregard the first message. Should the superintendent do as requested, or does she have a duty to address the matter raised?

Responses

Glenn "Max" McGee

Autofill is full of perils! While the Golden Rule should rule the day because there surely will be a time (or there has been a time) when the superintendent will want to recall a message owing to an autofill error, the superintendent cannot disregard the message.

As superintendent, she and all district employees are bound by school board policy, so she should turn over the e-mail to the human resources department to determine whether a violation of the district's acceptable use policy, civility policy, or any similar policy has taken place. The superintendent also should meet with the clerk in her workspace to explain the actions being taken and to encourage the clerk to discuss her concern face-to-face with her supervisor and/or union representative. Finally, the superintendent should toggle off her own autofill and show the clerk how to do the same.

Sheldon Berman

Once known, it's best the issues raised in the e-mail be addressed directly. People who are dissatisfied with their working conditions and their co-workers won't experience satisfaction in their jobs and won't create a healthy work environment for others. To address the issue, the superintendent should respond by expressing concern about the employee's dissatisfaction and indicate that she is forwarding the original e-mail to the person's supervisor so the two of them can discuss what might be done to improve the situation.

The superintendent also should remind the employee that district e-mail is a public record, at least in many states, and that this message can't simply be withdrawn and erased. Anyone interested in her communication could access it. If it was sent from a work e-mail address, this matter is more problematic since she should not be using work e-mail or work time for personal purposes.

If the employee is responsible and effective in her job as a clerk, this error presents an opportunity to initiate a problem-solving dialogue with her supervisor about how to improve the current work situation, perhaps leading to positive change. However, if the complaints she presents represent her own negative attitude toward her fellow employees and the district in general, this would be a good opportunity to either facilitate a transfer or to have her find another work situation outside the district. In either case, it is better that she confront the issues directly rather than remain disgruntled, which impacts the quality of her life and of others around her.

SNOOPING AT A SCREEN

> Scenario: When the middle school principal drops off a memo on the assistant superintendent's desk, she glances, inadvertently she claims, at his computer screen and notices her name. It appears in an e-mail to the superintendent blaming the failure of a recent initiative on her. The principal considers that an overstatement but wonders how to defend herself without admitting to the inadvertent e-mail read.

Responses

Maggie Lopez

It would be difficult for the principal to defend herself without admitting to the assistant superintendent what happened. If the principal believes it is essential to talk to the assistant superintendent regarding his perceived overstatement in the e-mail, then she'll need to admit to having read the e-mail.

Reading the email has placed her in a highly precarious situation because to address the concern over the e-mail, the principal also must admit she crossed a line of confidentiality. This may leave the assistant superintendent wondering about the principal's professionalism.

The principal preferably might wait to see if the issue is brought up to her by either the assistant superintendent or superintendent, at which time she can state her side of the story regarding the initiative. Whether inadvertent or not, her snooping may have provided her with information she wasn't aware of, but it also put her in a position that has given her little option to respond or defend herself without creating further questions from her superiors about her judgement or lack thereof.

Meira Levinson

Whether it was inadvertent that she noticed her name on the computer screen, she could not have inadvertently read the entire e-mail message. That takes intent. The middle school principal thus has two choices.

She can apologize to the assistant superintendent for violating his privacy by reading the e-mail on his computer screen and then explain why she believes she should not be held primarily at fault for the failed initiative. This is awkward but the most honest and transparent approach. Or she can remain mum but be attentive to comments from anyone who may have received the e-mail and explain her perspective on the initiative's failure when it comes up in conversation.

Finally, because it sounds as if the principal acknowledges that she bears some responsibility even if not the entire blame for the initiative's failure, she may wish to be proactive in developing a new approach. That might mean creating a proposal for a new initiative. She might be open about needing some personal professional development. For example, maybe she could ask the assistant superintendent to help her learn how to mobilize her staff around new ways of working together. Such actions may help the district leadership regain trust in her capabilities, without her having to discuss the e-mail she "inadvertently" read.

Chapter Six

Grading Practices

This chapter addresses the ethics of grading practices. The law accords school districts a large measure of deference to fashion their own grading practices, but within the bounds of the law there are still ethical issues that present themselves. The goal of this chapter is not so much to provide definitive answers as to help frame the right questions to help you think your way through to an ethical approach that reflects your district's values.

What are the ethical considerations around grades? To answer that, we must define the purpose they're intended to serve, how they're determined, how evenhandedly we apply the ground rules we've established, and what we tell the school community about those ground rules.

Whether students are locked in competition for the title of valedictorian or just trying to maintain a C average to stay on the football team, they all want to know how the teacher will be calculating their grades in a particular class. One might assume a grade reflects mastery of the subject matter, but that's not necessarily the case. As we know, many teachers consider factors having nothing to do with students' knowledge, per se.

Take, for example, awarding credit for class participation or effort, or deducting points for not turning in homework assignments. None of these factors has anything to do with how much a student knows or whether the student has mastered the material. In addition, students can try their hardest but still not learn the material because of the inaccessibility of classroom materials or teacher instruction. Meanwhile, a student with an innate math aptitude and interest may have already mastered the subject matter without even taking the course.

The problem goes beyond measures that are educationally meaningless. By reducing students' grades, or even giving a zero, for not turning in assignments on time, you're essentially imposing a disciplinary consequence. This cuts against the prevailing consensus that grades should not be used to discipline students for misbehavior; far better to require students to make up the work or otherwise drive home the importance of getting work done on time.

There also are fairness concerns about unduly emphasizing poor performance on quizzes, tests, or projects during the semester. As college basketball fans will agree, what's important is how your team is playing in March, not November. If the goal of grading is to assess a student's mastery of course material, isn't the true measure of success what the student has learned by the end of course? By assigning irreversible percentage allocations to poor grades along the way, or averaging them out, aren't we presenting an inaccurate picture of what students know or, even worse, discouraging them from learning from their mistakes?

The devil's advocate would raise the concern many have expressed about high-stakes tests generally: betting students' academic future on a one-shot assessment can be unfair to those who may just be having a bad day. This debate also implicates the longstanding controversy over the validity of the tests we use to measure mastery. Do they truly capture what the student knows, or are there baked-in biases that make them less-than-optimal measures of success? If students from one racial, ethnic, or socioeconomic group routinely perform worse on the tests we're giving, we certainly have an ethical duty to find out why.

As an alternative, the standards-based grading movement encourages schools and districts to use mastery of developmental standards as a means of providing meaningful feedback on student progress. The movement further recommends using separate accountability measures for participation or other behavioral elements the school deems important in order to provide greater clarity on students' achievement of academic standards.

Nothing brings the ethical issues in grading into sharper focus than the phenomenon of social promotion, which some detractors contend moves students along from one grade to the next simply for showing up—or, in some cases, without even showing up. Proponents claim it's beneficial for students' well-being and development to be with one's age cohort. They argue that variability is the norm in relation to student progress and that teachers need to personalize instruction and build from students' current level of skill development. Detractors claim it's a short-term high that destroys students' self-esteem once they emerge from school into the real world.

As we noted in the chapter on equal treatment, the law generally requires that government officials and agencies treat similarly situated people alike unless there's some articulable justification to do otherwise. When it comes to grading practices, determining what's evenhanded can be open to debate.

All would agree it's unfair to raise a low grade solely to appease assertive parents. On the other hand, if a student has the self-advocacy skills to persuade a teacher to correct a truly erroneous grade, is that student being given an unfair advantage or is self-advocacy yet another factor legitimately deserving recognition in itself? Is it fair to allow students to get "extra credit" for completing additional assignments above and beyond the prescribed curriculum when a teacher knows that affluent students with more resources at home may have a built-in advantage?

What about two sections of the same course—one taught by the "hard" grader and the other by someone who is more flexible? Is it fair to assign students to sections randomly? Or is it more equitable to acknowledge one section as more rigorous than the other, give students a choice, and weight the grades in those sections accordingly? On a broader scale, in a district with multiple high schools, do parents and students perceive that work that easily earns an A at one school would be found worthy of only a B—or even less—at a more competitive school? If so, what are the ramifications for high school transcripts and college applications?

Is it equitable to give the GPAs of special needs students the same weight as general education students if those GPAs were earned with accommodations? In one highly publicized federal court case, a school district attempted to keep a special needs student from being declared valedictorian because she had various accommodations and modifications in her IEP that some in the school community felt gave her an unfair advantage. When the district proposed a policy allowing for multiple valedictorians that year, the court put a stop to it, blasting the district for denying the student an honor she'd earned playing by the district's own rules.

There are no one-size-fits-all answers to these questions. The ethical approach to what's right will turn on the same principles that guide ethical decision-making generally: fundamental fairness that reflects the values of your school community, reasonable notice to affected parties of what's expected of them, and evenhanded treatment. The cases discussed in this chapter, once again drawn from real-life scenarios, offer helpful perspectives on a wide range of grading issues you may confront in your district.

A CEILING ON GRADES

Scenario: A high school art teacher doesn't give any grade above a 96 in her studio art elective because she believes there are always opportunities for improvement. A senior consistently on the school's high honor roll believes the 96 she earned fails to reflect her hard work and accomplishment in this course, thus leaving her with a lower grade than she believes she deserves. Is this grading approach appropriate?

Responses

Meira Levinson

This grading approach is not appropriate because it fails to fulfill any of the criteria for assigning grades. Broadly speaking, grades may be calculated on the basis of students' demonstrated mastery of learning goals, improvement over time, relative achievement in comparison to others, and/or effort to master the material.

No matter how the teacher constructs her own criteria for grading, however, little justification exists for her refusing to make available to students the 97- to 100-point range that report cards could include. It is unreasonable to set maximal mastery, improvement or effort goals that are impossible for students to reach.

That said, there is some rationale for the art teacher's goal of communicating to students that there is always more work to be done—and that they should be indifferent about whether they earned a 95 versus a 99 in a studio art elective. The question is whether grades are the right mechanism to teach this life lesson.

Because grades are used to communicate not only with students and parents but also with college admissions officers, employers, and merit scholarship evaluators, the art teacher needs to consider whether there are more effective ways to teach students about the never-ending horizon of improvement than to impose an artificial ceiling on numeric grades.

Sheldon Berman

Many problems exist with our grading and assessment systems, particularly ones using the 0–100 grading scale. However, this teacher's approach is particularly egregious. In essence, this teacher sees herself as an autonomous actor and her grading as her own private practice. She fails to understand that grades should accurately reflect mastery of a set of content standards and be applied consistently across courses in a school in order to communicate effectively about student achievement.

Grades should not depend upon which teacher a student has or how hard or easy that person grades. Students achieving at the same level in different classes should receive similar grades, and teachers across the school should apply similar grading practices. Although subjectivity and teacher discretion in grading will still exist, the more a school focuses on a consistent standards-based model, the greater the likelihood that grades will relate to mastery in a meaningful way.

Grades communicate to the student, parents, employers, and college admissions how well a student mastered the subject. A teacher who grades much harder than another or uses a truncated scale distorts the accuracy of that communication and compromises the school's consistency in grading practices. The teacher's point that there is always room for improvement will be the case in every course and on every task, not just her courses and assignments.

However, consistency in grading practices across a school doesn't necessarily mean that the school's overall grading system is fair or that grading practices are well designed to promote learning or reflect mastery. Leaders and researchers in assessment have pointed to numerous practices that undermine the value of various grading practices; for example, using zeroes as scores in a 0–100 grading scale when 70 is established as a passing grade, giving equal weight to scores across an entire course rather than focusing on mastery at the end of the course, or using cumulative grade point averages to establish class ranks.

Given that we should use grading systems to support learning and to reflect achievement on a set of content standards, schools would be well served to review their grading practices and systems to ensure these practices consistently encourage rather than undermine student achievement.

CHARITY FOR A GRADE

> Scenario: At New City High School, various clubs and organizations sponsor charity drives, asking students to bring in money, food, and clothing. Several teachers offer bonus points on graded exercises and final averages as incentives to participate. Some parents believe this sends a morally wrong message, undermining the value of charity as a selfless act. They've come to you to complain that the exchange of donations for grades sends the wrong message. What do you think, and how do you respond?

Responses

Sheldon Berman

The practice of offering bonus points on graded exercises and final averages may seem like a harmless vehicle for encouraging service to others, but the parents who are objecting are making a legitimate point. The issue, however, is a bit more complex than that simple framing.

One of the most important roles educators play is fostering the development of the skills, attitudes, and values of responsible citizenship. Central to responsible citizenship are an appreciation of the common good and a commitment to helping those in need. It is a responsible act for teachers to highlight issues within the community for which students can provide the kind of assistance that both helps address the need and encourages the development of an ethic of service. Therefore, the issue here isn't about whether the act of service is a viable one for educators to encourage but whether those acts should be rewarded through the grading system.

In order to address that point, it is important to understand that there is an essential difference between community service and service learning. Community service involves acts of service such as food and clothing drives or fund-raising for victims of natural or human disasters that are independent of the curriculum but are positive acts to engage students in support of the common good.

Service-learning activities, on the other hand, are acts of service deeply tied to the curriculum in which students study an issue and engage in service as an authentic avenue for demonstrating both their understanding of the issue and of ways that individuals can make a difference on that issue. Clearly, students can and should be graded when the acts of service are part of the curriculum and thus linked to learning.

Acts of community service are best encouraged when they aren't tied to a grade but instead tied to the achievement of some larger community goal, such as the number of grocery bags of food or a target dollar amount that students desire to raise for a cause. Therefore, it may be best to suggest to teachers that they not provide incentives within the grading system for acts of community service, but that it is fine to integrate service learning into the student accountability system.

The teachers who are providing the bonus points could make a viable counterargument that grades themselves represent extrinsic rewards and that we consistently use these extrinsic rewards to encourage participation in learning. Therefore, using extrinsic rewards for service through bonus points is not very different.

This raises a much deeper and more difficult issue about the meaning of grading. Hopefully, we are shifting our thinking about grades away from seeing them as extrinsic rewards to designing them as assessments for learning and as feedback to students so that they can advance their understanding. In this context, the addition of bonus points for community service does not enable students to better understand how they can advance their own learning while, alternatively, integrating assessment of service learning can serve that purpose.

Joan McRobbie

The teachers are acting on their impulse to ensure the greatest possible help for those in need. Admirable as that is, the parents are right in saying that it sends students an "end justifies the means" message. Moreover, in today's education world, where tremendous emphasis is placed on accountability for student results and stories in the news media describe teachers cheating to make student achievement look better than it is, the practice of inflating grades by donating to charity has the potential to be misinterpreted and go horribly wrong.

I would appeal to department heads to point out the problem to teachers and work collaboratively with them on creating a less fraught and more academically sound means of achieving their high-minded goal. Far better for teachers to construct curriculum-relevant assignments that help build student awareness of the problems the charity drives are addressing.

For example, teachers could assign students to read an article on the increase in families relying on food banks and write an essay about it. Math or economics students could prepare presentations—for class, schoolwide assembly or community or parent meetings—on the trajectory of poverty or joblessness in the community. Social studies students could interview local nonprofit officials and submit reports on the family impact of job loss. Granted, this would require teachers' time and thought. But the payoffs could more than make up for the effort.

Resulting student assignments would legitimately feed into grades, turning complaining parents into allies. Student interest in their subjects would likely get a boost from the real-world relevance. Pleased that their concerns prompted positive action, parents could also learn more about their own community by way of students' presentations. And the teachers' original intent —to spur more giving to worthy charities—would likely be fulfilled.

Should the media tune in, what might have been a story that no school wants would instead be one showcasing New City High as a place teaching strong academics while also promoting community values.

Roy Dexheimer

AASA's "Statement of Ethics" clearly states that educational leaders have an obligation to "provide equal educational opportunities to each and every child." Offering academic credit for charitable fundraising, however admirable that goal, is not an equal opportunity. Youngsters who, through personal circumstances, cannot participate are not receiving equal treatment. The charity drives, without academic grade incentives, seem like a good value to promote, but not at the expense of unfair advantages to some students.

THE $20 MOTIVATOR

Scenario: A high school English teacher shares with his principal the difficulty he experiences in motivating his students. For an upcoming unit exam, he wants to offer a $20 bill to the student scoring the highest grade and $20 to the student recording the biggest improvement over the previous exam. He defends the practice by arguing that if love of knowledge alone is the reward, why then do schools offer prizes for various accomplishments? Should administrators permit this teacher's attempt at motivating students?

Responses

Glenn "Max" McGee

This well-meaning teacher's idea is not inherently unethical, but the answer to the question must be a resounding, unqualified *No, Never.*

A significant body of research exists regarding the limited, temporal value of extrinsic motivation ($20) versus the deep, sustained value of intrinsic motivation (learning for the interest, curiosity, relevance, joy, and love of learning). In other words, working to win $20 for succeeding on one test may temporarily motivate some students, but it is not likely they will long remember much less apply the knowledge they were trying to acquire for the $20 or even continue to be motivated on the next test without a similar monetary incentive.

Another reason for denying the request is that this method will only motivate a few students—those who already are doing well and are likely to achieve the high score and those who are doing poorly and thus have the greatest room to improve. It also may foster unhealthy competition as those potentially high scorers can only win if someone else loses, and thus these students may be tempted to gain advantages through legitimate or illegitimate means.

In addition, this teacher is unwittingly encouraging sandbagging, that is, purposefully scoring low on one exam and thus making it easier to get most improved on the next one when $20 is on the line.

The $20 reward also raises expectations for future monetary rewards that, if not met, will alienate and probably anger students who, by the teacher's own admission, are already not motivated. Yes, those few for whom the $20 may be achievable may take more notes, participate frequently, do their homework and study harder, but the other students—arguably the majority of the class—will be even more likely to disengage at best and disrupt at worst as they perceive that the reward is not attainable and thus not fair.

The administrators should tell the teacher to motivate students through connecting with them, caring about them, making the subject matter interesting and relevant, varying methods of instruction, affording students opportunities for discovery and exploration, attending to different learning modalities, engaging individuals and small groups in purposeful problem solving, and restoring joy to learning.

Sheldon Berman

This strategy is ineffective and deflects attention from the real issue—the difficulty the teacher has in motivating students. First, the strategy is likely to be unsuccessful at motivating students who are not currently engaged. With only two awards, the one for highest grade would most likely go to a student who is already doing well in class.

Even if the award for greatest improvement went to a student whom the teacher considers unmotivated, that student, realizing the award could probably not be earned a second time, would revert to previous behavior. Other unmotivated students, understanding their slim chance of securing the prize, would continue their current detachment from the class.

Second, the teacher would become known for providing monetary rewards. This strategy would undermine his reputation in other classes, where his students would want similar rewards. It might also result in accusations of discrimination if the awards were not structured to accommodate students with special needs or students who are English language learners. Because cash awards are not an appropriate or allowable school or district expenditure, the funds would have to come from his personal resources, likely undermining relationships with colleagues whose students might also request monetary incentives.

Third, extrinsic rewards fail to engender long-term motivation. Given that extrinsic rewards have no connection with enabling the student to find meaning in the material, the rewards would not stimulate interest in the subject and may, in fact, trivialize the content that the teacher is trying to convey. Schools offer prizes for achievements in academics, athletics, and the arts, but these awards are acknowledgements of effort and excellence, not incentives to work harder.

Fourth, the teacher's attitude undermines the outcome he seeks. He has stereotyped a group of students as unmotivated and academically deficient. It is likely that he has either explicitly or subtly communicated that stereotype to them, making them more apt to see themselves in a similar light.

Given the dynamics of how stereotype threat operates, these students are not likely to respond to monetary incentives because they don't see themselves as being able to succeed in securing them, even if they were interested. He has characterized the students as the problem, rather than recognizing his responsibility as a teacher and owning the problem himself.

Finally, the real issue is the teacher's difficulty connecting with and motivating his students. Teaching is hard work and reaching all students is incredibly demanding. Instead of proposing simple but ineffectual responses, the teacher should seek assistance in developing approaches that have meaning for students and strategies that engage them in ways they find energizing and compelling. The question the teacher should be asking the principal is, Who can coach and mentor him so that he can help students make meaningful connections with the material he is presenting?

The teacher's desperate desire to motivate students may also indicate a more general schoolwide issue related to student apathy and disengagement, possibly reflecting the climate and culture of the school. If lack of motivation is a common issue for teachers at the school, the principal should begin a process to consider structural, cultural, and instructional changes that would promote student voice, agency, and engagement. These changes could include personalized learning, authentic project-based learning experiences, and social-emotional learning strategies that reengage students and enable them to find meaning in their schoolwork.

GRADING TRICKS

Scenario: After a new high school biology teacher assigned final semester grades, two students asked him to reconsider the C's he gave them. One got just what his test scores indicated. The other was close to a B-minus, and while he did poorly early on, he worked hard, sought help, and improved significantly. The teacher raised his grade to a B-minus but did not alter the other student's.

Nowhere in the course description or the district's grading guidelines does it state that improvement can be a factor in grading. The parents of the child with the C have come straight to the superintendent to complain. What position would you take on this issue, and how would you explain your position?

Responses

Joan McRobbie

The superintendent should explain to the parents that they need to talk directly with the teacher and principal. The superintendent's office should help set that up and then follow up to ensure that the matter had a satisfactory resolution.

The superintendent should talk with that principal and also take steps to reinforce the awareness of all principals and teachers of the need for transparency and fairness in grading. It's a matter of principle as well as a fundamental school responsibility. In today's high stakes climate, it's also increasingly a matter of public urgency.

Principals should ensure that every teacher has clear, written grading policies aligned with those of the school and district. Those policies need to objectively reflect student academic achievement, not subjective judgments of attitude or effort. Such traits are important and should be acknowledged, but separately. Grades are about providing students with feedback on what they know and can do as distinct from how hard they tried.

New teachers need guidance to ensure that grading policies are tied to clear academic goals and that the evidence and measures to be used are specifically delineated. They also need an awareness that the grading process must be the same for all students and clearly communicated to students and parents.

In this example, the principal needs to work with this new teacher and the complaining parents to resolve the problem, which arose because an inexperienced teacher with good intentions lacked support for thinking through grading policies and actions. The principal can use this experience as a prompt for strengthening and communicating fair grading practices schoolwide, thereby building community trust in the values that drive the school—an invaluable asset when difficulties arise.

Sheldon Berman

The first issue to be addressed is one of process. Grading is the prerogative of the classroom teacher, who is in the best position to make a judgment about student learning based on the student's performance. In some districts, board policies and teacher association contracts actually specify the teacher's ultimate authority in grading. Therefore, the superintendent should not take an immediate position on this case but instead ask the parents to speak directly with the teacher. If the issue was not resolved to the parents' satisfaction, they would then be referred to the principal. Only at that point could the principal's decision be appealed to the superintendent.

The second issue is whether the teacher was justified in changing the grade of one student but not the other. Unless a school has developed a consistent set of grading standards for teachers to use, different teachers will use different standards. Some will average the scores of assignments and tests, others will integrate multiple aspects of learning that could include effective participation in class, while still others will use proficiency-based practices designed to assess the degree to which students met the learning targets by the end of the term.

When it comes to grading, the qualities of fairness, consistency, and transparency are essential so that students and parents understand how a student's work is evaluated. By engaging teachers in determining the grading standards they will use, a school or district engenders greater consistency across classrooms and generally prevents situations such as this one from arising.

In this case, the teacher may not have been as proactive in preparing and sharing his syllabus as he could have been, thereby opening his grading to questions of fairness. It also might have been prudent for him to first consult with a more senior teacher, the department head or the principal for guidance on how to handle a student's appeal. It is fair for students to request reconsideration of a grade if they believe that there was some factor not considered or an error inadvertently made by the teacher. Although this should happen infrequently, it is reasonable for a teacher to change a grade if the justification is sufficient.

What appears to have been a factor in this teacher's decision to change the grade was the degree to which the student met the learning targets by the end of the term. Although a superintendent should be reluctant to interfere with teacher grading unless there is an egregious problem, if proficiency were the basis for the teacher's decision, the superintendent should support the teacher while ensuring that the teacher's decision was consistently applied to all the students in the class.

The superintendent should recommend that the principal meet with the teacher and ask to what degree this proficiency standard had been applied and whether it had been applied equitably so that no student gained an unfair advantage. The principal should encourage the teacher to make the best decision possible that could be upheld as fair and consistent across all students in the class.

Given that this is a new teacher who may not have a great deal of experience in grading, it would be important for the principal to work with him to refine the standards by which students are graded, and the delineation of those standards in the syllabus for the course, so that this circumstance is prevented in the future. More important, at the beginning of each term, each teacher should provide his or her supervisor and all students with a copy of the grading procedures and criteria for each course. To the extent possible, this information should also be shared with parents via open houses, parent-teacher conferences, online, and other means.

THE MANDATORY FIELD TRIP

Scenario: Early in the semester, the school's Advanced Placement English teacher tells her students they must attend an opera being performed about fifty miles away in the spring. Each student is expected to purchase a $65 ticket, though the school is providing transportation. The teacher asks each student to sign a "contract." Five girls on the lacrosse team discover a schedule conflict. They are told they will need to find their own transportation to the opera. Failure to attend will mean loss of the full year's credit. Parents are livid. How might you resolve this?

Responses

Paula Mirk

Side with the parents on this one. Immediately reverse the teacher's decision and make the trip optional. Then have a direct conversation with the teacher and the school principal.

A policy may need to be put in place requiring anyone to get approval from administration before expecting students to come up with cash for any purpose. It might also require that any extra costs be delineated before a student chooses to take a course. Some parents in this AP class already may have had to scramble to find the cash to pay for the typical AP costs that land on students. The opera ticket could feel like adding insult to injury.

There's a second layer to this story that is also an ethical concern. The English teacher needs to be aware of the possible conflicts—besides the monetary ones—her plan poses. Somehow, the school needs a system for making sure everybody is aware of students' co-curricular commitments, so that no student is forced to choose between a sports obligation and an academic obligation.

The AP teacher should be aware that some of her students are involved in lacrosse and should be scheduling with consideration or working with the lacrosse coach so they don't trip over each other. Expecting the students to find their own transportation is bad enough, but threatening "loss of the full year's credit" is totally unreasonable. While it is certainly right to provide interesting learning opportunities for AP English students, such as a night at the opera, it's also right to keep in mind family financial strains and conflicting student obligations.

Sheldon Berman

Attending an opera is a wonderful cultural experience that provides enrichment for students. However, it is unreasonable for a teacher to require all students to spend $65 and attend an opera 50 miles away, even if transportation is provided. It is also unjustified for the teacher to make full credit in the course contingent on attendance at the opera.

Any course encompasses an accumulation of knowledge and skills and is not dependent on one event. In addition, a student's high school experience is multi-faceted; scheduling conflicts such as this one will inevitably emerge and need to be resolved with respect for the student's commitments and evolving skill in decision making.

Faced with this situation, the superintendent should insist that the teacher ensure adequate scholarship resources for economically disadvantaged students and offer an alternative assignment for those unable to attend, regardless of reason, with no academic penalty attached for choosing the alternative.

CONVEYING CAVEATS ON EXTRA TIME

Scenario: The principal of a suburban high school with a popular STEM program has noticed a proliferation of students requesting extra time on exams because of disabilities. While harboring doubts about the legitimacy of some requests, the principal tells teachers to grant the accommodations. When these students ask for letters of recommendation, the principal thinks it is fitting to convey a caveat about the extended time, knowing it will affect performance in college and the workplace. Is it appropriate to do so?

Responses

MaryEllen Elia

These decisions should tightly align with district policy for all students. Simply put, an identified student need is met with a specific course of action. Any student with a learning disability would be supported through an individualized education plan, which documents the nature of the disability and related accommodations to ensure student success.

The criteria outlined in the IEP would be the only basis for any legitimate time extension and/or other accommodations. The premise that a principal would hold authority over the process and "grant the accommodations" is therefore flawed. Likewise, it would not be appropriate to mention this in any letter of recommendation, especially since the IEP is part of the official record that travels with the transcript. Any school or organization applied to would then have access to this information.

In this scenario, the implication is that the principal wishes to be additionally vocal about the accommodations as a proactive (and punitive?) counterbalance measure against perceived illegitimate requests. Because of the seriousness of learning disabilities and their related documentation, the principal's own intervention in this process is inappropriate and unwarranted.

Sheldon Berman

It is completely improper to convey a caveat about the extended time, whether in letters of recommendation, telephone conversations or other forms of communication. First, it's neither legal nor appropriate for anyone other than the student in question to publicly disclose a student's disability—be it cognitive, physical, or emotional, particularly in a context in which it could compromise the student's acceptance to a college.

Second, there is a well-defined legal process for determining whether a student may receive accommodations on exams and what form those accommodations may take. It is not the teachers' or the principal's prerogative to grant or reject requests for accommodations. If an accommodation is sought, it can be authorized only by the IEP team and must follow ADA or IDEA regulations and guidance.

The most egregious aspect of the principal's actions is the speculation that these students don't really need this accommodation and that it is giving them an unfair advantage on exams. Accommodations are provided to level the playing field so that all students can access the curriculum and demonstrate understanding, not to give a student an advantage. Accommodations provide a student with a disability the same opportunity as is already afforded a student without a disability.

Students may have reasons for requesting time accommodations for these particular exams. Perhaps the STEM program was not designed around the concept of universal design for learning.

Or perhaps the exams are being presented in a format that limits accessibility for students with disabilities. For example, the exams might entail multi-step operations that students with working memory challenges need more time to track; might require extended written responses that students with motor or organizational challenges need more time to format; or might include lengthy reading passages that students with reading fluency challenges or other print disabilities need more time to read and digest.

By acting on personal speculation, the principal would discriminate against students with disabilities and would likely cause the district to face unwinnable lawsuits from parents.

TWIN TROUBLE

Scenario: An assistant principal is a leading applicant to replace the retiring elementary principal. Her duties include students' grade-level assignments for next year. The PTA president, with twin first-grade girls, reluctantly acceded to the school's policy that twins be placed in separate classrooms. One twin is having academic difficulty and the teacher recommends retention.

The girls' angry mother demands promotion of both, blaming the teacher's performance for her child's difficulty. As a member of the site council that will recommend the next principal, she has begun to criticize the assistant principal's leadership without mentioning her personal circumstances. The AP fears her promotional chance is about to be extinguished. She seeks the superintendent's advice.

Responses

Sheldon Berman

Retention is a questionable practice, often resulting in negative social and emotional consequences without justifiable academic gains. In this case, the problematic nature of the practice is compounded by the recommendation to retain one of the twins. The recommendation raises questions about how the student's learning needs were assessed, the interventions that were provided to address the child's learning needs, the efforts of the teacher to involve the parent early when lags in the student's performance became evident, and the monitoring of classroom instruction by administrators.

The AP would also be well-advised to research the child's kindergarten experience and determine whether any learning difficulties had been identified prior to first grade. The AP should also investigate whether a referral was made for a special education evaluation and the results of any such evaluation. A retention decision should be made carefully, with ongoing family involvement, and only after other avenues have been exhausted.

The superintendent should meet with the AP and explore these questions as a way of helping her reflect on the decision. The retention decision should be based not on saving face or on simply supporting the teacher's recommendation but on the best interests of the child. The AP needs to understand thoroughly the reasons for the teacher's recommendation, while still helping the teacher understand that there are multiple factors that need to be considered before a final decision is made on retention.

If these issues have not been adequately addressed, it is not too late to reverse course and investigate ways to support the student in second grade. However, if the issues have been addressed and there are learning delays not related to a disability that could justify retention, communication with the family is vital to ensure a full understanding of the child's needs. Such a dialogue may yield appropriate ways of supporting the student that may or may not include retention.

The issue of communication with both the teacher and the parent is a significant one in this case. It is clear from the mother's angry response that she believes retention is not in the best interest of her child. The AP must take the lead in building positive communication with the parent, not because it would be advantageous in her application for the principalship, but because it is the only avenue to resolving this situation positively.

No matter what prior communication has occurred, this moment represents another opportunity to listen carefully to the parent's concerns and rebuild rapport and understanding. It may be beneficial to bring the teacher and parent together for a three-way dialogue to seek mutual understanding, defuse tensions that have emerged, and consider appropriate options to address the child's needs.

The true sign of whether an individual is ready for leadership of a school is in handling challenging issues like this one while at the same time building strong relationships with both teachers and families. In the end, the AP's ability to step back and either reverse this decision or gain the support of the parent is a meaningful test of her readiness to assume a principalship.

Mark Hyatt

There are two issues here. One is the possible promotion of the struggling twin and the other is the PTO president's gossiping about the assistant principal. Considering the unique circumstances associated with this dilemma, the parent's desire for promotion of both twins should prevail. The family dynamics of this situation are profound. Keeping the twins at the same grade level, if possible, is important. Possibly an individual education plan in second grade will help.

That said, the assistant principal should seek a moment of shared empathy in a meeting with the mother, witnessed by a neutral third party, such as the outgoing principal. If the mother has relevant issues with the assistant principal's job performance, then she can vent them in a constructive and direct way.

Chapter Seven

Student Discipline

Student discipline is one of a school administrator's most consequential duties. These decisions can have far-reaching effects on a young person's future and must be undertaken with sober reflection, a clear sense of purpose, procedural fairness and equity. But what is the essential purpose of student discipline? Is punishment always the appropriate consequence for student misbehavior? And what are the ethical considerations that come into play?

First and foremost, school administrators have an ethical duty to create and maintain an environment where students are physically and emotionally safe. Without that, learning cannot take place. This is not just a bullet point on your job description but an ethical imperative because, under our compulsory attendance laws, families without the resources to educate their children privately have no other option than the public schools. In other words, most students attending public schools are there whether they want to be or not, which imposes a heightened moral obligation to protect them while under the district's supervision.

Punishment is often the first thing that comes to mind when we think of a student disciplinary code. But the overarching purpose of discipline should not be punishing behavior that is bad, but using discipline to encourage behavior that is good. Here's where administrators need to be mindful of the allocation of responsibility between school and home.

School districts have no right to dictate to parents what is acceptable behavior when children are away from school under their parents' supervision, at least not when it has no direct impact on other students' school experience.

Within legal limits, however, administrators do have the authority, indeed the obligation, to establish guidelines for acceptable behavior at school. Because those standards may differ, the basic ethical duty of fairness requires administrators to place students on fair notice of what's acceptable behavior at school—to literally and figuratively "spell it out"—so they know the standards to which they'll be held accountable. Discipline only comes into play when those clearly defined expectations aren't met.

You also have an ethical obligation to respect students' legal rights when imposing discipline. Every state has its own procedures to be followed before a student can be suspended or expelled from school, but since the U.S. Supreme Court's 1975 decision in *Goss v. Lopez*, 419 U.S. 565 (1975), federal court decisions interpreting the Fourteenth Amendment's due process clause have recognized the bedrock principle that a public education is a valuable legal right and can be denied, even temporarily, only with procedures in place to assure fundamental fairness.

Due process is an elastic concept, and the formality of the process increases with the severity of the disciplinary consequences imposed. But students can never be suspended from school without notice of what's alleged and some opportunity to explain their side of the story.

Administrators also must be mindful of students' constitutionally protected right of free expression discussed in the chapter on First Amendment rights. Legal standards vary depending on whether the speech occurs at school-sponsored activities or off-campus on students' own time. Many states also restrict school districts' ability to impose consequences for off-campus conduct (as opposed to speech or other expressive activities), such as drinking or fighting, that does not have a direct impact on the school community. You should consult with your district's legal counsel to stay abreast of the latest developments in this evolving area of the law.

Another ethical duty is ensuring that students aren't singled out for disparate treatment based on factors that are irrational or perhaps even illegal. We all are products of our upbringing and come to adulthood with perceptions and stereotypes engrained in our psyche that we may not even be consciously aware of.

It's indisputable that, historically, students of color have received a disproportionate share of disciplinary sanctions. Whether that's the product of intentional discrimination, implicit bias, or other factors we can't substantiate, there's an obligation to ensure fairness, in appearance as well as in fact. To that end, administrators should press the pause button for a moment and conduct a quick mental audit to satisfy themselves there are no improper factors poisoning their decision-making.

In high-profile cases where student misconduct has become known in the community, you may find yourself under pressure to disclose details about the students involved and what disciplinary consequences were imposed for their behavior. Whatever those students may have done, they have privacy rights that must be respected, and it's incumbent on administrators to resist the temptation to violate those rights to appease an angry public.

"No comment" is never an appropriate response, but a straightforward explanation of the district's legal duty of confidentiality, coupled with an assurance that the administration has taken the matter seriously and culpable parties have been dealt with appropriately, may have to suffice.

High-ranking administrators typically don't conduct disciplinary investigations themselves but rely on reports from subordinates who've conducted the interviews, reviewed the video surveillance footage, scrutinized relevant documents, and made their own preliminary findings.

There is nothing unethical or improper about relying on second- or third-hand information gathered by competent staff with appropriate training in how to conduct investigations, but those responsible for the ultimate decision should make sufficient inquiry to satisfy themselves that the underlying investigation was conducted with due regard for the legal rights of the parties, with safeguards in place to ensure reliability of the fact-finding, and with fairness in appearance as well as in fact.

Administrators also must be mindful of their duty of protection toward students who may have been harmed by other students' bad behavior, even if the district itself is not at fault. In many cases, the offending student will be capable of making amends to the victim directly, but sometimes the district itself must step in with its own resources when the damage is something only the district itself can repair. In the end, it's your ethical obligation to ensure a just result.

The cases presented in this chapter address a wide range of disciplinary scenarios involving conduct, both active and passive, from bystanders who allow a fellow student to bully a helpless classmate, to student-athletes who put their college scholarships at risk by drinking off-campus. Each case finds the school administrator on the horns of an ethical dilemma, but the thoughtful perspectives shared by our contributors should help administrators think their way through to the right result.

IDLE BYSTANDERS

Scenario: A rural school sends youngsters with special needs to a shared program in a neighboring community. The youngsters wait for their transfer bus just outside the door to a school's wood shop classroom. A bullying lad from the shop class terrifies one of the students with special needs by threatening to feed him into a band saw. Punishment for the bully is a no-brainer. But what about the boys who stood by, watched the threat, and did nothing?

Responses

Sheldon Berman

This incident presents a valuable learning opportunity not only for the student who bullied the special needs student and the boys who observed it, but also for the class or school as a whole. Although punishment for the bully may be a "no-brainer," it will be important to go beyond punishment. This student needs to appreciate the impact of his actions, apologize to the terrorized student—and to other special needs students who observed the incident—in the presence of both students' peers, and appropriately demonstrate his sincere regret—preferably by way of a proactive and positive activity.

For the shop class students who observed the bullying, punishment hinges on whether they were actively involved, supportive or encouraging. However, passivity is no excuse in such situations. It will be important for an adult to work with these students to help them understand that by being a bystander, one is essentially endorsing the abuse. They need to learn why and how to be an "upstander" and acquire the courage to intervene on behalf of others who are being unfairly treated. Through dialogue with an adult, the passive observers can also find appropriate ways to express their regret to the student and to support him.

It will also be important for adults to process the experience with any special needs students who observed the incident since they, too, are likely to feel vulnerable as a result of having seen a peer threatened by another student. They need to know that bullying behavior is unacceptable, and that adults and other students will intervene to address it when it occurs. They also can learn how to bring incidents they observe to the attention of adults and to intervene in appropriate and helpful ways.

There is a growing understanding in the education community of the concept of "restorative discipline," in which the goal is not simply issuing consequences for inappropriate actions toward others, but recognizing the social contexts that condone such behavior, healing the damage that has been done, and building or restoring relationships and trust between students. For the student who bullied and for those who witnessed the bullying yet failed to intervene, finding ways to restore what is now a broken relationship and to build respectful relationships will be an important learning opportunity that could prevent similar incidents in the future.

For the class or school, this is a prime opportunity to more deeply understand bullying and the pain that slurs, threats, and derogatory actions create. It is also an opportunity to understand the issues faced by students with special needs, students who hold different beliefs, and students who are from diverse backgrounds.

The most effective prevention for bullying is creating an inclusive and caring community in which students support each other in facing academic and social challenges. This sense of community is built through class meetings and other community-building strategies in which students discuss issues, share their perceptions, find solutions, and strengthen relationships.

There are a number of highly effective programs to support the development of classroom communities, the prevention of bullying, and the nurturing of social skills at the elementary and middle school levels (www.casel.org). At the high school level, one of the most effective programs to address prejudice and intolerance is the Facing History and Ourselves curriculum (www.facinghistory.org). School districts need to develop their social curriculum and their academic curriculum with equal care, pursuing social development and prevention strategies on a consistent and coherent basis from pre-kindergarten through twelfth grade.

The overall goal in responding to this incident should be to turn it into an opportunity to cultivate understanding, tolerance and a commitment to inclusiveness, kindness, and fairness. For the school and district, it should prompt a review of the social curriculum to ensure that a coherent and comprehensive set of social development and prevention programs is in place.

Sarah Mackenzie

Because this incident occurred in a different district, one would hope and expect that the woodshop students who were bystanders to the incident would be counseled regarding what happened. First, they should be questioned as to the facts of the situation. This action alone may help them to realize what they witnessed and their role in it. Some may have actually assisted in the bullying; at the very least, they provided an audience for the incident. Some may have wanted to counteract the bullying but may not have known what to do.

Even if a school has a bullying prevention program, these students need a more focused understanding of the role of bystanders, specifically their culpability if they do nothing to protect others or prevent bullying behavior. Ideally, these students need to understand the consequences if they fail to act in the future. Of course, any future punishment in a situation like this depends on the policy of the school and district.

Mark Hyatt

Did the boys from the shop class who stood by feel empowered to take action to protect the special needs student? If not, they need to know they are the protectors of everyone in their community—and have permission to stand up and speak out. Culture provides a level of risk prevention that cannot be attained with rules and regulations. Culture provides greater discipline than disciplinary action.

If the students in the scenario knew that tolerating bullying behavior was wrong, then there is a much better chance that the boys who stood by would have said something. It's tough to stand up for what's right, but if good school culture is reinforced daily starting at the top, it's much easier for everyone to stand up, speak out, and maintain a safety-supportive school culture.

AN ACCIDENTAL DRINKING DISCOVERY

Scenario: A high school coach returning to his small community after the year-end holiday break stops at a restaurant in a neighboring town, where he spots three of his senior basketball players enjoying a beer. These are upstanding students (one is the son of two teachers in the rural district), and it was purely coincidental that the coach stopped there. The students had signed a preseason pledge to not drink during the season—which up to that point was an undefeated season, in a basketball-crazed town. What action should be taken by school or district administrators?

Responses

Sarah Mackenzie

Rules are rules, and pledges are pledges. The point of committing yourself to a team and to the attendant responsibilities will be lost on these students if the coach does not share the information with administrators so he and they can mete out the appropriate consequences.

There is no way the responsibility for disciplining these students, which likely will result in their being suspended from some number of games at the very least, should be evaded. Furthermore, if the coach were to neglect his responsibility and pretend he didn't see them at the restaurant, he would be in even more serious ethical trouble. Tantalizing as it might be to slip out of the restaurant so the students wouldn't see him, the coach must act. He is the enforcer of the rules and a role model for the students on the team and all the students in the school.

Even if the coach is not a teacher at the school, he still has to recognize he is an educator whose job is to ensure that students learn important lessons. And they won't learn them if their teachers and coaches are swayed by a citizenry who seem to care only about success on a basketball court.

We can imagine that the students and their parents may argue that this incident was a one-off, that the students should be given a lighter penalty or even simply a warning, that they will know better next time. The coach and the school administrators need to stand firm for the good of the students and the community that nurtures them. Students' understanding of their obligations and the meaning of commitments cannot be sacrificed to a winning season no matter how much it might help the morale of the town and the reputation of the school in the town.

Sheldon Berman

Understandably, the families, school staff, student body, and community will be disappointed to learn these three student-athletes violated their pledge. Despite the fact their transgression was discovered purely by accident, these players need to face the same process and consequences that any other student-athlete would confront in similar circumstances, most typically suspension for several games. It is the obligation of the coach to report what he saw, just as it is the obligation of administrators to ensure that due process and appropriate consequences are administered based on the school's and district's codes of discipline.

Even in a basketball-crazed town whose school boasts an undefeated season, it is important to deliver a consistent message both to athletes and others that underage drinking is unacceptable, as is the failure to honor one's commitment.

In the long run, this situation will work out for the best and serve as a teachable moment if the athletes acknowledge and apologize for their violation and if the community supports the coach who reported it and the administration as a way to deter other students from committing similar violations.

A PRANK GONE WRONG

Scenario: As a "senior prank" two weeks before graduation, about twenty students drive four cars onto the high school athletic fields, causing $20,000 worth of damage to the infields and turf. Cameras record license plate numbers. Ten seniors confess and implicate a dozen others plus ninety plotters on a Snapchat network. The school board president's twin daughters were in one of the cars but not driving and the president plans to hand out their diplomas at graduation. As superintendent, what do you do?

Responses

Maggie Lopez

The superintendent needs to use the entirety of his/her communication and leadership skills with the board president and the board so that they clearly understand how the superintendent will process her decision regarding the consequences for this action. This is one of those times when the relationship (positive or negative) between the board and superintendent will shine through to others.

The superintendent needs to communicate clearly with the board president that whatever consequences these students receive, those consequences will apply to his daughters as well, as they were in one of the cars and participated in the prank. Therefore, the superintendent cannot guarantee the board president will be handing out diplomas to his daughters. The superintendent should help the board president (and other board members) understand how important it is to stay as neutral as possible and allow her and staff members to do their job.

These students' actions were of a very serious nature, resulting in major destruction of public property and the distinct possibility the students will be barred from participating in graduation. The superintendent and staff must talk to law enforcement, examine relevant district policies and state statutes, and review suspension and expulsion options.

Whatever consequences result for these students, it will be a political football for the board and the superintendent. The political ramifications of the decision will be exacerbated if the board president continues to insist that regardless of what happened, his daughters will get their diplomas on stage from him.

Like the board president, these students' parents may oppose any consequence that would prevent graduation participation. Some parents may question any consequence and contend this was just "kids being kids" and recall that they, too, participated in senior pranks in high school. They will need clear communication from the superintendent and the board that today these activities are viewed differently, and that policies and statutes often define consequences.

Sheldon Berman

The good news is that with two weeks until graduation, there is time for discipline, restitution, and the potential to walk at the ceremony. The primary responsibility for addressing this situation rests with the principal. The superintendent can support and advise the principal on process but should not play a major role because any appeal would need to be heard at that level.

The incident—far more serious than a "prank"—violated the law, and the principal needs to file a police report. The individuals involved likely will be charged with malicious and willful destruction of property and face court-issued punishments. While the police undertake their investigation, the school should proceed with its own probe.

The students' flagrant misconduct caused serious damage to the school's property, disrupted important culminating athletic events, disrespected the community that invested in these students' education, and demonstrated thoughtlessness and destructiveness by many senior class members as they prepare to transition into adulthood. All students who participated need to accept responsibility, and they and their parents need to be involved in addressing the damage done to the fields.

The negative impression this incident attaches to the school and its students will take years to erase. It is important the students understand the long-term consequences of their actions and express remorse in a way that demonstrates to the community the lessons they have learned from this incident.

The initial task for the principal is to distinguish the categories of responsibility among the drivers, passengers, and plotters. The punishment for each may be different. Discipline could range from detention and community service for some of the plotters, to suspension from school and senior activities, community service and restitution for those more actively involved.

The drivers will face the most serious punishment, although passengers were, in effect, accomplices to the destruction of property. The most important consequences for all involved are that they share in the cost of repair and offer a public apology to the community as a prerequisite to walking at graduation.

As part of the disciplinary process, the school administration needs to meet with the parents of these students to discuss the seriousness of the incident and the requirement that each student contribute to the cost of the repairs prior to graduation. In addition, the students need to commit to comport themselves at the graduation in a manner that reflects positively on the class and makes the ceremony a meaningful one for all. The board president's daughters should face the same consequences as any of the other passengers. It doesn't matter who the parent is. What matters is the role the student played in the incident.

Walking at graduation is a privilege, not a right. Still, graduation is a very important rite of passage. While the consequences should reflect the seriousness of the incident, administration should provide students with an opportunity to make amends for their error so that they can participate in the graduation ceremony.

At a more fundamental level, however, this incident raises several questions that parents and the school administration should ask themselves as they reflect on why this may have happened. Is there something about the school or community culture that fostered an attitude among students where destruction of property was simply viewed as a prank? Given how many students were involved, why didn't one or more students come forward to express concern to an adult or voice objections to fellow students? How can parents and the school join forces to change students' attitudes or perceptions so that an incident like this won't happen again?

The answers to these questions will be more important in the long run than the specific consequences experienced by students in this senior class.

A YEARBOOK YIKES

Scenario: Three months after the yearbooks are distributed, a parent meets with the high school principal and superintendent to complain her daughter's photo had an offensive word superimposed in her hair. While it's difficult to spot, everyone in the small, rural community is aware of it. The mother wants a total recall of the yearbooks and a 100 percent reprint of books, paid by the school district, for eventual exchange.

Based on modest returns after a month, the superintendent realizes the impossibility of retrieving every yearbook and wants to order a third of the original number. The mother of the distraught girl is threatening legal action. How should the district respond?

Responses

Mark Hyatt

Mistakes are excusable if we own up to them and make the damaged parties whole. Yes, this will cost money, and most school districts don't have surpluses, but being the leader means we must "do the right thing." As leaders, we strive to operate in good faith with parents, so we must accept responsibility for the oversight and reprint the yearbook.

An apology from the superintendent and principal to the student and her family is appropriate. A letter to the community with an offer to replace 100 percent of the yearbooks is fitting. Our first duty as school leaders is to "do no harm to students." This student was harmed.

Roy Dexheimer

The district has an obligation to make every effort to identify the person(s) responsible for the offensive photograph and to administer consequences. The superintendent also should make it known that reprinted versions of the yearbook are available for exchange. The district should make an official apology to the student and the family.

Sheldon Berman

Although it means additional costs and increased effort on the part of the staff, it is appropriate for the district to work with the victim's family to find an acceptable solution. The family's concern is understandable, and the school's responsiveness is important in allaying their distress.

The probable reason for the low exchange rate is that students treasure what other students have written in their yearbooks. As an alternative, the district could offer to replace that one page or place the correct photo on a sticker over the altered picture. To encourage more students to participate, the district could provide a small financial incentive to students to take the time to bring in their yearbooks for correction or exchange. As long as the district makes a good faith effort to correct the problem, it is unlikely to be legally liable.

It is appropriate for the district to order enough books, pages, or stickers and to make contact with all the students and families who received the yearbook. Given that students received the yearbook only three months prior to the discovery of the superimposed word, it is reasonable to expect that almost all the yearbooks can be replaced or corrected.

What may be most important in this case is that the thoroughness of the district's effort communicates to parents its commitment to respectful treatment of all students. Even if it requires personal phone calls to students' homes, the district's commitment to correct this situation demonstrates it won't accept disrespectful and personally damaging conduct. The district should investigate how this transgression occurred and also determine how it could be prevented in the future, if those responsible could be charged for the replacement costs, or if there are other appropriate consequences.

DELINQUENT ADVOCACY

> Scenario: A twenty-year educator now working as a middle school principal has served as a character witness and written letters on behalf of students who have been arrested, sometimes on charges of violent offenses. Because court proceedings take place during the day, the principal must ask others to cover his duties.

Some colleagues take issue with this advocacy. Is it ethical to support students charged with violence?

Responses

Maggie Lopez

The principal is a twenty-year veteran who believes that the students for whom he is providing advocacy deserve to have their story told. These are middle school students who are young and may not fully comprehend the serious consequences of their actions. There may be extenuating circumstances (e.g., bullying) that drove the students to their poor choices.

By speaking on behalf of these students, the principal is not dismissing the bad choices the students may have made, but rather providing information from the school's perspective that may provide further context for the court. Who better than the school to provide information on the students' school life and their patterns of behavior?

It would be helpful for the principal to have a frank discussion with his staff and clarify his decision to support a student who may have committed a violent act. How does he make that determination? What is the staff's role in this process? Why is he the one required to go to court? Is it a principal's obligation? He needs to work with his staff so they may better understand and support advocacy for these students. It also may provide the principal a chance to clarify with staff why he believes it is important to have a commitment to all kids, even in the case of a student being charged with committing a violent act.

The principal should provide as much lead time as possible when he is going to need to be in court. Hopefully he is not in court on a frequent basis. He needs to develop a plan that is the least disruptive for his school, while also trying to fulfill his school duties when he goes to court. Planning ahead to have several staff members who can take turns stepping in would alleviate just a few people having to always be the ones to cover for him.

Sarah Jerome

The middle school principal is supporting students who have demonstrated poor decision-making skills. These students clearly need to be guided by caring educators to make better choices in their lives. The principal is going the extra mile to reach out to these students in their time of need. It is ethical to support students charged with violence based on the knowledge that education and guidance from caring adults can change lives and help students become better citizens in society.

A despicable action is not necessarily a path for life. When the principal demonstrates his own belief in these errant students, it opens a door of opportunity for them to believe they can be better. Everyone needs to have someone who believes in them.

This principal is an advocate in school, in the community, and in court for students learning to be the best they can be. Letters and appearances in court are important and surely colleagues can find a way to rotate coverage if the principal is scheduled for a court appearance during the school day.

COLLABORATION OR SHARED ANSWERS?

Scenario: A high school junior lends his completed homework to a friend for the purpose of illustrating for him the general approach to the assignment. The friend winds up copying a portion of the work and submitting it. After the teacher discovers this, the accused plagiarizer confirms the original arrangement. The teacher adds a critical note to the first boy's student file. His parents complain first to the teacher and then to administrators that the note may discourage other teachers from writing letters of recommendation for college applications. Did the teacher misstep?

Responses

Louis N. Wool

As with all ethical dilemmas, it is sometimes easy to be distracted by concerns raised by the aggrieved parties—in this case, the parents' concerns that teachers will be unwilling to provide college recommendations because of the negative note attached to their son's permanent record.

The school leader's work is to explore more significant ethical questions: Is this punishment warranted and appropriate, and what values does enacting the punishment convey or reinforce? Was the student treated fairly and was the punishment appropriate and within the parameters of the student code of conduct?

Suppose we accept that the student's intentions were honorable—to provide a prototype so that his classmate might better understand how to represent information in the assignment. In that case, this punishment not only seems to be disproportionate but unwarranted and discouraging students from meaningful collaboration.

A regular part of a rigorous academic college experience often includes study groups, note sharing, providing sample papers, and even outlines of critical ideas. Are we to assume that most college students who engage in beneficial scholarly collaboration do so merely to plagiarize and reduce their responsibility for learning?

The school leader should ensure that the note is removed from the student's permanent record and should undertake a review of the code of conduct and its interpretation. A student was punished with scant evidence that his intentions were anything but honorable. The punishment discourages scholarly collaboration.

Finally, building leadership and faculty should determine how best to illuminate to students the values of appropriate scholarly collaboration, clearly delineating the difference between plagiarism and the powerful outcomes that are possible when students support each other in their learning.

Sheldon Berman

The teacher may not have erred if the student handbook and school procedures indicated that this was an appropriate way to handle such incidents. However, the teacher missed an important opportunity to help the student understand the boundaries between assisting a fellow student and being complicit (even unwittingly) in plagiarism.

If the student was sincere in his desire to help another student better understand how to respond to the assignment, he was doing what we hope students will do in working with each other. In that case, a dialogue with the student and a warning may have been more fitting than a critical note to the student's file.

However, the parents are raising an important point that is less about the teacher than about school procedures. To prevent promoting bias against a student, it's best to provide some confidentiality around discipline records, through either maintaining a separate file for these records or limiting access to student files. Only administrators, not teachers, should have ready access to student discipline files. If a behavioral incident emerges, administrators can check the files to determine if it is a first occurrence or a repeated incident that calls for more significant consequences.

Teachers should write references based primarily on their personal engagement with the student in class and through extracurricular activities, not on incidents experienced by other teachers. At the very least, administration should establish a procedure for maintaining confidentiality around discipline.

The case also raises a deeper issue about the school's approach to homework and to students learning from each other. Although grading needs to be based on individual demonstration of learning, schools can create a climate in which students learn collaboratively—conferring with each other, doing homework together, and assisting a peer who is confused or lacks understanding of the material.

Although plagiarizing isn't an acceptable way to demonstrate understanding, it may be highly appropriate and beneficial for students to help each other by sharing their work products and discussing answers to questions and problems posed by the teacher. In that kind of climate, homework may be low-stakes in terms of grading but high-value in terms of students taking risks to struggle with and put forward ideas of their own or of their collaborating group.

Given those parameters, the first student would not be violating a norm. The second student could be helped to recognize that plagiarism doesn't facilitate understanding. He could then be assigned to revise the homework in his own words to demonstrate his grasp of the material.

The concept of plagiarism can be somewhat difficult for students to decipher, particularly at the middle school and high school levels when a student must adapt to the expectations and procedures of multiple teachers. Students need a chance to discuss what plagiarism is before they cross the line, especially when some classrooms promote collaborative work and some don't.

The point is to foster students' love of learning so they will keep striving. To that end, administrators should encourage teachers to have a frank discussion with each class about collaboration and plagiarism and how students will be expected to demonstrate their individual mastery of the content matter.

Chapter Eight

Hiring, Résumés, and References

Building a competent and cohesive team to implement your district's educational mission is one of your primary duties as a school administrator. This chapter focuses on the ethical issues you may confront in the hiring process.

In the chapter on discrimination, we discussed your legal obligations to members of certain protected classes, but for most employment decisions you'll have a wide breadth of discretion largely unfettered by legal constraints. Still, there are ethical duties you owe to your district, to prospective candidates, and to other employers conducting reference checks.

It's easy enough to say you have a duty to hire the most qualified candidates, but it's not always that straightforward. What if you're faced with a "package deal"—a woman who's head and shoulders above the other candidates but will only accept your offer if you also hire her husband? Or a candidate who's slightly less qualified than another applicant but has longstanding connections with a charitable foundation prepared to finance important district projects? In such cases, are compromises unethical if they promote the greater net good—or are they prohibited by community standards?

Nepotism, of course, is an age-old ethical challenge for school administrators. It's plainly improper to hire an unqualified individual solely to appease a board member whose vote you may need for your own upcoming contract renewal. Yet why should a qualified candidate, perhaps even the most qualified, be denied employment simply because he's the board president's son? Is it fair to presume someone is unqualified or had an unwarranted advantage simply because of a familial relationship?

The guidepost should always be the best interests of the district. All things being equal, suitable candidates should not be denied employment solely based on whom they're related to. But when candidates, for whatever reason, are so controversial that it would undermine their effectiveness if hired, or their appointment by you under the circumstances would make them so, you are certainly free to factor that into your decision whether to recommend them.

Some states have made administrators' jobs easier by adopting laws barring the appointment of otherwise-qualified candidates who are related to board members. New Jersey, for example, prohibits the hiring of over twenty categories of relatives by blood or marriage except on a showing of necessity as determined by state education officials. Whether this strikes the right balance or not, there's much to be said for uniform guidelines that spare administrators this undue pressure.

Is it ethically appropriate to consider candidates' private lifestyles in determining their fitness for employment in your district? Some aspects, such as same-sex relationships, may be off limits for consideration in the hiring process under anti-discrimination laws applicable in your jurisdiction. A growing number of states have also adopted legislation barring negative consideration of a wide range of legal activities in one's private life. So, for example, if your state permits recreational marijuana use, you may need to disregard your own personal view of how that activity reflects on a candidate's suitability.

Candidates' privacy has other ethical implications as well. Many applicants will not want their current employers to know they are looking for a position elsewhere. There may come a point when you need to secure information from their current supervisors, but only once the applicant is comfortable with your doing so. A harder question is what to do if you learn one of your high-ranking subordinates has his résumé on the street. Is there anything unethical in letting the employee know you know and offering to discuss any dissatisfaction with the current job? Probably not, as long as it wasn't a "heads up" shared with you in confidence.

The digital age has introduced additional ethical concerns into the hiring process—most notably, how far you can go in researching a candidate's online presence. Any information that's publicly accessible on the internet is generally considered fair game, but be careful not to accept at face value information not posted by the candidates themselves. Just as with a Yelp review, supporters or detractors may have hidden agendas of their own.

It's clearly unethical to bluff or hack your way into a candidate's private social media group, or to ask others to do so on your behalf. It may also violate the federal Stored Communications Act of 1986. In some states, it's illegal to ask candidates to provide their social media passwords even on a voluntary basis, so it's important to familiarize yourself with your state's restrictions.

Is it possible to know too much for your own good? What if your online research discloses political affiliations or other legal but controversial activities that play no part in your decision not to hire the individual? If it ever comes to light you were aware of this information, you may find yourself subject to unfair criticism or even litigation and may have difficulty proving it was not a consideration. That's why some employers use firms that conduct social media searches limited to factors, such as illegal drug use or violence, having a legitimate bearing on fitness for employment.

What are your obligations when a candidate's résumé is incomplete, misleading, or downright false? To begin with, you have a duty to confirm, by independent verification if necessary, that all candidates meet the minimum qualifications legally required to perform the job. Whether your job posting requires an electrician license or special education certification, if you don't take steps to confirm an applicant's representation of having it, your district will not be getting the service it bargained for and, even worse, could face liability for any harm suffered by placing an unqualified individual in the position.

Depending on your state's professional licensure procedures, you may also have an obligation to report to the appropriate authorities outright falsehoods that may reflect on the candidate's fitness to be employed by any district in the state. Résumé fraud discovered after an employee is on board could also serve as grounds for termination. Even if not, some states recognize a false résumé as a defense to backpay claims in wrongful termination suits if the falsehood was discovered during the course of the litigation and would have been good cause to terminate the employee at that point.

What are the ethical considerations in responding to reference checks of current or former employees? In times past, off-the-record inquiries of candidates' former employers were one of the most common methods of getting the real scoop. However, modern tools of forensic investigation, the digital footprints we often leave without realizing it, and our highly litigious environment make this time-honored practice riskier than ever.

In some jurisdictions, even a plain-vanilla reference can support a defamation claim if you're damning someone with faint praise. For this reason, many employers have adopted a strict "neutral reference" policy, limiting responses to confirmation of dates of service, positions held, and compensation paid. If you do choose to share more information on a reference check, be sure to say what you mean, mean what you say, and avoid gratuitous comments that may be taken out of context later.

One of the most prominent ethical concerns in hiring these days is what to do when asked to give a reference for an employee who's a poor performer, or even worse has engaged in serious misconduct, and needs to go. Is it unethical to give a recommendation to a prospective new employer that "highlights the positives" without disclosing the bad stuff? After all, you're not lying—or are you?

Courts in many jurisdictions have recognized the doctrine of misrepresentation by silence, so the truthfulness of your comments may be judged by the overall context of the conversation. The problem is the uncertainty around whether the information you're sharing is enough, not enough, or too much. It's one thing to disclose a formal finding that an employee engaged in sexual misconduct with a student. It's quite another to pass along unsubstantiated speculation unless your state law requires it. Ask yourself whether you're satisfied that, by an objective standard, your response is accurate and balanced overall.

The 2015 Every Student Succeeds Act requires school districts receiving federal funds to implement measures to prevent predatory teachers from working with students elsewhere. Several states have even adopted laws requiring disclosure to potential future employers of criminal conduct or sexually inappropriate behavior by former employees.

An effective hiring process is essential to providing quality educational services, but filling vacancies can be a minefield for the unwary. The cases discussed in this chapter probe the ethical issues of hiring in several different settings you could well encounter in your own district. Reflecting on these cases may help you chart your own course in the hiring process.

THE DOUBLE-HEADED JOB SEARCH

Scenario: After a lengthy search for a deputy superintendent with both budget experience and knowledge of curriculum and instruction, you find a "perfect" candidate who appears ready to relocate. At the final negotiation, the candidate indicates that because the spouse would be quitting her teaching job to relocate with him, his acceptance is contingent on giving his wife first consideration for a position somewhere in the school district. The human resources director balks at the request, but you are reluctant to lose this candidate after such an extended search. What's the right thing to do?

Responses

Sheldon Berman

In today's highly competitive job market, the employer is prone to think only about how well the applicant meets the demands of the position. Family issues are often irrelevant, especially when the candidate is local, and the spouse is already managing his or her own career and personal interests. From this perspective, we live in a highly autonomous world where the individual and the organization look out for their own interests. However, that approach may not be the best one in all employment situations, particularly when the organization is interested in hiring someone who would have to relocate.

Although one could say that the individual chooses to move and must accept the consequences of that choice for spouse and family, there is a better, more humane point of view that serves the organization as well as the individual and his or her family. That approach is to provide support, within bounds, to assist the spouse and the family in relocating.

From this perspective, it is reasonable for a prospective employee to request assistance and for the organization to provide some level of support for the spouse's search. There is no obligation on the part of an organization to employ the spouse, and there are limits on the extent to which an organization should help in the job search of a spouse. It is also reasonable for the prospective employee to indicate that his or her acceptance of the position is contingent upon the spouse obtaining a suitable position in the same locale, even though that stipulation may eliminate the individual from consideration for the position.

In this case, the human resources director and the superintendent should have had the foresight to consider family-related issues early in the candidate review process, thus preparing themselves to address these contingencies during negotiations. Assuming the district wants the new deputy superintendent to be a stable and long-term employee of the system, Human Resources should try to accommodate the interests of both working members of the family, while adhering closely to legal and ethical standards opposing preferential treatment.

Given that financial demands often require that both spouses work, and given that both may have serious professional interests, school districts need to respect the value of finding solutions that strengthen the ties of the family to the district and the community. Having the foresight to address this as an integral part of the hiring process keeps it from becoming an issue raised by the candidate in the final stage of the negotiations.

In the case at hand, depending on the size of the district, district policies, and reporting relationships within the district, it may not be appropriate for the wife to be offered a teaching position within the district. If it is accepted practice that spouses of district-level administrators may work in the district, the spouse should be given the option to interview for an open position within the district.

However, it would not be appropriate to guarantee selection for such a position, nor to create a position for the spouse in order to close the deal. Such a step would be tantamount to increasing the compensation package for the advertised executive-level position—at the taxpayers' expense.

It would certainly be appropriate for the district to alert the spouse to potential classroom openings in surrounding districts, as well as non-teaching positions in other companies or non-profits that might match the spouse's interests—especially given that such positions in the business world are not always advertised, but instead are filled through organizational networking. The district is not obligated to employ the spouse or to find a position for the spouse but has an organizational interest in aiding with the spouse's search for employment.

In today's corporate world, it is commonly understood that when you recruit someone for an important position, you are extending an offer that impacts the entire family. If an organization is requiring an individual to relocate, it is viewed as appropriate to think about a suitable position for the spouse and educational arrangements for children. However, in the field of education, many superintendents and board members have not yet embraced this approach to recruitment.

Public school leadership is a demanding field at both the local school and district levels, and strong, qualified candidates are in short supply. It is naïve to think that top-tier candidates can be identified and hired within a short timeframe with no consideration given to the welfare of the applicants' families. We in education espouse the concept of the total child thriving as a result of the support given by the entire family-school partnership. Applying this same philosophy of support to our employees is a logical extension that entails understanding and creativity but should not and must not cross the boundary of professional ethics.

Roy Dexheimer

The AASA Code of Ethics echoes the "do no harm" guideline of physicians. It says: "The educational leader makes the well-being of students the fundamental value of all decision-making."

Therefore, the request of a "perfect candidate" for a critical position in the district—someone who will affect the lives of students, staff, and community—is perfectly reasonable. The challenge of a trailing spouse can be addressed by trying to find a position for that spouse in the district or a neighboring district, or in other jobs that match the career of that spouse. When you ask an exemplary candidate to leave a job and move a family, plus give up spousal employment, this effort seems appropriate.

There are, of course, ethical dimensions to the process. No current local teacher may be displaced for the spouse, either by release from a job or forced reassignment. All collectively bargained contractual obligations must be met in good faith, including an interview and reference checking. Salary placement must conform to the usual protocols for teaching staff. And the superintendent has an ethical obligation to keep the Board of Education fully informed.

Finding strong "perfect candidates" with experience and knowledge of instructional strategies is crucial to the district's success. If you can add what is likely to be an effective teacher to the staff or the region, so much the better.

A CHALLENGED HIRING

Scenario: The son of an assistant superintendent applies for a job as an elementary school principal in the school district. Of the two leading candidates, he is clearly better qualified with relevant experience, and an unofficial decision is made to select him. But before school board action is finalized, word leaks out. The other candidate—who on paper meets all the qualifications for the post—says he believes he was passed over because of nepotism. How should the superintendent respond?

Responses

Paula Mirk

Forms of favoritism, such as nepotism, can seem—and sometimes are—a violation of fairness, one of the core ethical values most human beings share worldwide. But reverse favoritism can be just as unfair. If the assistant superintendent's son is clearly the better candidate, specific documentation should back that up in every step of the process.

As a matter of course, because of the optics but also because of the real bias of parents, the assistant superintendent should not be involved in the hiring process. The process should be "blind"—without names—to the degree possible, ensuring candidates are compared only on the merits. While both candidates may meet the qualifications, presumably the final choice is the better candidate.

The superintendent should be apprised of all this evidence and completely confident about the choice. The superintendent also should protect the privacy of all candidates in any public or private response (such as in reviewing the process with the unsuccessful candidate). Generally, that means describing the step-by-step hiring process to demonstrate it was fair and effective, providing assurance there was thoughtful and in-depth discussion at every stage, and proclaiming support for the final decision.

Sheldon Berman

A response to this case hinges in part on the size of the school district. In a small district, the assistant superintendent might supervise principals directly or be in a line relationship to the person who would supervise the son. It would be difficult for staff to have confidence that a fair and credible supervisory relationship exists, which in turn would make it challenging for both the principal and the assistant superintendent to be effective in their positions.

By contrast, in a large urban or county district, an assistant superintendent might have supervisory duties at another level, in another section of the district or in a completely different department. This separation would lessen the perception of possible bias or influence and would facilitate supervision from a neutral perspective.

In the scenario above, if the school district is small and no official decision has been made, the superintendent should not accept the recommendation of the hiring committee. While the recommended candidate may have the potential to be a terrific principal, the personal circumstances could seriously compromise his ability to lead. It is not worth the risk for the candidate, the assistant superintendent or the district. However, the superintendent could offer to write a letter on behalf of the candidate if he chooses to apply for a principalship in another district.

On the other hand, if the school district in question is large, before making a final decision the superintendent could review the process thoroughly to ensure that nepotism had not influenced the decision and that there would be sufficient organizational distance between the two parties.

POACHING PREVENTION

Scenario: To combat the ongoing loss of its best teachers to neighboring school systems with higher salary schedules, a metropolitan district puts in place a policy developed by the human resources department. When teachers receive contracts in March, they must sign a stipulation to pay a liquidated damages fee of $750 in recruiting costs should they break the contract by June 1. Those resigning after June 1 are assessed the fee and reported to the state for abandonment of contract.

Several teachers complain to the school board when asked to pay the penalty, saying they should be released from their contracts since they are paying a penalty. What advice does the superintendent give the board?

Responses

Mario Ventura

Each year, school districts fill teacher vacancies by seeking to employ the most highly qualified teachers and to ensure students have the best learning experience possible. Historically, economically disadvantaged urban school districts have experienced teacher turnover rates that are higher than suburban and rural school districts. There are costs associated with the recruitment, hiring and training of newly hired teachers.

In most cases, a teacher resigning or asking to be released from their contract in late spring is a manageable situation for a human resources department. By June, the teacher pool of available candidates has been depleted and many of the most qualified teachers have been placed under contract, which in turn creates a hardship for the school district. In this scenario, the school district decided that creating a policy to apply liquidating damages for breaking a contract and to report teacher unprofessional conduct, such as job abandonment, is an effective way to discourage teachers from breaking their contract.

Teachers have the professional responsibility to follow state statutes, education codes and school district policy. Breaking a contract is viewed as unprofessional conduct and the school district has the right to report the teacher to the state for job abandonment. The state could impose disciplinary action against the teacher. The policy needs to clearly state that assessing liquidating damages for a breach of contract is meant to cover loss incurred by the school district and it should not be defined as a penalty.

The superintendent should advise the governing board to seek legal counsel to assist in the evaluation and possible revision of the existing policy and the teacher contract. The policy should be clear in its intent—to recover monetary losses incurred by the school district due to the breach of contract. If the policy indicates or implies the fee is a penalty for breaking the contract, then it could be deemed unenforceable.

Legal counsel can assist to ensure the language in the new policy is clear and aligned to other existing policies and procedures for reporting job abandonment. The teacher contract should contain all the terms of the agreement between the teacher and the school district. Adding the liquidation damages terms to the contract is better practice than having a stipulation.

A change that affects teacher working conditions, such as signing a stipulation to pay liquidating damages, should be communicated and explained prior to releasing contracts. This would allow ample time for teachers to consider their options for employment and the repercussions associated with breaking a contract.

Sheldon Berman

Policies such as this one arise from districts' frustration over losing high-performing teachers at a time when it is very challenging to secure replacements. Such provisions may deter teachers from breaking their contracts but are not the best way to retain people in a competitive environment.

Clearly, it is unprofessional to sign a contract for continued employment and then resign to take a more lucrative job elsewhere. Such shopping for positions does not speak well of the individual. However, it may be preferable that disaffected employees leave rather than stay in the district and potentially spread their dissatisfaction to others.

Some state teacher licensing agencies provide that it is a breach of professional standards for a teacher to depart from employment without providing adequate notice. Where state law permits, a district may report such teachers to the licensing agency for abandonment of contract and/or breach of professional conduct. However, in the end, districts really have no way to legally compel teachers to remain in their employ indefinitely, nor would it foster positive employee-employer relationships to do so.

Regarding the liquidated damages policy, the district should do its homework, consult with its lawyer, and proceed cautiously. Whether the $750 liquidated damages clause is enforceable would depend on state law and the circumstances of the case. Generally, a liquidated damages clause provides that because it would be difficult to determine the actual damages of a breach of contract, the parties agree that "X" dollar amount is a reasonable estimate of damages if a breach were to happen in the future.

Before entering into such an agreement, the district would want to ensure it has proof that the damages that would result from the teacher's breach of contract would be difficult to calculate, and that $750 is a reasonable estimate of the loss. Further, some states have specific laws prohibiting contracts that require teachers to repay any portion of their compensation. There are also collective bargaining issues to consider. In most unionized states, the policy being implemented in this scenario affects the compensation of teachers and would require bargaining with the teachers' union.

Finally, one must consider the negative impact on employee relations in the district. The district would be better served by offering positive incentives for continued employment rather than setting a punitive tone or taking punitive actions. Metropolitan or urban districts should be seeking individuals who are deeply committed to making a difference with urban youth. Individuals leaving for more lucrative positions may not have that commitment.

If a district can't offer a salary that compares well with neighboring districts, it should highlight advantages that others might not make available, such as greater opportunity for growth and advancement; access to special resources; participation in strong induction, mentoring and professional development programs; and/or access to the metropolitan area's social and cultural resources. The district needs to promote its advantages to teachers rather than try to contain employees through punitive measures.

Providing a positive and enthusiastic start to each year in a district is critical, even if it means losing some people to other districts that are paying more or have a less challenging classroom environment. The board should have administration review the policy and recommend changes that will address the teacher retention issue in positive ways. The superintendent should then work with the human resources staff to formulate an alternative to the existing policy.

A FAILURE TO DISCLOSE

Scenario: A candidate for school district communications director with an impressive résumé touting thirty years of public relations experience does not mention a pair of noncriminal state ethics commission violations for a conflict of interest and lobbying incident almost a decade prior. A few days after his hiring, a local newspaper discovers via a Google search the individual had been assessed a $14,000 fine for the earlier acts. He submits his resignation to the superintendent the next day. Should the superintendent promote a statute of limitations on past mistakes?

Responses

Sheldon Berman

The issue is not whether an individual can overcome past mistakes, but whether it is appropriate and responsible to reveal these past mistakes to a prospective employer so that an appropriate decision can be made prior to the individual's hiring. In this case, the candidate took the right action in resigning immediately. The superintendent would be wise to accept that resignation because the candidate's lack of candor about the earlier ethics violations compromises the integrity that a school communications director needs to demonstrate to be credible in the eyes of the press, community and general public.

The position of communications director is a very sensitive, highly public position. If the candidate had revealed the violations earlier in the hiring process, the superintendent would have had an opportunity to consider whether they were sufficiently egregious to disqualify the individual simply based on the facts in that situation.

Depending on the circumstances of the violations, had the candidate provided some evidence of his integrity in addressing them when they occurred and in his years of experience since, the superintendent could have chosen to make a case that the individual's impressive record, openness, remorse and length of time since the violations provided sufficient justification for offering the candidate the director position. However, such a stance would present a significant risk to the credibility of the superintendent and the district.

The superintendent needs to have the utmost confidence in the trustworthiness, credibility and competence of the district's communications director. In this case, the candidate demonstrated poor judgment and insufficient ethical standards in not being straightforward about the earlier violations and thus further compromised his career.

Karl Hertz

It is always kind to give a person a second chance. However, in this case, one needs to dig deeper to find out what questions the candidate was asked before he was hired. It is common today to ask if a candidate has legal actions from the past or other matters that may be embarrassing to the school district or the candidate.

In this scenario, the ethics violations of the past have been labeled "non-criminal," but they certainly are embarrassing both to the candidate and the district. Otherwise, the candidate would not have resigned the next day. For leaving out this piece of history, he is going to have to live with the loss of the position. He would be wise to candidly and immediately inform future employers of his problem in the ethics case.

A NUANCED RECOMMENDATION

Scenario: The superintendent occasionally is asked by a teacher or principal to serve on a doctoral dissertation committee at the local university, where he serves as an adjunct professor. He has come to know one advisee as a conniver who uses his intelligence to manipulate people who don't know him. The superintendent wonders how to respond to his requests for letters of recommendation for positions in neighboring school districts. Is the superintendent obliged to find some good points to share?

Responses

Maggie Lopez

A letter of recommendation is a professional courtesy that we are afforded by our colleagues indicating support for our work and our character. The superintendent is not obligated to write a letter for this individual if he does not feel he can support his candidacy for other positions.

The superintendent has worked with this individual through dissertation process and has obviously observed some behaviors which he does not condone. The fact that the superintendent is questioning the request, and whether he can respond to it, is an indicator that he does not have real enthusiasm for supporting this advisee's request for reference letters as he seeks positions.

A letter from a superintendent typically carries strong influence in the hiring process. Follow-up reference calls to the superintendent, should the individual become a finalist, could create a difficult situation for both the superintendent and applicant.

Though he could focus just on the positive aspects he observed as his dissertation adviser, ultimately he may be asked, "Would you hire this person?" It appears the superintendent's answer may very well be "No," in which case it would create a difficult situation for the superintendent who has written a letter of support for someone he would not himself hire, and for the advisee who thought the reference letter indicated support.

Mario Ventura

The request for a letter of recommendation by a less-than-deserving advisee draws focus to an ethical dilemma that many educators can unexpectedly find themselves in when one's dual professional roles cross paths.

In this scenario, the superintendent serves in two roles—one as a school district superintendent and a second as an adjunct university professor. Careful consideration should be given to potential conflict that may arise between the two professional roles. As a school leader, one of the responsibilities of the superintendent is to support the advancement of qualified leaders. The responsibility of an adjunct professor is to promote the learning of doctoral students. The conflict lies in the student wanting to take advantage of the professor's second role as superintendent.

Though the superintendent has knowledge of the advisee's poor character, there is limited knowledge of the advisee's professional experience, abilities and skills. Supporting the employment or advancement of a less than qualified individual is unethical and could tarnish the superintendent's reputation. Therefore, the superintendent should not feel obligated to comply with the request.

Chapter Nine

Employee Discipline

This chapter addresses the ethics of employee discipline. Unlike student discipline, where the primary focus is educating impressionable children on the ground rules of good behavior, the purpose of staff discipline is to motivate mature adults to honor their professional and contractual obligations, and to terminate their employment relationship if it becomes unsalvageable.

As with all aspects of school administration, the ethical duty to follow the law is paramount. This is especially so when disciplinary actions affecting an employee's livelihood and reputation can expose you and your district to significant liability if not handled correctly.

In the chapter on student discipline, we discussed the Fourteenth Amendment's due process clause, requiring government agencies and officials to provide advance notice and an opportunity to be heard before depriving citizens of property and valuable benefits. Public employees also are entitled to due process when subjected to disciplinary actions affecting their compensation or job security.

The elements and formality of that process vary depending on the severity of the deprivation involved. In addition, state laws or provisions in your district's employment contracts may superimpose additional procedural protections for employees that must be observed. Those protections may include a timeline and format for prior notice of a proposed disciplinary action, specific grounds for particular levels of discipline, rights of appeal, and other important matters.

Fundamental fairness dictates we ask the threshold question whether discipline is necessary to accomplish our objective. Before needlessly tarnishing an employee's reputation and future marketability, consider whether an alternative approach would get you there. If a non-tenured employee commits a minor infraction, demonstrates poor judgment, or fails to meet professional expectations toward the end of the school year—something that warrants severing the relationship—would simply non-renewing his annual contract, or offering him the opportunity to resign, suffice in lieu of placing an involuntary mid-term termination on his record?

Of course, these non-disciplinary options would be inappropriate for more serious misbehavior. However, allowing employees the opportunity to leave with their reputations and dignity intact may be the more ethical course—and pay dividends in the long run in terms of your standing as a tough but compassionate administrator.

Your choice of whether to pursue your objective through disciplinary or non-disciplinary means has other implications for your district. For example, if the affected employee is covered by a union contract with a grievance and arbitration clause, pursuing a disciplinary path may result in adversarial proceedings and litigation expense that could have been avoided.

Let's say, for example, an employee engages in behavior that's unacceptable but could be addressed adequately through forward-looking, counseling-type comments in an annual performance evaluation as opposed to a formal reprimand. You may find you can accomplish your objective just as effectively without creating a disciplinary event that could mire the district in time-consuming and expensive grievance proceedings. This approach might also boost morale by conveying to your staff that your goal is to compassionately support their professional growth, not to tarnish their record.

If you do choose to move forward with discipline, the ethical precepts of fairness and evenhandedness discussed elsewhere in this book govern here as well. In the world of labor and employment relations, those principles are subsumed under the rubric of "just cause," the standard most frequently applied in challenges to an employer's disciplinary actions. The term has come to be synonymous with a multi-factor test almost universally invoked by arbitrators in grievance arbitration hearings.

The "just cause" standard focuses first on whether the employee had reasonable notice of the employer's expectations. Some transgressions are so obvious they don't need to be spelled out, but most aren't.

Let's say you assign a high school teacher to teach a course called "Controversial Issues" with no advance guidance from administration on what's too controversial, and the teacher delves into subjects you consider too edgy for teenagers. Or an employee fails to report misconduct by others where you feel there was a duty to do so. It wouldn't be fair to discipline staff members for crossing boundaries or failing to live up to expectations you didn't apprise them of in advance.

Next, "just cause" considers whether the rule or expectation violated was a reasonable one. Naturally, if it's an infringement of employees' legal rights, it's unenforceable. For example, in our earlier discussions of First Amendment rights as well as the hiring process, we noted some limitations on districts' jurisdiction to impose consequences for employees' behavior in their private lives. But a rule isn't reasonable just because it's legal. If the standard in question is arbitrary on its face or isn't one the employee could have reasonably been expected to meet under the circumstances, it's unlikely a disciplinary sanction would hold up.

Did you conduct a timely and fair investigation? "Just cause" requires that as well. The starting point for any disciplinary process is nailing down the relevant facts. If you've had bad experiences with an employee in the past, or the school community is pressuring you to resolve a high-profile scandal, there may be a temptation to rush to judgment. You must resist that temptation and conduct an investigation that's thorough and impartial—in appearance and in fact. That includes interviewing witnesses with first-hand knowledge of the events, reviewing available documents or video surveillance recordings, and following up on leads.

The next step in the "just cause" analysis is whether the evidence substantiates the allegation. Here, you have some flexibility on how rigorous a standard you choose to hold yourself to.

The "preponderance of the evidence" standard is the one most commonly used in non-criminal proceedings, which is a fairly modest burden of proof—whether it's more likely than not that a certain event occurred. Your state law or local contract provisions may impose the higher "clear and convincing evidence" standard for more serious disciplinary consequences, so be sure to check. A helpful yardstick may be to see if you, or perhaps a small focus group of your inner circle within the administration, would be convinced, if you were the judge or arbitrator on the case.

Is it unethical to impose discipline when there is little hard evidence, but you have a strong belief the employee engaged in wrongdoing? Not necessarily. It would be unprofessional to punish an employee based purely on speculation, but where there is a good faith basis to believe she is guilty, you're free to assess the pros and cons of expending district resources on a disciplinary proceeding and to move forward if you believe the district's best interests are served by doing so. There are occasions where the greater good is served by sending a clear message that certain behavior will not be tolerated, even if you don't have a "slam dunk" case.

The final step for consideration is the appropriateness of the disciplinary sanction imposed. In other words, "Did the punishment fit the crime?" Termination is rarely seen as an appropriate consequence without a prior history of progressive discipline, unless the misbehavior is so egregious that it warrants the ultimate sanction. The trend toward restorative justice may also persuade you to require the employee to make amends by remedying the harm caused by her misbehavior.

A relevant consideration is whether you're dealing with an otherwise responsible employee who had a momentary lapse of judgment, acknowledges his wrongdoing, and sincerely expresses remorse—or a defiant employee who still "doesn't get it." Judges, arbitrators, and other reviewing authorities will surely take these factors into account, so you'd be well advised to do so up front.

The diverse set of disciplinary scenarios covered in this chapter put the different elements of "just cause" to the test. The cases are divided into two sections: the first, dealing with misappropriation of district resources, and the second, addressing misconduct that poses a risk of danger to the staff member or others.

Misappropriation, as used in this chapter, involves far more than the theft of district funds per se. When employees fail to perform their assigned duties, wrongly take credit for colleagues' ideas, or otherwise shirk their responsibilities, that's tantamount to a misappropriation of district resources, and the cases in this chapter treat it as such.

Hopefully, the contributors' insights on the following scenarios will challenge your thinking about employee discipline and provide helpful perspectives that guide you toward the right answers for your own situations.

A PENALTY ON THE HANDOFF

> Scenario: The wife of a high school assistant football coach who was terminated from his coaching position makes copies of the football team's playbook and mails them to several upcoming opponents on the football team's schedule. The wife is a teacher at the high school that had employed her husband. The varsity football coach is furious about the unauthorized playbook distribution and complains to the central office about punishing the offending teacher. Is disciplinary action warranted?

Responses

Sarah Mackenzie

This teacher performed a startlingly vindictive act, one that would certainly mean she would lose the respect of her colleagues. More important, she presents a terrible lesson for students. It's hard to imagine that she thought she had any right to act in this way. And one wonders how she would justify the action if the story were to be published on the front page of the local newspaper. (In fact, it may have been.) It certainly violates the ethical rule of publicity, as well as the golden rule.

As a member of a couple, both of whom work for the same school system, she and her husband had an obligation not to let their relationship interfere with their professional responsibilities. Not only has she violated her teaching responsibilities in the school, but also the expectations of good sportsmanship.

The penalty for a team member who lost his position on the team for some reason and who compromised the team's success in this way would be severe. For a teacher to engage in this kind of behavior is a significant offense, and the resulting discipline for her must be emphasized to underline for students and the entire community its seriousness. At the very least, suspension without pay for a period of time is warranted. Her judgment and professionalism are in question, so the consequence might likely be dismissal.

Sheldon Berman

This unauthorized use of district property constitutes unprofessional conduct by a teacher who seeks to retaliate against the district by undermining the success of the football program. In the end, her behavior hurts students who are giving their best effort to represent their school and brings disrepute to herself, her school, and the district.

If the playbook was developed by the assistant coach prior to his employment with the district, he may have some property rights in its ownership and use. However, his wife's distributing it to opposing teams would still constitute unprofessional conduct.

It is more likely that the playbook was developed collaboratively among the coaching staff and that these individuals were paid with district funds to perform their coaching responsibilities, thereby giving the district ownership of their work product. If that is the case, her unauthorized taking of the playbook belonging to the district, and her apparent intent to deprive the district of the value of its property, may also represent a property crime, depending on that state's law.

Although the teacher and the assistant coach may have a sincere grievance about the assistant coach's dismissal, distributing the playbook is neither an appropriate nor proper manner to address that grievance. Her action embodies conduct unbecoming a teacher, who instead should be modeling ethical behavior for her students. It undermines the confidence students may have placed in her and the respect they have for her as an individual who acts with integrity. Disciplinary action is warranted, although it legally may not rise to the level of dismissal.

The teacher, school, and district should take other actions beyond discipline. A key purpose of high school sports is not about winning but about building character and a sense of teamwork and fair play. Most schools and coaching staffs understand this concept.

The varsity coach probably learned of the playbook distribution from an opposing coach who received a copy. If the other schools in their conference were contacted by the principal or superintendent, it is likely that they would refrain from using the playbook and would destroy any copies they received. Such support for the integrity of the game and the well-being of all students could be an important demonstration of character and honesty for staff and students.

In addition, the district should provide some additional resources to the coaching staff to revise and update the playbook to give the team the best chance possible on the field. If students on the team and their parents are aware of the distribution, the principal should meet with them to discuss the incident and the actions the school and district are taking to support them. Most important, the teacher needs to accept the consequences of her actions and formally apologize to students, parents, and colleagues if she is to re-establish her credibility within the school.

THE SLACKER AND THE SELF-STARTER

> Scenario: Two K–12 directors responsible for math and literacy curricula in the school district often must work together to get a common project completed. One director is a self-starter and routinely works extra hours to do a job well. The other makes contributions but is a 40-hour-a-week person who is content to let her colleague shoulder most of the load. Should the superintendent continue giving extra assignments to the self-starter in order to get work done and meet timelines? Or will this lead the strong performer to burn out or transfer to another school district in the region?

Responses

Sheldon Berman

It is the responsibility of the superintendent to set high expectations for all district leaders. Effective leadership means taking charge and moving the district forward. District leaders must be self-starters and devote whatever time is needed to ensure the job is done right and that projects go smoothly and are completed on deadline. If an individual is not meeting those expectations, it is essential to have the difficult conversation about why that slippage is occurring and how it can be addressed.

Granted, it is important and reasonable that district leaders have a balanced life and that the demands on them are manageable. However, if the superintendent in this scenario is aware of the habitually disproportionate effort and ignores it, he or she is shirking the responsibility to develop professional behavior within the staff.

In this case, the superintendent needs to make expectations clear and assign projects that can be equitably balanced between the directors. If the forty-hour-a-week person still doesn't step up and meet the expectations for shouldering a fair share of the workload and responsibility, it is time to have a respectful conversation about taking a different position that requires less initiative and a more routine schedule. The 40-hour director need not be made to feel guilty about doing less work than the colleague but must choose among priorities and make a decision that addresses the needs and expectations of the district.

Karl Hertz

Every sizable organization has "forty hours and out" people. The superintendent might well start by deciding whether the curriculum projects needed to be shared. This in itself could give relief to the more dedicated director. There are many ways to reward the more productive person. They could include pay, recognition, and advancement. The key is not to have hard workers feel they are being exploited.

The superintendent may wish to give the shirker a less than glowing evaluation. It is important that people clearly know there is dissatisfaction. When friction exists, it is often helpful to have both individuals meet with the superintendent, put the leader's impressions before them, and let the dialogue develop. In this circumstance, doing nothing is not fair.

RECORDING SURREPTITIOUSLY

> Scenario: During a meeting of the superintendent's cabinet, a department head places his cell phone on the table and records the discussion without anyone else knowing. The next day he transcribes what everybody said as a way to hold the superintendent and others accountable for action items discussed. Was the department head obliged to get permission of all those at the table in advance for the recording? A meeting participant complains to the superintendent about the surreptitious recording.

Responses

Mario Ventura

The department head was obligated to obtain permission from all individuals present at the superintendent's cabinet meeting prior to the recording because the act infringes on a person's privacy rights. The recording of an individual's or group's conversation without disclosure that a recording is being made is unethical and, in some states, illegal.

As a district leader and professional educator, the department head is responsible for developing and maintaining trust with all stakeholders of the organization. Though the purpose for recording the superintendent's cabinet meeting may have been to improve follow-through and completion of action items that were discussed, the recording of the meeting without disclosure or consent could very likely adversely affect the relational trust within the group and their effectiveness to work as a team.

The department head also should consider the ethical use of technology and the impact of creating and distributing sensitive information. Once information is captured with a district-owned technology device such as a cell phone or if information is transcribed and stored as a document using a district technology device, the information could be considered a record under the Freedom of Information Act and state public access laws.

The department head should consider taking a professional approach to addressing the issue by bringing the concern to the superintendent or the group and proposing an inclusive process toward reaching a resolution. Taking a more reasonable and collaborative approach will promote trust and increase the executive cabinet's professional effectiveness.

Sheldon Berman

The actions of the department head are, at the very least, a breach of trust among cabinet members and may be sufficiently disrespectful as to warrant discipline. Surreptitiously recording conversations is not only a violation of typical group norms and district policies, but, in many states, recording a meeting without the consent of the parties is illegal. A number of states explicitly require consent from all those who are party to a conversation.

It is unlikely that cabinet meetings are open, public meetings at which a recording would be permissible. In superintendents' cabinet meetings, there is generally an expectation of privacy so that people can feel free to present options, offer perspectives, and take risks in suggesting ideas that may later be rejected. Even if the department head thought the transcription would be helpful to others, his actions reflect poor judgment in not seeking the consent of the superintendent and cabinet prior to recording the meeting.

To record and transcribe a meeting for the purpose of holding others accountable is not within the purview or authority of any department head. It expresses a profound lack of trust in others and in the superintendent to follow through on tasks or commitments. It also undermines whatever spirit of cooperation exists between the department head and other members of the cabinet.

If the department head has sincere concerns about the follow-through of others, including the superintendent, these concerns need to be brought to the attention of the superintendent first in a private conversation and then more publicly at a cabinet meeting, framed as a question about how the group can be more effective in moving plans forward or meeting deadlines, not in the confrontational manner of delivering a transcribed recording.

The superintendent should meet with the department head to discuss the concerns that led to the recording and determine if there is something that the superintendent can or should do to better address those concerns. At the same time, the superintendent should make clear the negative impact the department head's actions have had on the relational trust present with other cabinet members and discuss actions the department head might take to reestablish some level of respect and trust, including, at a minimum, a verbal apology to the meeting participants.

Based on the results of that conversation, the superintendent needs to consider possible discipline and whether the department head should continue as a cabinet member.

DECEPTIVE ILLNESS

Scenario: One of two support personnel in the superintendent's office announces she has a medical condition that would leave her vulnerable to contracting the COVID-19 virus. She takes a four-month medical leave, leading to most of her duties being added to the colleague's platter. When she returns to work, it's discovered she faked the medical claim, yet is allowed to return to her job. The office colleague feels betrayed by the deception and the inaction of the administration. Should some action be taken?

Responses

Sheldon Berman

Medical and personnel issues should remain confidential. Only management and the individual have a right to know what was involved in this situation, whether the leave was faked, and, if so, what action was taken to address the falsification. On the surface, lying to secure a medical leave is a fraudulent act and should result in termination. It not only put additional burden on her colleague but cost the district four months' salary.

It appears there were multiple management failures in the superintendent's office. Vulnerability to COVID-19 doesn't necessitate a leave when the individual could work at home. If her duties required presence in the office, the superintendent could have distributed them among personnel and assigned the individual other tasks that could be done at home. In addition, the superintendent could have provided temporary office help to reduce the burden on remaining staff. Another mistake was not requiring medical certification prior to or at the beginning of the leave, thereby potentially preventing the lengthy absence.

Lack of termination could indicate a failure by management to hold the individual accountable. However, the colleague should not assume that the leave wasn't necessary or that consequences weren't imposed. Perhaps there were consequences that others are not aware of or there was another explanation for leave that requires confidentiality.

Regardless, the superintendent's mismanagement has now been exacerbated by leaving ambiguity around how a person could retain employment after faking medical leave. If the leave was legitimate, once aware of the office friction the superintendent should take immediate action to address rumors and allay staff concerns while protecting confidentiality.

If the superintendent does not act, the colleague faces a difficult choice: either remain silent or raise questions about the superintendent's management and potentially jeopardize her position and relationship with the superintendent. Silence won't heal the division between these two employees or restore trust in the superintendent.

The colleague could speak with the district's human resources director. The HR director may not be able to reveal the circumstances around the leave or the actions taken, but still could hear the colleague's concerns and either reassure her that appropriate action was taken or follow up with an investigation without identifying who brought this matter to the HR department's attention.

MaryEllen Elia

I don't blame the colleague for feeling deceived—after all, she was deceived. I can't think of an instance in any context where faking a medical claim is not unacceptable and unethical at the least, if not legally fraudulent. In this case, I must believe that employee policy is clear around medical claims, related leaves, and all of the compensation and other details surrounding them. The redistribution of work during an employee's absence is common practice, but an absence taken on false pretenses that unfairly burdens coworkers is sure to create feelings of betrayal and resentment among staff.

So, then, how to handle such a mess? If the staff member is allowed back to work, I would hope that a well-documented review of all the facts surrounding this issue takes place followed by some resultant action—a letter in the employee's file detailing missteps and the terms around future discipline/dismissal, transfer to another (lesser) position, and so on. But if no action is taken, then the staff is undermined, sending the wrong message around what is permissible and eroding the culture of the workplace.

THE SLACKING STAFFER

> Scenario: A long-term support staff employee in the school district has two years remaining before he's eligible for full retirement. He has been a valued employee. In recent months, he frequently has been late to work and no longer performs work to standards. Others in the department are tired of carrying this person's load and want him fired or transferred to another department. How should you proceed?

Responses

Paula Mirk

While the staffer must be recognized for his years of service, he also must maintain performance and expectations like everyone else.

Immediate communication with the staffer is in order. Why is he burning out and what can take place to help him? The staffer must be made aware of the impact of his behavior on others (while not spelling out their wish to fire or transfer him), and specific, reasonable goals must be established within a satisfactory timetable.

Sheldon Berman

The first step is for the department head to meet with the employee and have an honest conversation about the changes that people perceive. The tardiness and other behaviors that are affecting his work could have many causes.

It is important to understand the employee's personal situation and to determine whether specific factors might be addressed. For example, there may be a health- or family-related explanation that could be acknowledged and temporarily accommodated. Alternatively, the district may have a suitable vacancy in another position that would re-kindle the employee's career interest and enable him to work until his full retirement date. On the other hand, the individual may essentially be ready to retire. A conversation with his department head could help clarify his interest in an earlier retirement.

As a valued, long-term employee, he should be treated with respect, dignity, and honesty so that he can understand the impact his work-related actions are having on others. Correspondingly, and in fairness to the district and his co-workers, he is responsible for cooperating with his department head to devise a plan that ensures he either meets the expectations of his assigned position or sets an imminent date to retire.

PUNISHMENT FOR A PILFERER

Scenario: The bookkeeper at the school district's high school is found to be pilfering small amounts of money, now totaling about $500, from the student activity fund. The fund consists of money collected by various student organizations and contributions from parents. It does not include public tax dollars. The bookkeeper is a single parent with a good work record over seven years and no criminal history. In the past year, her preschool-age daughter was diagnosed with brain cancer and needs expensive treatment and medical travel not covered by her health insurance policy. Should the school district press charges?

Responses

Sheldon Berman

Although the bookkeeper has a good work history, her recent acts of theft betrayed the trust that parents, staff, and the district placed in her. Granted, she faces challenging family circumstances and may have made a poor decision out of a sense of desperation. However, an employee's personal situation does not justify the appropriation of even small amounts of funds that were intended to benefit students.

Indeed, had she asked colleagues and others for support during this difficult time in her life, it is likely many would have offered assistance. The fact money was stolen on multiple occasions points to an unacceptable pattern of behavior. While one cannot help but feel compassion for the daughter's medical condition, at this point a simple expression of remorse by the bookkeeper would be an insufficient response.

The public trust has been violated, and it is neither just nor appropriate that the bookkeeper remain in her position. The district has an obligation to press charges that will likely result in a misdemeanor offense and, potentially, restitution of the funds.

Karl Hertz

When weighing the ethical question in this case and discerning the greater good, one is confronted with a relatively minor offense being compared with the consequences of the woman losing the position. If we assume the offense is not public knowledge, then the secondary effects of this decision about pressing criminal charges become relatively insignificant and a simple relocation to a position where the person does not handle money could occur quietly.

If, on the other hand, there is public knowledge of the offense, then concern over secondary effects becomes a factor. For instance, if children know about what has happened and are given the notion that stealing will be forgiven the first time, another variable comes into play. In such a scenario, there would have to be ramifications of the pilfering, even if there were no formal charges.

The preceding cases dealt with employees whose offenses involved some form of theft of district resources, whether that be funds, intellectual property, or simply paid time for work that was not performed. The next set of cases revolves around the administration of discipline for employees whose transgressions could present a threat of physical danger.

TOP-RANKED BUT SUSPICIOUS

> Scenario: Jack Reynolds, in his eighteenth year as superintendent, was upset about dealing with a teacher with thirty years in the district who had been accused of battery on a fourth-grade pupil. An arrest warrant was signed by the parent. "You know if I ranked all my teachers from top to bottom, she would be one of those least likely (to hit a child)," Reynolds told a colleague. He placed the teacher on administrative leave even though the only evidence was the child's claim. Did the superintendent act properly?

Responses

Maggie Lopez

The superintendent acted appropriately. When an allegation is made against an employee, the prudent action is to put the employee on administrative leave. Although the superintendent is hesitant to believe the accusation is true, the correct protocol has been followed.

This is apparently going to become a police investigation (owing to the arrest warrant), and the school district should work with the police to provide whatever information is requested. The district's legal counsel can provide any legal support the district needs. Because an arrest warrant is a public document, as are police reports, the information could be accessed by the news media.

The superintendent needs to work with the teacher's principal and legal counsel to be ready to address the student's and family's concerns, as well as staff and community needs as they arise. The district also must remember this is a personnel matter. Any information not cited as public must remain confidential.

Sheldon Berman

Placing the teacher on administrative leave while the charge is pending investigation is appropriate. Despite the superintendent's perceptions of and confidence in the teacher, an accusation of battery must be taken seriously. The involvement of police and the issuance of an arrest warrant make this a more problematic matter to resolve and a public issue that will likely be covered by the media. To not act with sufficient caution could result in the school district being accused of putting children at risk, even though the teacher may have an excellent reputation.

The district will need to initiate its own investigation into the allegation and work alongside the police department without interfering. Interviewing the parent and the student as well as the teacher is a critical start to the investigation. It is essential that the teacher be offered the opportunity to have legal or union counsel present at the interview.

If the incident occurred in school, it is likely that other students or adults observed the event. A nurse may have documented any physical evidence, such as bruises or other marks. If the incident occurred outside of school, the district may have to rely on the police investigation for a determination. The superintendent needs to remain neutral and objective throughout the investigation.

This situation is difficult for both the teacher and superintendent. If the superintendent is correct and the teacher is innocent, the allegation itself may have damaged the teacher's reputation and the community's perceptions of her. In that case, the superintendent can serve the teacher best by expressing his confidence in her as she returns to the classroom and by allaying the fears of parents while not demeaning the student. If, on the other hand, the teacher is found to have struck the child, then administrative leave was the right action prior to disciplinary action by the district.

PRECEDENT WITHOUT POLICY

Scenario: A much-loved high school history teacher is arrested for driving under the influence. It's his second arrest for drunk driving, with the previous arrest taking place more than ten years prior. The district has no policies on dealing with misdemeanor arrests of staff, and the state board tells the school district the matter should be dealt with locally. The superintendent is left worrying about what precedent to set with any decision he makes. How should he proceed?

Responses

Sheldon Berman

Driving under the influence of alcohol is a troubling and potentially dangerous offense, one we continually counsel students against. Being arrested twice for this offense, even though the arrests were years apart, may indicate the teacher has a serious problem with or addiction to alcohol. At the very least, it is evidence of extremely poor judgment.

At this point, the teacher's use of alcohol apparently has not been evident in the classroom. However, news of his arrest will probably travel quickly, undermining his standing among students and parents. His position as an authority figure and role model will likely be diminished. In addition to having a negative impact on his professional and personal life, the arrest is apt to result in the loss of his driver's license, making it harder for him to meet his responsibilities at school and at extracurricular activities.

The superintendent and the principal must begin an investigation that includes reviewing the police report on the latest arrest and then meeting with the teacher to hear his perspective. They will need to determine whether this incident represents a potential addiction to alcohol.

Because alcohol abuse or addiction is considered a medical problem, they may need to make a referral to an Employee Assistance Program or an addiction treatment center and provide a medical leave of absence if the teacher undergoes treatment. Even if addiction isn't present, the teacher's irresponsible use of alcohol necessitates a referral for therapy or counseling with the understanding that another alcohol-related incident, even some years in the future, could jeopardize his career and employment.

As for setting a precedent, the superintendent will want to treat this case as a medical or mental health issue, taking steps that will enable the teacher to resolve the alcohol use or addiction problem and return to teaching, with the understanding that another similar event could end his teaching career.

Sarah Jerome

The superintendent should proceed on two courses of action: investigation of the history teacher and creation of a policy to guide practice in similar future events. The first step in the investigation is to examine the facts, provide due process, determine whether the misconduct has a relationship to the person's ability or fitness to perform assigned duties, and determine the impact on the school and educational community. The superintendent may want to consider a leave of absence for the teacher so the teacher can be assessed and receive treatment as warranted by the assessment.

The district needs a policy to guide practice in this matter and all similar situations in the future. The bottom line is that teachers are held to a higher standard of conduct than the general public, and if the community is offended by the conduct of the teacher, it is likely that the teacher will either resign or be released. The consequences for each misdemeanor increase the likelihood of license suspension or revocation. Drunk driving is a serious matter and must be treated seriously by the district. The job of protecting students and encouraging quality educators is paramount.

HUNTING HE WILL GO

> Scenario: A middle school teacher plans to leave from school on a Friday afternoon for a weekend deer hunting trip. As such, the teacher leaves his new .50-caliber rifle displayed on a gun rack inside the rear window of his pickup truck, which is parked in his space outside the school gym. Parents who notice the gun tell the principal, who asks the teacher to immediately move the gun out of sight and then contacts the central office the following Monday for help in dealing with the matter. Is punishment against the teacher warranted?

Responses

Mario Ventura

Punishment against the teacher is warranted if an investigation finds a violation of the law and/or school district policy related to firearms on school property. The teacher's actions may be found to be within the acceptable boundaries of the law and school policy. However, they may not be within the boundaries of the school community's sociocultural norms in relation to school environments.

In some parts of the country, keeping a rifle in a truck gun rack may be acceptable, and in other parts of the country it may not. An ethical educator considers how parents, students, and staff might react to seeing a rifle in a parked vehicle on school grounds. Could storing a gun in a parked vehicle on a school campus cause emotional and psychological distress to members of the school community? Could this action be problematic by adding risk factors to student and staff safety that the school administration is not aware of?

Sheldon Berman

Gun laws vary widely nationwide, from allowing individuals with permits to carry guns on campus to the strict prohibition of any weapon on school property. Local attitudes and community values play a role as well. Attitudes toward the appropriateness of this teacher's action in a rural community where hunting is widely accepted may deviate greatly from attitudes in an urban environment troubled by gun violence. Therefore, it is important to understand relevant state laws, municipal regulations, school board policies and community mores before taking action.

We expect schools to be safe and secure environments, yet that sense of safety has all too often been undermined by gun violence on school grounds. In this case, parent expressions of concern about the rifle in the truck reflect a realistic fear that children may be in danger, not just from the gun owner, but potentially from someone who might break into the vehicle and remove the rifle from the rack. Most school districts have a policy that prohibits bringing a gun onto school grounds. If a school district lacks such a policy, it should adopt one.

School policy and state law notwithstanding, the action of this individual reflects poor judgment. He has placed his own convenience above the interest of campus safety. Recognizing others' concern for school safety, he should have left his rifle at home, even if it meant a later start to his hunting trip.

Although state laws may vary in terms of whether this teacher's action was legal, a school district has the right to regulate employee behavior. Even if the laws and community mores tolerate guns on campus, at the very least the teacher should be reprimanded. If existing gun laws and policies prohibit the possession of guns on school grounds, much more serious discipline, including possible termination, is appropriate.

Gun violence in schools across the country has created justifiable concern for the safety of our children. As school administrators charged with protecting the emotional and physical welfare of students, staff, and visitors, we must do all we can to ensure safe and secure school environments.

THE PRIVATE POST-PROM AFFAIR

Scenario: A teacher and her husband hosted a post-prom gathering at their farm for their son and his date plus a handful of other prom couples. The number of participants grew larger than expected when uninvited guests turned up. When the teacher suspected alcohol use, she collected car keys, and she subsequently shut down the event when she witnessed a few students consuming beer. The teacher did not make a report to anyone in the school district until someone else divulged information several days later. Should action be taken against the teacher?

Responses

Maggie Lopez

Prom night can be a challenging time for students, parents, and school staff. Planned, positive, after-prom events have become a good opportunity for students to have a more appropriate choice of activities following prom. This was a well-intentioned parent (who is also a teacher) who was attempting to offer a positive after-prom venue for her son and his friends. The teacher acted responsibly by collecting keys and ending the party when she observed alcohol use.

It would have been prudent for the teacher to have informed the district (e.g., principal, central office) of the occurrence in the spirit of "no surprises." Follow-up discussion with the teacher would be appropriate. Although this was a private event, it might be warranted for the district to follow up with students and parents (e.g., the athletes' code of conduct/expectations). If there is policy specific to staff role in the occurrence of such events, it would be important to ensure all staff members are informed on the policy.

Sheldon Berman

This situation is particularly challenging because the host of the party viewed herself in the role of a parent, while most of the attendees, their families, and the community see her primarily as a teacher. Depending upon the state's social hosting laws, she and her husband could have been held liable had a student been injured as a result of alcohol use at the party.

Given the small number of invitees, the teacher's first mistake was allowing intruders to enter and remain at the party. The intruding students acted irresponsibly and disrupted an otherwise positive event, prompting the teacher to take action. She did well to collect students' car keys and end the event.

We assume that she called all the students' parents to pick up their own children and that she informed the parents of those students observed consuming alcohol so they could address the matter individually. Because she controlled the situation, she may have deemed police intervention as unnecessary, instead allowing parents to pursue appropriate discipline of their children.

However, her decision to treat the occasion as a private and non-school event to be handled by parents, without informing the school or police, did not take into account the public nature of her position. Even before the age of social media, such incidents have always been shared among students and parents. That disclosure could compromise her professional reputation and come to the attention of the school administration.

By proactively informing the administration, she could have prevented the principal from being blindsided and enabled the principal to quell rumors, correct misinformation, and defuse criticism of the teacher. In addition, if the students involved in drinking were underage, athletes, or involved in activities in which they had made a commitment to refrain from drinking, it was her obligation to report these students to the administration, if not the police.

The district is not liable because the teacher was not acting within the scope of her employment. However, at a minimum, the teacher should have immediately reported the incident to the principal. Depending on the teacher's past performance, this episode may or may not merit discipline. Either way, the principal should make it clear to the teacher that she must proactively inform the administration of any incident involving students and alcohol and that it is her obligation to report those students she observed drinking.

A THREAT ON RECORD

Scenario: The high school principal is well-respected and credited with disciplinary reforms that led to a forty percent reduction in suspensions and fewer expulsions. But the superintendent receives an audio recording in which the principal, who is also an assistant varsity football coach, can be heard threatening a fourteen-year-old special education student. He is heard on the tape telling the teen, "I'll knock your (expletive) teeth down your throat."

Legal counsel advises the superintendent the tape cannot be used against the principal for criminal or potential disciplinary proceedings because state law prohibits recording someone without permission. How should the district proceed?

Responses

Sheldon Berman

By being given the tape, the superintendent has been alerted to a serious incident and has an obligation to investigate. Although the tape cannot be shared or used as evidence, the superintendent can indicate that she has received a report of an incident. Then she or her designee can interview the student, his parents, and others who may know about this or other incidents where threats and intimidation were used.

The student may not have come forward for fear of retaliation. It is important to treat this matter sensitively and ensure that the student is protected and supported. If the investigation reveals that the principal threatened the student, the student's statement or evidence other than the tape can be used in a disciplinary proceeding.

If the superintendent can't confirm the incident through an investigation, it would still be appropriate for her to meet with the principal and let him know that she received a report that he had threatened a student. The principal can deny the incident happened, but the conversation would still put him on notice of the unacceptability of that kind of behavior. Or the principal can admit it, offer some explanation as to the circumstances, and accept the disciplinary consequences.

This incident should also give the superintendent pause to think about the actual disciplinary reforms put in place by the principal. If he has threatened one student, other similar circumstances may reveal a troubling pattern of discipline based on fear and intimidation. Even if the student or others are unwilling to come forward, the superintendent is forewarned to look more carefully into the disciplinary reforms and approaches the principal uses with students or condones among his staff.

Anonymous letters, statements, or tapes present challenging dilemmas for administrators. We may be inclined to ignore or discount them. While many are erroneous, some point to serious issues presented by an individual who is afraid to step forward publicly. The superintendent can't simply ignore information when issues have been raised. Even if a tape or anonymous material can't be used, a separate investigation may reveal evidence that requires an administrative response or disciplinary action.

Meira Levinson

No school principal should tell a student, "I'll knock your (expletive) teeth down your throat." It doesn't matter how effective he is at reducing suspensions and expulsions or at coaching the football team. Nor does it matter whether the student he is threatening has been diagnosed with special needs. Children should not be threatened with physical violence nor should they be cursed at by school personnel. If this is how the disciplinary reforms—or football victories—have been achieved, then they are not worth the cost.

Because the superintendent cannot legally use the tape to initiate formal disciplinary proceedings against the principal, she must decide how to proceed informally. Confronting the principal about the tape could enable a productive conversation about leadership expectations and anger management.

On the other hand, it might risk exposing the student to retaliation and expose whoever made the tape to risk criminal prosecution for illegally recording the incident. Perhaps the superintendent could encourage the principal to rethink his approach to students without directly discussing the tape—through professional development or district initiation of a school culture survey.

In deciding whether to disclose the tape and how to engage the principal, the superintendent will need to conduct an informal analysis of the likely pros and cons of disclosure and engage in some creative thinking about leadership and personnel management.

At the same time, the district leadership team should take a hard look at the cultures surrounding school discipline, athletics coaching and special education throughout the district. Rather than being a "bad egg," it's quite possible this principal is simply reflecting a more widespread culture of disrespect toward students in one or more of these arenas. Overcoming this risk should be of highest priority to the superintendent and her team.

SAMPLING VINTAGES OVERSEAS

> Scenario: A high school teacher serves as a chaperone of a school-sponsored trip to Europe with a dozen students during spring break. During the trip, the educator and several students who were of legal age consume alcohol in the country they are visiting, sampling a few varieties of wine. Students' parents learn of the consumption following the trip and complain to the high school principal, who advises the superintendent of the matter. How should the administrators handle the complaint?

Responses

Kelly C. Henson

Because it is a school-sponsored trip, the consumption of alcohol by both the teacher and the students must be addressed. It is understood that, in many countries, the consumption of alcohol by students of this age is perfectly permissible, and certainly in countries such as France and Italy the sampling of wines is a cultural experience. However, that cannot supersede the fact that the consumption of alcohol by the teacher and students is not permissible. The educator not only consumed alcohol in the presence of students, but also allowed students to consume alcohol.

The administration must make it clear that an educator's responsibilities do not end when crossing state lines or leaving the country with students. Regardless of where an educator is with students, the educator must comply with applicable policies and laws of the state and school district.

Certainly, the district must do a better job making teachers aware of policies that govern off-campus and out-of-country experiences. And the superintendent must communicate to principals to be aware of these types of activities and appropriately guide teachers. This guidance will help prevent situations such as the one in this scenario where no one is pleased with the outcome.

Sheldon Berman

Wine sampling by students who meet the legal age of the visited country may seem innocuous, just part of the country's culture. However, it is a serious error of judgment on the teacher's part that should result in significant discipline, if not dismissal. The drinking age in the host country is irrelevant.

As a chaperone and district employee, the teacher is responsible for ensuring that students are safe and avoid the use of alcohol or drugs. The rules that students and parents agreed to when enrolling in the trip almost assuredly specified that students follow school rules and not use alcohol during the trip. Even as a cultural experience, the consumption of wine violates those rules. In the United States, purchasing or providing alcohol for underage youth, or even attending an event where alcohol is being consumed by underage youth, is illegal and would end a teacher's career.

As educators, we want students to experience other countries' cultures; but we also carry our own cultural guidelines with us, particularly when it comes to an activity that would be illegal or simply against school rules in the home state. There may be some mitigating circumstances, such as inexperience, to justify something less than dismissal of this teacher. However, the seriousness of the incident leaves administrators with few options.

Chapter Ten

Relationship Boundaries

Is it acceptable for teachers to "friend" students on Facebook? Or for a coach to give a team member a lift home in her personal vehicle on a rainy day? Is it unprofessional for co-workers to date? How about for the PTO president to have the principal's personal cellphone on speed dial? This chapter will focus on the boundaries for acceptable relationships between members of your school community—and your obligations when those boundaries have been crossed.

The education profession has long struggled with the appropriate balance between formality and familiarity in relations between staff and students. All adults in the building are expected to function as role models and authority figures, which necessarily requires that those relationships be somewhat at arm's length. But we all remember that teacher, coach, or bus driver with whom we had a closer relationship—the one who took a personal interest in our well-being and was a formative influence in our lives.

We also know, from the headlines, about personal involvement between students and staff that went horribly wrong, including sexual relationships and other predatory behavior.

Some boundaries are spelled out clearly in the law or your district's policy. Sexual harassment and bullying are two areas where this is often the case. But staff's interactions with students, parents, and each other occur in many different structured and unstructured settings where the ground rules aren't so clearly defined or have traditionally been left to each individual's common sense—sometimes with unfortunate consequences. What rules should govern in these situations, and, just as important, who gets to decide?

Instant access to others through smartphones, email, and social media has made it more challenging to define the proper boundaries and to monitor compliance with them, but even before the digital age the lines could be blurry. In times past, school employees were more likely to live in the communities where they worked, and there was a greater chance they'd have independent relationships with students and co-workers outside of school as neighbors, scoutmasters, "rec" coaches, or relatives.

Today, staff are more likely to commute some distance to their jobs. The odds are greater their initial contact with students and parents stems solely from their employment relationship with your district, but the opportunities for unsupervised electronic interaction are greater. Each generation has faced its own unique challenges in defining and enforcing acceptable boundaries.

It's often said that legislatures and the courts lag behind society in developing legal mandates or prohibitions. That's certainly true for the sort of boundaries we're talking about here, where the law or district policy hasn't explicitly addressed the matter—in large part because there's no broad consensus on where many of these boundaries lie.

For example, take social media contact, sharing personal cellphone numbers and email addresses, texting, and other electronic communication. Opinions vary from one community to another on what's appropriate, and there are even sharp disagreements among stakeholders within school districts.

In keeping with the ethical duty of fairness which grounds much of the discussion in this work, it's crucial that your district leadership develop acceptable ground rules and communicate them to your school community so all involved have fair notice of your expectations. Given the divergent views on the matter, this is one area where leaving it to each employee's common sense alone will invite trouble.

An example of an enlightened approach is the legislation adopted in New Jersey, requiring school districts to develop written policies setting acceptable boundaries for all manner of electronic communication between staff and students. The statute doesn't dictate what those boundaries should be, just that they be developed with input from stakeholders in the school community and shared with anyone affected by them.

This legislation has generated many lively discussions in the development of these policies. Is it acceptable for coaches to text their team members on a weekend to let them know a game's been canceled? Should a troubled student be allowed access to her counselor's cellphone number in case of after-hours meltdowns? Or should electronic communication on personal devices outside of school hours be forbidden altogether?

There is no one-size-fits-all set of "best practices," but there are some strategies districts have used to take advantage of the benefits of this technology while limiting the potential for abuse. For example, some districts permit teachers and students to text each other, but only regarding homework assignments. Coaches' texts to the entire team are appropriate to reinforce logistical arrangements for games. Some districts require that a supervisor, parent, or where appropriate the entire class or team be copied on electronic communications.

"Friending" students on social media sends all the wrong messages. Instead, with administrative approval, a teacher may wish to create a class Facebook page, but without the capability for real-time conversations. The right answer should reflect your school community's values; but in any case, those rules should be conspicuously circulated so everyone's on notice.

Romantic relationships between staff and students are clearly unethical, if not illegal. All staff exercise some level of supervisory responsibility over students, and the notion of a "consensual" relationship is illusory. Some employees are under the misguided impression that once a student reaches adulthood, there's no longer a moral or legal impediment. It's true that, in some states, the law regarding so-called "statutory rape" does not apply once all parties are adults; however, such a relationship with any student, regardless of age or maturity level, is unprofessional, unethical, and should be grounds for dismissal.

What about physical contact that isn't intended as sexual? The answer may depend on whether it's a football coach patting a team member on the back after scoring a touchdown, or a teacher putting an arm around the shoulder of a high school student who appears upset. It would be an overreach to suggest that even the slightest physical contact between staff and students is always inappropriate regardless of the context; however, staff always must be mindful of how protective many students are of their "personal space," and how innocently intended gestures can be misconstrued if a student objects to being touched.

What about boundaries between staff members? There's confusion there, too. For example, society hasn't fully come to grips yet with the ethicality of the office romance. Experience tells us that if it works out, everyone wants to be at the wedding; and if it doesn't, people will tend to blame one party or the other for behaving badly. That's hardly a guideline to help staff plan and monitor their behavior.

As discussed in the chapter on hiring practices, the law is trending steadily in favor of protecting employees' lawful activities in their private lives as long as they don't conflict with job duties. For example, the chapter on conflicts of interest mentioned activities, such as private tutoring of district students, that can be regulated or even forbidden if the district so chooses.

But when it comes to staff relationships, a school district seeking to forbid consensual, non-abusive romantic relationships between co-workers across the board would generally find itself on thin ice legally, unless the district could demonstrate some compelling operational need. That need would be unlikely for relationships between teachers and other non-supervisory staff. On the other hand, such relationships between a staff member and a supervisor, or where one employee has access to confidential information the other doesn't, may require rearranging reporting relationships or other protective measures.

The law in some states will permit you to forbid romantic relationships between co-workers altogether if you believe it's warranted, as long as there's advance notice to the staff. Some employers have tried to straddle the line, permitting such relationships if they're registered in some form with the HR office. This requirement invariably creates awkwardness for all concerned, especially when those relationships end, and is generally not a constructive way to address the matter.

Personal boundaries must also be set, and respected, in dealings between parents and staff. Romantic relationships can create the appearance of favoritism, and it would be manifestly inappropriate for a staff member who is personally involved with a parent to have any supervisory responsibility over that parent's child.

On the other hand, when parents confront school personnel with complaints about grades, discipline, or other issues of concern, they are entitled to be advocates for their children's interests, even if that advocacy can get heated at times. But staff should be protected from conduct by parents that's intimidating or abusive, and you have a duty to protect them when that line is crossed.

Measures available to curb abusive behavior by parents include limiting contacts to designated administrators or, in extreme cases, barring parents from school property. These steps are to be implemented only as a last resort, after all attempts to "lower the temperature" have been exhausted, and with care to assure that the children do not suffer from their parents' misbehavior.

In this chapter, our contributors offer their take on a series of cases exploring boundary issues in a wide range of settings.

OUTING A PARENT OFFENDER

Scenario: An elementary school principal learns, through the local police website, that the father of a girl at his school has confessed to paying for sex with a teenage prostitute after an undercover sting. The man's name does not appear on the county's database of sex offenders because the father is considered at low risk to re-offend. In a meeting with the man and his wife, the principal insists he may not volunteer at the school or be on campus during school hours. The principal does not share any information with the school's parents. Should the parents be told about him?

Responses

Maggie Lopez

By informing the parent that he cannot volunteer at the school or be on campus, the principal has taken the necessary steps to protect the students in his charge. If the police did not find the parent to be enough of a threat to be placed on the sex offender list, then it is not the principal's place to further publicize the father's offense to the parent community.

It is important to note, however, that the father's offense does constitute a public record that is accessible to anyone in the community. The principal may want to consider communication with staff members who have a need to know about this parent not being allowed to volunteer or be present on the campus. This would allow others in the school to be watchful as well.

Sheldon Berman

The precautionary action of barring this father from the school campus and school activities is appropriate and sufficient. For meetings essential to the daughter's education, the principal could hold them online or after school if he is accompanied by another adult. To ensure the precautions are comprehensive and taken seriously, the principal could issue a no-trespass notice through the police department outlining the terms of access to the school.

The local police department already has made the arrest information available to the public and, in many communities, that information will circulate among parents. The court, after fully vetting the crime and the individual, has not required him to register as a sex offender and has determined that he is at low risk to re-offend.

If the court, which has the authority to make such a determination, has not required that he report as a sex offender, then it would be problematic for the school to overreach in its notification. On the one hand, such action could open the school up to civil liability. On the other hand, it could set a precedent under which parents would expect the school to disseminate controversial information that came to its attention in the future. Exercising discretion in this current situation will better serve the family, the child, the school, and the community.

THE DELAYED DISMISSAL

> Scenario: The superintendent discovers a female teacher may be having an affair with an eleventh-grade female student. The initial confrontation with the teacher elicits a denial. After a weekend of thinking about the consequences, the teacher confesses. The superintendent's first inclination is to fire the teacher on

the spot. But only four more weeks remain in the school year, including exam preparation. Would it be a better, less disruptive plan to insist the teacher leave the profession when the school year ends in another month, forbid the teacher to have any contact whatsoever with the student and begin a quiet counseling process with the student?

Responses

Sheldon Berman

A teacher who is having a sexual relationship with a student—be it physical or via telephone, Internet, or social media—presents a very serious ethical and legal problem. The teacher has abused her authority, misused her position and, depending upon the state, may have committed a crime. A superintendent faced with this kind of information must first ascertain that the information is credible. If it is, the superintendent's response should be neither to confront the teacher nor to contemplate "low keying" the situation until the end of the year.

The appropriate legal and ethical response is to place the teacher on administrative leave while an investigation is conducted, notify the student's parents of the information that the superintendent received, and contact the appropriate legal authorities so they can pursue an investigation. Each state has laws about reporting sexual misconduct. Although these laws may differ in detail, they generally require immediate reporting to law enforcement and child protection agencies whenever a mandatory reporter has reasonable cause to believe that a sexual crime has been committed against a child.

There is little question about what latitude a superintendent has in this kind of situation. As disruptive and as painful as it may be, the superintendent and the district have an obligation to act immediately and allow the legal system, with its higher standards of due process, to take its course.

It is very disturbing when a teacher violates the basic trust invested in her or him by parents and the public, and the district bears direct responsibility for responding promptly and decisively. Also, in many states, when the superintendent reasonably believes that a teacher has engaged in acts of gross neglect of duty, including any sexual conduct with a student, the superintendent must report it to the teacher licensing board promptly in order to permit the licensing board to consider disciplinary sanctions against the teacher.

Once these initial actions have been taken, the superintendent can then focus on working with the student and her parents to determine how the district can best support them. The superintendent also needs to ensure that an effective substitute teacher is in place as quickly as possible and that staff members are prepared to handle student/community reaction if the news becomes public. Should it eventually be determined that no laws were broken and that the justice system has no penalty to impose upon the teacher, it then falls to the district to follow its own policies, which will almost certainly result in the teacher's resignation or termination.

Because such incidents have the potential to significantly disrupt a school's educational process, it is essential to manage the situation thoughtfully and pre-emptively. A strong and immediate response assures students and the community that the district will not tolerate abuse of students and helps restore the school's focus on its academic mission.

Joan McRobbie

The superintendent needs to let the teacher go. Immediate action sends a strong message that the teacher's behavior is a major ethical breach and will not be tolerated. The student should go into counseling, and the superintendent should work with the principal and faculty to create ways to help all affected students deal with the issue as well as overcome this huge distraction and prepare for exams.

The alternative plan of waiting a month not only hedges about the seriousness of the teacher's actions but is unlikely to curb disruption. The teacher's continuing presence would create an environment of extended speculation among students, staff, and parents about what happened. As a news story, it could take on a life of its own, with reporters and cameras showing up daily. An already bad situation for the student in question could become considerably worse.

Removing the teacher deflates the sense of ongoing drama. But in the aftermath, people will want the superintendent to address their concerns, which may range from, Are our children safe? to, The district discriminated unfairly against a wonderful teacher because she's gay.

Internally, the superintendent needs to ask, is this an isolated incident or a culture problem? Assuming the former, there nonetheless needs to be faculty-wide discussion. Externally, personnel policies constrain district leaders from discussing the particulars, but the superintendent can convene parent/community meetings to discuss policies, school values, and the safeguarding of students.

Particularly important is ensuring that students have ways to air their reactions face-to-face with key teachers or counselors who can facilitate dialogue about teacher-student relations, sexual preferences, and "how we treat each other in this school community." Especially for the sake of the student victim, it's critical to address social media and seek and support student leadership in averting the potential for destructive consequences.

A SURPRISE IN STORAGE

Scenario: A teacher lends his personal jump drive to students in his Advanced Placement World History course so they can use material stored on the drive for a major group project. The students open a written document that contains sexually graphic themes. Several students are exposed to the material. Their parents learn of the discovery and complain to the principal. What actions are warranted?

Responses

Sheldon Berman

The teacher may argue that the jump drive was personal equipment and not school property, that the students were supposed to access only particular files, and that the material was not pornographic but simply contained sexual themes. However, none of these arguments meet the standards teachers must maintain in their work.

First, the teacher should not have provided his personal jump drive with personal documents to students for use in a class project. He could have relayed files to students in numerous ways without incurring the possibility of sharing inappropriate or personal material.

Second, because he used the drive instructionally, the documents on the drive are now reviewable by the administration for their appropriateness. Given that the class is an AP World History course, it is unlikely that the document mistakenly accessed by students is germane to the subject or part of the curriculum.

Finally, it is highly inappropriate for teachers to provide sexually graphic material to students, unless it is in an approved part of the curriculum such as a health class on human sexuality. The material may be legal, in the sense that it does not contain pornographic images. However, it was inappropriate for students to read, and the teacher may have created a sexually charged environment that crossed the boundary of appropriate relationships with students. It also undermined, potentially permanently, students' and parents' confidence in and respect for the teacher.

The administration needs to pursue a thorough investigation, including searching the teacher's school computer to determine if there are other similar documents stored on school property. The findings of the investigation are likely to result in discipline that could rise to dismissal.

The degree of discipline depends on: the history of the teacher's performance, particularly around using inappropriate materials in class; the nature and explicitness of the material accessed by the students; and the extent to which the teacher assumes responsibility for his error. If the circumstances indicate that the teacher can effectively continue in his position, the teacher should strive to regain the respect of his students by first acknowledging the error and then apologizing to the students and their parents.

Maggie Lopez

The principal, having informed his supervisor and having reviewed district policy related to the incident, needs to meet with the teacher and talk to him about the complaint that has been lodged. The teacher may choose to talk to the principal or may request representation before talking to the principal.

The teacher needs to be placed on paid administrative leave and an investigation needs to be conducted. The principal needs to talk to the teacher, students, and anyone else involved or having information related to the matter. The jump drive needs to be reviewed by the principal and the instructional technology director to determine the nature of the content that has been called into question. Human resources, IT, and legal counsel can provide support in this process.

Finally, the principal needs to review the documentation from parent calls. After talking to all involved and reviewing all data and applicable policies, the principal may need to have an additional conversation with the teacher or others involved for clarification.

Upon review of the information collected, the critical questions to be considered are: Was the content on the jump drive simply inappropriate or was it of a pornographic or illegal nature? If illegal, law enforcement would need to be involved. Did the teacher break policies? If policies were broken, which policies, and were they serious enough to constitute reprimand or termination?

Ultimately the principal will need to determine, based on his data, what action to recommend. Depending on the outcome of the investigation, actions could include follow-up discussion with the teacher, the teacher being reprimanded, or the teacher being recommended to the board of education for termination. Follow-up with students, parents and/or staff will need to be determined, while also taking into account that this is a personnel matter.

MR. M'S SHOULDER MASSAGE

Scenario: The newly hired high school principal comes to the superintendent because a new guidance counselor tells him a student confides she is uncomfortable with Mr. M, a math teacher, giving her a shoulder massage, as he apparently did to several other young women during a senior class meeting. The student tells her counselor she does not want the counselor to tell anyone and does not want the teacher to be confronted as she is certain he will fail her in advanced algebra. How should this proceed?

Responses

Meira Levinson

It sounds as if everyone needs a refresher course on handling sexual harassment allegations and other concerns about inappropriate teacher behavior toward students.

The counselor should have well-developed practices for informing students that while he respects and protects their confidentiality, he also is responsible for protecting students from harm, which includes reporting potential illegal behavior. He and the high school principal also should well know the district's policies addressing reports of inappropriate teacher behavior.

For the sake of students and staff, the district should have clear procedures spelled out in advance for reporting of confidential information; the investigation process; monitoring, reassignment, or suspension of adults during the investigation; student protections including reassignment of classes if needed; and guidelines about resolution options and appropriate protections of students and staff moving forward. Due process cannot be ensured ad hoc.

Sheldon Berman

Students need to feel physically and emotionally safe in school, particularly in interactions with adults where a difference in power, authority and age could exert undue and inappropriate influence on a student. The counselor made the right decision in coming forward to inform the principal, as did the student in coming forward to the counselor.

The counselor needs to reassure the student that she was right to bring this incident to the attention of another adult. The counselor can reassure the student that she will do her best to protect the student's identity, while explaining that the school must ensure that Mr. M does not continue to make her, or other students, feel uneasy. If there is scheduling flexibility, the counselor may also offer to make a schedule change and transfer the student to another teacher's advanced algebra class, without identifying to Mr. M the real reason for the change.

It is important for the student to understand that the school needs to document this and other incidents to protect all students from inappropriate behavior. The counselor should encourage the student to report any other past or future concerning actions or statements made by Mr. M.

The principal has an obligation to investigate further and determine whether disciplinary action is warranted. Although the teacher may not have had ill intent and may have meant the shoulder massage as a gesture of support, it is not appropriate to touch students in this manner, regardless of the student's or teacher's gender. Not only can this conduct make students uncomfortable, but, viewed through a different lens, such touching could be a form of grooming behavior by a child predator.

Because both the principal and the guidance counselor are new, they may have no knowledge of any prior incidents involving Mr. M. Therefore, the principal needs to begin the investigation by examining personnel records and incident reports that may reveal a pattern of behavior.

Because this behavior occurred at a senior class meeting and other young women may have had a similar experience at other meetings, the principal needs to interview teachers who were present at this and previous meetings that Mr. M attended. Because the student reported that other students had been similarly touched, the principal needs to interview any student who was reported as having been touched. The interviews must be carefully crafted to solicit information while not creating rumors that could unduly damage the teacher's reputation, particularly if this was a first and isolated incident.

Based on his investigation, the principal needs to meet with Mr. M, after recommending that he bring either union or legal representation, to make clear the inappropriateness of touching students and the resulting discomfort that undermines the teacher-student relationship. If documentation reveals a student's name, Mr. M should be emphatically advised that any attempt at retaliation will be severely punished. If the investigation reveals a pattern of misbehavior or gives rise to greater concern, disciplinary action or dismissal may be appropriate.

PUNISHING THE HARASSER ... OR NOT?

Scenario: The superintendent is dealing with a sexual harassment allegation involving a principal and an office staff member—something the superintendent characterizes as "one person's word against the other." The school board's attorney recommends allowing the alleged perpetrator to come back to work with a sternly worded letter of reprimand. The superintendent believes the principal should remain on leave for the duration of the year but has some doubt, admitting, "It was clearly my opinion that the alleged person did cross the line." How might you proceed?

Responses

Sheldon Berman

Sexual harassment involves a range of behaviors from indirect comments that make a person uncomfortable to quid pro quo solicitations of sexual favors from a subordinate. Although the reasons for the allegation in this case are not specified, neither a letter of reprimand nor continued leave will resolve the issue.

If the superintendent believes the principal crossed the line, returning the principal to the school with a reprimand, even later, will not allay the victim's concern. Leaving the situation as one person's word against another's demeans the victim and perpetuates a hostile environment.

The superintendent may not have done a sufficient job of investigating the allegation. Evidently, the principal disavows any wrongdoing. Given all the training in harassment that administrators receive, the principal should be aware of the laws and the implications of his alleged actions.

At this point, the superintendent should press the issue with the principal to determine whether the principal denies the incident(s) ever happened—or will acknowledge that statements or actions occurred that could have been interpreted or even misinterpreted in a way that made the office staff member uncomfortable. While outright denial may mean the principal fails to recognize the impact of the statements or actions and thus should not return to the position, acceptance of responsibility raises the possibility of a resolution.

The superintendent also must interview the victim to uncover additional evidence. In situations like this, the individual often confides in close friends or colleagues, and they may be able to confirm that the victim shared these concerns. Since harassing behavior is often evident to observers, the superintendent must widen the net and interview others who may have observed the alleged behavior.

At the same time, the superintendent must remain open to the possibility that other circumstances may have motivated the complainant and that the principal's denial is truthful. It is important to complete the investigation in a timely manner because many people are affected, and the ramifications can escalate over time.

If a thorough investigation confirms that one or more incidents of harassment did take place, the principal cannot be permitted to return to the position. If the incident was a misunderstanding and the principal is willing to acknowledge this and address it directly, the superintendent may want to determine whether the two individuals can work together again effectively.

One initial step is to directly ask the victim what he or she would like to have happen. Honoring the victim's perceptions and supporting that individual are critical not only to that employee but to the entire staff. How the superintendent manages the situation will make a clear statement as to whether this kind of behavior will be tolerated, whether people will be respected and protected, and whether the working environment will be free of harassment.

Maggie Lopez

A sexual harassment allegation is a serious matter. Consequently, the superintendent should adhere to the specific district policies and procedures that address sexual harassment allegations.

The superintendent needs to take this allegation seriously and direct the human resources department to investigate the alleged sexual harassment claim against the principal. Without an investigation where the facts can be reviewed under the guidance of legal counsel, no further decisions can be made. Until the investigation is completed, the principal should not return to the school.

Once the district completes the investigation on the claim filed, then the facts should direct the superintendent, with direction from legal counsel, to determine the next steps. These steps may include a reprimand with a plan to address resolution between the principal and staff member, dismissal or resignation of the principal if the facts warrant such action, or any other prudent and reasonable actions that ensure the concern has been appropriately and legally addressed.

WITNESS FOR DUBIOUS CHARACTER

Scenario: The superintendent of a small school district is approached by a neighbor whom he has known for about ten years. The neighbor, fifty-four, says he was recently convicted of unlawful contact with a minor, a felony, in a case that involved sexually touching an eleven-year-old boy through his clothes. This happened in a community in a bordering state where the neighbor was working at a university. He asks the superintendent to serve as a character witness at his upcoming sentencing.

After obtaining support from his school board, the superintendent agrees, saying he doesn't condone the behavior "but feel that it was my obligation to offer what I knew of him so the judge could make the very best decision he could." Did the superintendent compromise his leadership duty?

Responses

Maggie Lopez

The superintendent will compromise his leadership role and duties by testifying. His actions, regardless of intent, will send a message he can look beyond the neighbor's abhorrent behavior and still offer him support. He has no obligation to be a character witness for his neighbor when the individual has violated a child.

Additionally, the superintendent should not have put the school board in a situation where they had to respond to this request. This is poor judgment on the part of the superintendent. Aside from the ethical message the superintendent will send by serving as a character witness and the fallout it will have for the district, the superintendent should have considered the hurtful message this will send to students and families who have experienced similar trauma.

Glenn "Max" McGee

The superintendent should update his résumé. While he may have obtained board support in closed session or through individual conversations with members, there was not a public board vote. It is highly unlikely board members will stand by a leader who publicly supports a convicted child sex offender at sentencing.

Cases like this are high-profile in the media, and the fact the superintendent will speak in support of the felon's character will likely receive significant media attention. The term "guilt by association" may be an unfortunate perception, but in public life the adage "perception is reality" is all too true. Actions matter more than words, and his support will be perceived as de facto condoning of his neighbor's felonious activity.

SHIELDING FROM DANGER?

Scenario: A high school student tells a teacher she does not want to go home the day before winter break because she fears her mother's boyfriend. The teacher takes the student home with her, then contacts the mother, who insists her daughter be brought home immediately. The student calls her father living in a bordering state, who promises to pick up his daughter the next day and grants permission for the daughter to remain overnight with the teacher. Following the break, the principal and superintendent learn the father has taken his daughter to his residence. The mother is livid. What actions should they take?

Responses

Sheldon Berman

The teacher's compassion and the trusting relationship she has developed with the student are commendable. The student's alerting the teacher to her fear of the mother's boyfriend was an important first step in securing assistance to address the situation. Ethically and legally, the teacher had a responsibility to help ensure the child's safety. However, there are serious problems with the way this teacher chose to respond.

Schools and other institutions that work with children and youth are generally required to provide all staff with training on mandated reporting. As a mandated reporter, the teacher has a legal responsibility to report to the school principal, the police, or the state's child welfare department as soon as she is aware that a child is at risk of physical or emotional injury or neglect. In this case, the teacher faces repercussions for ignoring her obligation to report, thereby violating school procedures and administrative policies. Her failure to report has left her vulnerable to such consequences as the loss of her teaching license, fines, or even prison.

There are good reasons for these reporting requirements. The teacher is not an investigator. Although she may think she understands the situation, she does not have the background, training, or authority to appropriately investigate the student's allegations or address her concerns.

In fact, the teacher's actions could have inadvertently placed the student in even greater jeopardy. It is possible that a family court had considered the evidence before and either awarded sole legal custody to the mother or placed limitations on the father's contact with his daughter.

In addition, taking the student home without consulting her administrator or other authorities and against the will of the mother leaves the teacher open to legal claims. The school does not have custodial rights and, by taking this action unilaterally, the teacher has inserted herself into a family situation without knowing the legal relationships among family members and with no authority to intervene.

Although the teacher may have had the best of intentions, her action could be considered kidnapping or custodial interference by the parent and/or by law enforcement. Acting as a school employee, she has also placed the school and district at risk of liability. The teacher's concern for the student's welfare was admirable. However, taking the student home with her reflected poor judgment, a lack of professional boundaries, and disregard for state laws and administrative procedures.

Upon hearing the student's apprehension, the teacher should have immediately met with the principal, guidance counselor, school social worker or nurse to report what she had learned and discuss how best to support the student's safety. If those individuals were not available, she should have contacted the police or the state's child welfare agency. Depending on the degree of risk the student was experiencing at home, community resources might have provided assistance or lodging while the home situation was properly investigated.

The principal, having become aware of the situation after the fact, needs to immediately file a report with the appropriate state authorities. The principal should provide the teacher with the opportunity to explain her decisions and discuss with her the inappropriateness of her intervention. It is highly likely that the principal will also need to take disciplinary action. The state may pursue its own action against the teacher, including the possible revocation of her teaching license.

Kelly C. Henson

The first issue that must be addressed is the educator's lack of proper action regarding the student's assertion that she fears her mother's boyfriend. The teacher should have immediately reported the information to the principal or principal's designee. The principal is charged with reporting to the proper social service/child protection agency and/or law enforcement—whatever is required by state code and/or board policy. Disciplinary action against the teacher is warranted in this case as failure to report is a serious violation.

The second issue is the teacher's decision to take the student home with her and likely ignore a custody agreement by allowing the father to take the student to his home. Both choices represent serious errors in judgment by the teacher and, at a minimum, require disciplinary action. Law enforcement also may have interest in the teacher's decision to take the student home and the fact that the teacher's actions led to the father (presumptive noncustodial parent) taking the student to his home. The fact that the father lives out of state makes this a potentially even more serious error in judgment.

Chapter Eleven

Funding

In this chapter, we examine the ethical challenges in acquiring, and prioritizing delivery of, goods and services in your district. School administrators are charged with responsibility to line up the talent and other resources necessary to fulfill the educational commitments your district has made to the community. In doing so, it's your obligation, as steward of the district's finances, to secure the biggest "bang for the buck" while remaining faithful to your district's vision of its role in the local community.

As we've discussed in earlier chapters, a cornerstone of your ethical duties is compliance with the law. The philosophy underlying most government procurement laws is that the public is usually best served by paying the lowest price. Of course, that's not always the case. Maybe you've heard the joke about the astronaut blasting off into space, hoping his capsule wasn't built by the lowest bidder.

To be sure, pinching pennies can sometimes cost you more in the long run if the cheapest alternative isn't up to your standards. That's why, if you're bound by a public bidding law requiring you to award a particular contract to the lowest bidder, you have a duty to be sure the specifications precisely and completely convey your expectations for quality and performance.

Many procurement decisions entail some measure of subjectivity where uniform specifications and awards to the lowest bidder aren't feasible. The most common examples are legal, architectural, or other professional services where intangible factors such as trust level and relatability play a crucial role. Of course, whenever contracts are awarded without formal bidding, there's always the prospect that political pressure or undisclosed personal relationships may infect the process. In the end, it's your ethical obligation to ensure that these decisions are made on the merits.

Be mindful of appearances that can be deceiving. Let's say you're comparing the hourly rates of vendors seeking your district's business. A lower rate is meaningless if the individuals assigned to the project are so inexperienced that you're paying for their learning curve. A professional with the wisdom and experience to justify the higher rate may cost less in the long run. Again, your obligation is to pursue the highest quality at the most advantageous price overall.

Oftentimes there will be confusion among your staff about who's authorized to make contractual commitments on the district's behalf. You may have a high school principal who's under the misimpression he can sign a contract to rent a catering hall for the prom, not realizing that his school is not a legal entity in itself but merely a building owned and run by the school district. All staff must be informed that legally binding commitments for the district can be made only by those explicitly authorized by law or board policy to do so.

A prime example of how good intentions can lead to trouble is the common practice of teachers, with the best of intentions and entirely on their own, downloading educational apps from the internet onto their personal smartphones for classroom use. From an educational standpoint, if the content of those apps hasn't been approved by curriculum supervisors, they may conflict with your district's educational philosophy. And when those teachers "agree" to online vendors' terms of service, they may be unwittingly obligating themselves, or even the district, to legal or financial obligations no one in a position of authority has seen or approved.

Sometimes, the pursuit of economy will collide with other values that are important to your district. Take, for example, two scenarios discussed in this chapter examining the appropriateness of paying more to "hire local," or using unpaid volunteers who may cost full-time employees their jobs. There's nothing inherently wrong in doing so if it's in furtherance of the district's vision of its role in the community; however, it may conflict with other values and priorities that could present ethical dilemmas in making these choices.

Along the same lines, questions often arise about the appropriateness, and even the legality, of donating district funds or resources to individuals or groups in the community. Most would agree that donating public funds for private purposes is wrong, and some states have constitutional provisions or statutes explicitly prohibiting it. But is it unethical to provide free meals to students and their families who lost their homes to a tornado? Or to voluntarily raise the minimum wage for part-time recess aides to help them make ends meet? Or to purchase a district table at a community benefit dinner to raise funds for an important local cause?

The answer depends on whether you can articulate a legitimate institutional interest for engaging in this activity. Today, our public schools do far more than teach "the three R's." Many offer before- and after-school programs, school-based mental health clinics, breakfast programs, summer camps, and other non-educational services to meet the needs of the families they serve. In our chapter on board relations we'll discuss who's responsible for conceptualizing your district's mission. But once it's been developed, your ethical duty is to align your handling of the district's finances accordingly.

What about the standards you apply when accepting donations or advertising from outside individuals or organizations, or even from booster clubs, PTOs and other support groups loosely affiliated with the district? Does it matter if the new turf field at the football stadium is underwritten by the alcohol, tobacco, or firearm industry? Or if the band parents want to use the muscle of their fundraising prowess to influence your selection of the new band director?

In the next chapter we'll discuss in more depth the implications of taking stands on controversial issues; but suffice it to say, for now, that how you handle these matters can be perceived by some in the community as endorsing or rejecting others' politics, values, or priorities—so be sure your messaging to the community is clear on these matters. In fact, it is helpful and advisable to have board policies outlining appropriate relations with outside or affiliated groups and addressing these boundary and donation issues.

Equitably allocating resources among the schools or constituent groups in your district also presents challenges. In earlier chapters we've emphasized the importance of treating similarly situated individuals equally, unless there's good reason not to. The same holds true here. The quality of students' educational experience shouldn't depend on which of your three middle schools they attend. Decisions regarding staff-student ratios, school construction, available technology, and even sports equipment should reflect that commitment to equity.

You may face the dilemma of individuals or organizations associated with a school in your district raising funds or securing donations on their own—to benefit just that one school. These well-intentioned efforts can create disparities from one school to another that put some students in your district at a disadvantage. Things can get further complicated when those raising the funds, or making the donations, insist they be used for purposes that don't necessarily reflect the district's priorities. Maintaining control of your district's operations without alienating these stakeholders can be a delicate matter.

As we've also noted earlier, perception can be as important as reality. Even though you're acquiring and allocating district resources properly, some sectors of your school community may not see it that way.

In many districts, there's a misguided belief that schools are "better" on one side of town. Naturally, students' overall school experience can be shaped by socioeconomic and demographic factors at work in their neighborhoods that you have no control over. But if the quality of education is uniform throughout the schools of your district and the data backs that up, it's important to shape your messaging and present an accurate picture to dispel the myth of disparity. If there is a disparity in quality, it's important to correct any inequitable distribution of resources.

The cases discussed in this chapter are divided into two parts. The first set focuses on obtaining resources. The second addresses how they're allocated within the school community. Our contributors offer their take on ways that responsible school administrators should tackle these complex issues.

OVERVALUING VOLUNTEERS

Scenario: Community members have responded to their town's worsening budget situation by volunteering at the libraries in each of the school district's six schools. They commit so many hours that the district has laid off a couple of long-term, full-time employees. Having fewer employees means a slight reduction in property taxes, but it harms those left jobless. Should the school district's leadership reconsider the extent to which it relies on volunteers?

Responses

Sheldon Berman

Communities want quality schools. In their compassion for children, community members often step forward to fill gaps emerging from schools' financial difficulties. Bringing volunteers into the school in support roles builds on individuals' generosity in a way that clearly benefits students and staff. It also educates citizens about the challenges teachers, schools, and the district face in hard economic times.

Faced with declining revenues, many schools reluctantly reduce or eliminate media specialists and other special area staff. Class sizes increase and support services to children decline. Using volunteers as a stopgap measure is an acceptable response until conditions improve. However, volunteers should not be used to intentionally replace employees in order to reduce taxes. If labor reductions are necessary, they should be made thoughtfully, systemically and ethically, not opportunistically.

Taking advantage of volunteers' generosity in order to replace employees compromises the community's well-being and quality of life and its sense of fairness to individuals who serve the common good. It replaces professionals qualified to offer exemplary services with well-meaning but untrained individuals who cannot provide students with a comparable level of service and reliability.

Taxes sustain our common commitments and the common good. The district's role is to maximize opportunities to improve the success of children and to present the community with a realistic request for funding that best meets students' needs. When the community's economics seriously compromise its ability to raise sufficient revenues, schools must adjust, but these decisions should be based upon students' best interests. The district should not replace employees with volunteers simply as an expedient way to reduce taxes.

Nevertheless, this district should seize the opportunity to welcome and encourage volunteers. Volunteers can supplement, rather than supplant, the support provided to students through alternative uses of their time and energy that do not entail taking employees' jobs. The district has an opportunity to provide added support to children, while educating the community about the importance of adequately funding schools so that students have the learning experiences necessary for success.

Roy Dexheimer

Volunteers are wonderful. They often perform tasks others don't have time to do, and they can be great ambassadors for school support in the community. However, they are not necessarily dependable or even knowledgeable about protocols in some instances. There is skill required in managing a library, and while extra hands are welcomed, sometimes you need more, not less, professional time to oversee volunteers' efforts.

Volunteers are not replacements. This isn't so much a matter of ethical behavior as much as it just isn't smart management. Would we lay off police officers or firefighters and replace them with eager but untrained volunteers? Not likely.

SOLICITING FOR HER STUDENTS

Scenario: A teacher submits a request through DonorsChoose, an online tool to solicit funds for targeted projects, for a class set of twenty Chromebooks without seeking authorization from the school district, which is identified in the request along with the school, grade, and teacher. The district's policy, which is not mentioned, requires that gifts become school district property. The teacher also communicates to the parents of her students: "In lieu of small holiday gifts, please contribute to the DonorsChoose request." Should the solicitation be allowed to proceed?

Responses

Sarah Jerome

The teacher is to be complimented on her ingenuity and interest in providing technology opportunities for her students. The adage "where there's a will, there's a way" comes to mind. However, she is not in a one-room school but likely working in a school district with multiple schools and grades. She is part of a bigger picture. The school district is likely to have a board-approved technology plan with a strategy for resource distribution based on grades, curriculum, and teacher training. The solicitation should stop.

The teacher will need two approvals: one for the purchase of the Chromebooks and one for the source of the funding. The district is likely to have board policies on each area. The appropriate steps to seek school authorization for solicitation of funds or other gifts must be followed. Those policies are in place to protect both the district and the teacher.

There are many questions that will need to be answered before the twenty Chromebooks are approved. Are the Chromebooks part of the district's technology plan? If so, is there a sequence for distribution by grade level, by school, by subject area? Does this acquisition disturb the equitable distribution of the approved tech plan? Does this addition create a "have" and "have not" problem within the school?

Before the teacher proceeds with the funding request, the district will need to decide if DonorsChoose is an acceptable option. If it is, would the district encourage all the teachers in the school to fund Chromebooks for each class in the same manner?

Maggie Lopez

The solicitation should proceed. However, before moving forward with the request, the teacher should take some additional steps.

The teacher needs to discuss the funding request with the principal/district. DonorsChoose has specific expectations and protocols for funding recipients. It is important for both the teacher and district to have knowledge of these expectations for funding. There also should be some coordination with the IT department to ensure the Chromebooks are compatible with district specifications for technology.

This district's policy on gifts is "gifts become district property." If the teacher receives the funding for the Chromebooks from the DonorsChoose project, the Chromebooks are in essence a "gift" or donation to the classroom and would become district property. Regardless of the policy, it is typical practice that resources garnered for classrooms and students, through grants or charitable organizations, become district/school property.

There are some exceptions when the grant or charitable organization dictates that items awarded (e.g., books) are to be distributed to the students for personal ownership at the end of the project. Something to consider is whether the Chromebooks would follow the teacher if he/she were to change schools or grades within the school since the request is for a specific school, grade level and teacher.

It is important for the teacher to clarify with parents that there is no expectation for them to give a holiday gift. The e-mail request issued to parents, saying they could donate in lieu of giving a holiday gift, is not an appropriate request. One guess is that the teacher was only intending to garner parent support for the DonorsChoose project.

It would have been more appropriate for the teacher to simply inform parents that she posted a request on DonorsChoose for Chromebooks and that there is an opportunity to donate but that it is not an expectation. The teacher could provide information through a link on the DonorsChoose program to offer more information on the request she is posting and on the DonorsChoose program.

This is a good opportunity for the students in this classroom to receive technology that will support learning and for the teacher to receive technology that can help her better serve the students. The teacher's good intentions in trying to secure additional resources for students should be acknowledged.

With the dwindling resources classroom teachers experience, the DonorsChoose program attempts to make a positive difference for students, teachers, and classrooms across the United States. It is a great resource for teachers to get support for their classrooms. The program was started by a teacher who needed a set of classroom books!

QUID PRO QUO DONORS

Scenario: When the school district passed an austerity budget that cut interscholastic sports, community members started a GoFundMe drive to restore them. One active parent couple urged others not to donate, fearing that private fundraising would encourage further budget cuts. The couple also heard reports that coaches might make a family's donation a factor in who makes the team roster. Should district leadership take any actions?

Responses

MaryEllen Elia

Many communities have booster clubs of parents who are involved in supporting interscholastic sports, theater, and band activities. They might work the concession stands, drive equipment to away events, or fund facilities associated with the programs. Whether a GoFundMe drive, a booster club, a parent organization, or a district foundation that supports programs for students, these funding efforts occur in many school communities.

District leadership should establish rules on how the money/support comes into the district and how it is distributed in an equitable way to schools and programs. This should be part of a district plan related to contributions that then takes away the emphasis on "who gave what." It is naive to think that contributors are unknown; but an ethical approach related to decision making should provide guidelines for all staff in the district.

Sheldon Berman

The couple's concerns about fundraising for interscholastic sports supplanting district expenditures and influencing roster decisions need to be taken seriously. In a situation like this, school board policies on fundraising are critical in providing guidance to district leadership and the community.

Many districts, to address the financial pressures on their budgets, rely on booster organization contributions, gate receipts, and athletics and activity fees to underwrite or offset expenditures for extracurricular programs. To a large extent these sources have become institutionalized as regular revenue, without which the programs could not exist.

Although historically, athletics and other extracurricular activities have been important elements in building strong school cultures and a sense of connection for students, legally they are discretionary programs. Districts can legitimately charge fees and seek other revenues to underwrite these programs. The school board is the critical decision-making body in the area of budget. At this time the board may not be able to predict whether these reductions should be sustained, increased, or eliminated in the future.

Fundraising by community members may, of necessity, become a critical resource to support extracurricular programs. Therefore, urging others not to donate may have the unintended impact of eliminating or severely shrinking the schools' extracurricular programs, rather than forcing the board to identify alternative areas of district expenditure for reduction. However, if the school board is willing to accept fundraising and gifts to underwrite extracurricular activities, the board should refine its policies to avoid any potential conflict of interest or influence on coaches' decisions about rosters or playing time.

As a basic policy, such funds should be subject to review and/or acceptance by the board, in accordance with state regulations and accounting procedures, and distributed equitably among activities. The policy should also dictate that booster organizations shall not solicit donations or engage in activities that could lead any person to believe there is a conflict of interest or that a donation may influence rostering, playing time, or other student participation decisions.

Finally, the policy should prevent funds from being allocated to any particular team or used to pay stipends for particular coaches. In fact, to avoid any allegation that funding sources influence team decisions, no coach or member of a coach's immediate family should know how much any individual donated or be involved in the activities of booster organizations, including fundraising, promotion, and maintenance and expenditure of funds.

If a school district doesn't have such policies, the board should enact them prior to accepting funds raised by the community for extracurricular activities.

BUMMED BOOSTERS: "NO RAH-RAH"

Scenario: The high school's student newspaper staff wants to begin livestreaming home varsity football and basketball games via Facebook so people can watch from any location at no charge. Several school board members, long active in the athletic boosters, object, contending the remote viewing will depress needed revenue from admission and food/beverage sales at home games. The athletic director takes no stance, leaving the decision to the superintendent and the board.

Responses

Sheldon Berman

Livestreaming games could be a win-win for the student newspaper, the athletics program and its boosters, and the community at large. Just as the broadcasting of professional sports enables people to follow their favorite teams and adds to the excitement of attending games, livestreaming could have a similar impact on the school community.

It would enable a broader audience to watch the game—from the extended families, friends, and neighbors of the athletes to alumni who still feel connected to their alma mater and their sport to interested community members who might be out of town or otherwise not able to see a game live. Making school news and events more accessible to all can heighten interest in the livestreamed sports as well as in the band, cheer team, dance team, and other participatory components of these events.

The superintendent could explore ways to allay boosters' concerns over potential revenue losses. For example, in addition to broadcasting the game, the programming could promote spirit wear, booster membership, and attendance at sporting and school events. It could feature video segments on the role of the boosters and how their support is making a difference for the athletes and the school as a whole. It might also offer personal interest pieces on coaches, students, volunteers and involved parents.

If the board approves commercial advertising by local retailers and businesses for these programs, livestreaming may represent another revenue source for athletics and student activities. If the livestreaming of football and basketball proves successful, it could be extended to other sports and other student activities. With the right approach, livestreaming could both expand support for school activities and enhance school spirit within the broader community.

Maggie Lopez

It is time that the school board enter the twenty-first century! Whether or not they like it, digital access/social media for schools is here to stay and on-demand streaming is expected by many of their patrons. If they are concerned about physical attendance and food/beverage revenues going down at these events, they certainly could increase the athletics budget.

Greater access could become a marketing tool for the school district and, in the long run, create increased revenues and support for the district. Livestreaming has the potential to broaden viewership. The athletic director needs to get onboard and encourage this opportunity and get the superintendent and school board to see the benefits of social media access for viewers. It is an excellent way to promote the many activities and programs the district offers students, not just in these two sports but overall.

There could be short clips during game breaks to show snippets or interviews with students, parents, staff, or even board members about the good things happening in the district. Those watching might be inspired to donate to the Booster Club and be more aware of what the district does for students when the next bond/millage election comes around. This is a perfect scenario for the superintendent and athletic director to help the board see "the glass as half full and not as half empty."

NOXIOUS BEYOND THE ODOR

Scenario: The cash-strapped school district has a middle school that borders on a construction waste dump generating obnoxious odors that the Environmental Protection Agency has been investigating. The corporate owner approaches the school board offering $125,000 a year and property the district needs for constructing a new athletic field in return for a promise not to file an official complaint unless the company acts illegally. Should the superintendent advise the board to accept this offer?

Responses

MaryEllen Elia

This proposition seems like a disaster waiting to happen. Such a "gracious" and preemptive offer reeks of questionable motives—ones that a school should not become embroiled in. Whatever short-term fix the proposed arrangement might appear to offer cannot supersede the long-term needs of the middle school and its community.

It would be irresponsible and financially and ethically inappropriate to engage the corporate owner with full knowledge that an EPA investigation already is underway and that a potential judgment looms. The fact the EPA is actively involved to begin with indicates that a high degree of concern exists, enough to warrant its intervention, and that a significant problem is at least possible, if not likely.

In superfund sites across the country (West Virginia and Niagara Falls, to name two), contamination seriously affected schools and their communities. If these examples tell us anything, it's that there's a strong possibility that this school will need to be completely rebuilt based on the EPA's investigation, with a cost that could total in the tens of millions of dollars.

To sign this agreement is to sign away the school's rights and future ability to hold the company fully responsible for the effects of its actions. The superintendent should therefore advise the board to decline the offer, file their own complaint if they so choose, and allow the investigative and legal processes to take their course.

Maggie Lopez

Steer clear of this deal and find another way to fund the projects and land you need. Agreeing to these terms would be like making a pact with the devil and eventually will catch up with the district. Long term, this would be a public relations mess and might make your community wonder what other under-the-table deals the district has been involved in that might make others question the district's integrity. Districts always are looking for partnerships that will benefit students and bring more resources to help kids. This is not one of those partnerships!

The superintendent should advise the board against even considering this option and include legal counsel in the discussion so that legal aspects can be reviewed with the board should one of the board members question the recommendation. All the parameters for this scenario point to exchanges that could not ethically be explained to the taxpayers the board represents.

This offer looks more like a payoff for the district to keep quiet even when it is obvious inappropriate actions are occurring, being ignored by the landowner, and apparently are serious enough that now the EPA is involved. It appears the owners have something to hide, and it would be unethical for the district to assist them in sweeping it under the rug.

A DUBIOUS DONATION

> Scenario: The education foundation in a school district is raising funds to renovate art and technology classrooms badly in need of updating in several schools. A local businessman with known connections to organized crime offers the district's education foundation a substantial gift. Should the district's leadership recommend the foundation board turn down the donation?

Responses

Sarah Jerome

One might read this scenario and immediately think there's a simple solution. Just decline the money. Why take the risk? But through conversations with several heads of foundations and agencies dependent on donations, greater complexities became evident. These are the questions that arose.

What are the foundation guidelines/criteria for accepting donations? Are specific ethical standards spelled out? Is the donor suspected of "known connections" to organized crime or has a court found him guilty of wrongdoing? Is there proof of wrongdoing or just a rumor? If one decides not to take the money, what does one say to the donor as a reason his money is unacceptable?

Has the foundation ever accepted an anonymous donation? If so, was there a background check to determine the acceptability of the donor? Can the police or other judicial authorities endorse the acceptance of these funds? Will other donors be discouraged from future donations if this donation is accepted? Will they view it as an unsavory entanglement or an embarrassment for the foundation?

In addition, foundations must establish standards and guidelines for donations and donors. The foundation board will need to wrestle with this opportunity, weighing carefully the good the money could do for children who need it versus the ethical dilemma of accepting a donation that some will view as tainted. It is a thorny issue.

Sheldon Berman

Education foundations should have policies for making judgments about gifts. In the private school and university world, most have adopted fundraising policies such as those modeled on the website of the National Association of Independent Schools. Its standards include this: "The school accepts only gifts that support its mission, character, integrity, and independence." This standard would enable a foundation to reject a gift from an individual or corporation associated with crime, pornography, alcohol, tobacco, guns, gambling, or other activities that may not be aligned with the character or mission of the foundation.

In this case, the foundation could and should unambiguously reject the gift if there is a clear and publicly documented connection to organized crime through a criminal record or public scandal. However, often there isn't such clarity, and the stakes may be substantial.

On the one hand, the gift may be of such significance that it could make major improvements in the district's classrooms. If the businessman's association with organized crime is only a rumor, it may not be true. Acting without a factual basis could alienate a valuable donor as well as others in the community.

On the other hand, if there is some credibility to the donor's association with organized crime, the foundation's reputation, its status in the community and its good work could be compromised by accepting a gift from a socially unacceptable source or, worse, by having to return the funds at a later point if the individual is tainted by scandal or it is determined that the funds were obtained illegally.

Connection is an ambiguous term. Organized crime boss James "Whitey" Bulger's brother was William "Billy" Bulger, the longest-serving president of the Massachusetts Senate and president of the University of Massachusetts. While it would have been an easy decision to reject a donation from Whitey, it would have been more difficult for Boston's public education foundation to reject a gift from Billy, simply based on his family connection. Therefore, the foundation will need to do the research necessary to assess the validity and degree of connection between the individual and organized crime, as well as the legitimacy of the gift.

Public education foundations don't have the luxury of keeping this kind of decision secret. If the foundation doesn't currently have a policy that sets standards, now is a good time to develop one. As superintendent, urge the foundation to conduct thorough background research and act with caution, even to the extent of opening a conversation with the donor about the implications of his reputation for the foundation's decision and its future. The best gift he could give to the foundation may be to withdraw the offer.

The previous section of this chapter addressed several avenues that districts may encounter for increasing the diversity and amount of resources available to them. The next section deals with decisions districts must make in how those resources are prioritized and allocated to meet district needs.

BANKING ON THE HOMETOWN CHOICE

Scenario: The Board of Education is about to award a contract for the district's banking services for the coming year. Two proposals are submitted—one from a local bank, the other from a bank in a nearby community. The local bank has had the district's business for years and performed well. The bank in the neighboring community offers investment services not available locally. That bank also provides a better interest rate on day-to-day investments. At the board meeting, the local banker urges keeping the contract with the bank that employs constituents and taxpayers. The board president asks the superintendent for a recommendation.

Responses

Sarah Mackenzie

The superintendent in charge of making a recommendation must first consult existing policies for awarding contracts to ensure any decision is in keeping with them, for example, policies and principles related to comparing competing proposals.

Then the superintendent must make it clear that the school system must be mindful of its responsibility to the community to seek the best financial arrangement it can. Granted, those school system employees engaged in deliberations about contracts may consider past performance and reliability of a vendor or provider, but that does not mean considering who is employed there. In fact, such considerations might be considered conflicts of interest.

As long as the decision is in keeping with existing policies, the superintendent should not be swayed by the urgings of a person who has an interest in keeping the contract if there is a better offer available. Furthermore, the superintendent has an obligation to all the taxpayers in the community—not just those who work for a particular organization or company—to be fiscally responsible.

Sheldon Berman

The key to making a fair and objective choice among vendors is establishing a clear set of criteria within the request for proposals (RFP) that provides a way to value various aspects of the proposals, either through a point or priority system. In this case, much depends on how the RFP was written.

For example, one criterion might be that the bank has multiple branches for accepting schools' deposits. Banks with a local presence would fit that criterion very well. On the other hand, banks with few local branches might offer technology solutions or courier service to improve their scoring in this area. Such creative approaches may gain them some additional points, but they would not rate as highly on this criterion as would a bank with many local branches.

Although including a local preference among the criteria used to evaluate RFPs for contracts and services may be a strategy for public agencies to stimulate their local economy and support their community, only some states allow that preference and only in limited circumstances. The district is primarily responsible to the community for managing its finances efficiently and for exercising sound stewardship of limited funds.

In the case at hand, because changing banking services has a significant impact on the district's finance office, the superintendent should ask the finance staff to evaluate the two proposals against the criteria set in the RFP and provide their recommendation. If allowable and if it is delineated in the RFP, the review can take into consideration the value of local preference, along with the value of various service options, the quality of service, revenue from interest rates and other factors.

If the RFP requested independent bids on particular services and the bids demonstrated that it was advantageous to split services between the two vendors, it may be possible to contract for services with both banks, thereby continuing the basic banking service with the local vendor and contracting for specific investment services from the other bank. However, this option would have to be carefully evaluated because dividing services between two banks could create greater complexity for the finance office and increase its workload.

To provide a strong justification for the decision, the superintendent's recommendation to the board should be based on the findings and evaluation of the finance office staff against the criteria within the RFP. However, if the RFP didn't delineate criteria sufficiently, the superintendent can recommend rejecting both bids and issuing a new RFP that provides the district with the greatest flexibility to assess quality and cost-effectiveness of services and the potential benefit of a local preference priority if allowable.

COSTLY COOKIES?

Scenario: Central office administrators and principals in a school district routinely use their funds, which come from tax dollars, to provide beverages, snack foods, and cookies at after-school meetings and at work sessions during the workday. A director of homeless shelters in the community privately questions the superintendent about whether this practice is appropriate and should be condoned.

Responses

Sheldon Berman

The question raised by the director is both ethically and logically problematic in that it redirects attention away from the real issue and presents a false choice between snacks for public school educators and meals for the homeless. The question frames the problem as one of appropriate expenditure of limited public resources when the real ethical dilemma is the failure of our society to adequately fund two societal obligations—high-quality education and the eradication of homelessness.

The fact that the wealthiest society in the world neglects to provide a safety net of social supports and economic policies to address poverty and eliminate homelessness is in itself a serious ethical issue. Regrettably, the rise of selfishness as a justifiable ethical position and its expression in "no tax" policies have served to escalate rather than address homelessness, as well as to wrongly pit valuable social programs against one another.

In addition, the question raised by the director suggests that public servants who are doing their best to educate most of the country's poor children should somehow bear more responsibility than other groups for addressing homelessness. Would the shelter director equally indicate to the Chamber of Commerce, other business associations, or private schools—all of which provide refreshments at meetings as standard practice—that such snacks are ethically problematic and that those funds should be donated to the homeless shelter instead?

In addition to this potential double standard, the director's question implies a false choice since any decision to not expend resources on snacks would have no direct impact on funding for homelessness.

The question of whether the provision of refreshments at meetings is a justifiable expenditure of public funds can be a sincere one. School districts offer refreshments—if they can afford even a minimal level of such hospitality—because the meeting or workshop asks staff to go beyond their normal classroom duties and to participate in after-school activities.

Teachers and administrators work an exhausting daily schedule. If a modest beverage or snack enables people to participate more fully and enhances their productivity, then the small investment of resources is well worth it and is entirely ethical. However, to focus on schools' provision of simple snacks, rather than on the root policies that allow homelessness to continue, misdirects our attention away from the real issue and supports an attitude of disrespect for public educators.

Maybe the shelter director should raise the larger ethical issues surrounding homelessness—and raise them with an audience of community leaders that extends beyond the school superintendent who is dedicated to serving much of the same clientele. Rather than quibbling over the disposition of limited public funds, the superintendent and shelter director could instead join forces to advocate for a full array of social services including what is needed in schools, particularly for social supports for homeless children, and for jobs, food, and shelter for the homeless of all ages.

Karl Hertz

This scenario brings to mind what is described as "unintended consequences." When school people use tax dollars for refreshments at meetings after the students' school day, it is likely they hope to build morale. There is no devious intention.

However, the tax money that is sent to the schools may not be seen by the average taxpayer as being used for refreshments for the staff. Now, here come the unintended consequences. School people doing their best to have a creative, motivated atmosphere may find themselves defending a no-win situation.

Roy Dexheimer

Wrong dilemma. The school is not responsible for poverty in Haiti or hunger in the Congo. The more relevant dilemma is to justify the cost of these goodies (which can be surprisingly high over a year) if the school district has cut art supplies for students or musical instruments or library books. Then, despite the goodwill and friendly tone refreshments bring to a meeting or a workshop, it isn't right.

ADVOCATING ARTS OR ATHLETICS

> Scenario: The district faces a tough budget decision between two cost-cutting proposals. One calls for eliminating the arts program in three elementary schools. The other would end organized sports at the one middle school. The board president's elementary school-age daughter is an avid artist who has won several awards. The board rejects cutting sports because of its impact on students' physical health. On the arts cut, the board members are split 2-2 (with one member absent). The members ask the superintendent, what would he prefer to cut?

Responses

Sarah Mackenzie

Although one could claim the board member with the elementary school daughter who is an artist is biased, one could say that about any board member. It is certainly not a conflict of interest. Any concern about the president's position is a non-starter.

Assuming this vote occurs midway through the budget process, the district board has been working on proposals for a while and presumably still must please other stakeholders—especially governing bodies representing the town or towns—so there is no need to force a vote or decision at this point. The first thing the superintendent might say is, "Let's wait so the absent board member can weigh in on these proposals."

Even with the opportunity to wait for a decisive vote, the superintendent would be wise to suggest the board reexamine the figures and see if there is a way to meet needs, with some adjustments to both programs.

Is there a way to pare down the arts program but still have viable offerings that keep elementary students progressing in their artistic interests? Should they consider focusing on organized sports that include the most numbers of students rather than sponsoring as many sports as they do presently? Or, if the goal is to maintain or enhance student health in the middle school, perhaps they could consider intramural sports rather than teams that compete interscholastically.

The point, then, is to have the superintendent attempt to have board members consider a "both/and" approach to the budget rather than making "either/or" decisions. This requires more work and more conciliation, but in the long run, it could pay off in terms of student needs and in terms of elected officials recognizing there are creative ways to solve what seem like insurmountable impasses.

Sheldon Berman

Choosing which programs to cut because of inadequate funding to education is a no-win situation. However, a decision needs to be based on assessment of data and options, not on personal advantage for board members. Given the division on the board over which program to cut, and the need to demonstrate that students come first, it may be wise to review data on both programs and explore other options.

How many students are involved in each program? What is the per-pupil cost? Are there ancillary benefits such as preparation time for classroom teachers when students are at art or active engagement of students with academic and physical challenges in the athletic program? Can modest reductions be made to both programs that would achieve the same financial savings? Are there fundraising possibilities that could sustain some aspects of the sports program? With support, can art be well integrated into daily classroom instruction?

The superintendent needs to gather the data, weigh the options, and then make a recommendation to the board that offers the greatest advantage possible for the most students.

WHO PAYS TO BE AT THE TABLE?

> Scenario: In the name of networking and building positive relationships with community partners, school district department heads routinely purchase tables at fundraising dinners for other community organizations. These tables are filled mostly by school board members and top-level administrators in the district. Is this expenditure of public funds appropriate?

Responses

Paula Mirk

Strictly speaking, it's not ethical to do this if the money used to purchase a table is taxpayer money. Notwithstanding the importance of networking and of building positive relationships with community partners, any time taxpayer money is involved, we must be cautious of slippery slopes. There are many ways to network and build relationships, after all. If a department head truly felt a community organization could advance the learning of students in that department, it might be wiser to organize a way to raise funds for the table.

There is also a question about "school board members and top-level administrators" enjoying these events. If the department head wants to serve the students, is the logic for superintendent and school committee participation clear? The "headline test" could come in handy for this purpose. Could it read "students, parents, teachers and leadership all enjoy a community organization event" instead of "top brass once again get to sit at the table?" That would be a factor to consider on many levels, not least of which is this: How are our students best served in this case?

Sheldon Berman

This situation presents a common but uncomfortable challenge for district administrators and boards of education. Districts often are asked to purchase tables for a wide range of events, such as dinners in which an organization awards student scholarships, events honoring local legislators for their contributions to education, and events raising funds to support programs for youth.

The occasions often serve as public acknowledgement of the important relationship between the community organization and the school district. The events allow the organization's members to see district leaders participating as a community partner, and they enable district leaders to demonstrate publicly their support for these causes.

In some communities, governmental agencies such as the mayor's office, county government or public utilities also purchase tables at events, and the citizens view this practice as an appropriate way to demonstrate the partnership between the private nonprofit sector and the public sector. At some events, the keynote address or other program component qualifies as professional development for district leaders or board members.

The way these tables are purchased also varies. Some districts purchase tables from district funds to show their support for, partnership with or cosponsorship of community organizations that assist young people. Other districts may coordinate the purchase of tables on behalf of the board and district leaders, but those who attend pay for their seats with personal funds. Still other districts rely on funds raised by local education foundations to purchase tables at important events.

Regardless of the potential benefits that can be derived from supporting community partners by purchasing tables at their events, some districts believe this practice is—or their community would construe it to be—a misuse of public tax dollars and so avoid it completely. This perception is even more likely to be the case in difficult economic periods, such as those occasioned by a nationwide recession or the shuttering of a major local employer.

In these districts—indeed, perhaps in many districts—it is advisable that board members, administrators, and other district staff purchase the seats from their own personal funds rather than from district funds and rotate representation among district leaders to preclude anyone from incurring excessive costs.

However, even in those communities where the purchase of tables is accepted as a reasonable way to demonstrate the partnership between the private nonprofit sector and the public sector, specific guidelines should be enacted and enforced to avoid even the appearance of impropriety. For example, decisions about purchasing tables should be made through an open process at the district level, not by individual departments. There must be sufficient oversight and a system of checks and balances to prevent the potential misuse of district funds.

Most important of all, if a district chooses to underwrite the cost of tables at organizational events, complete transparency about these transactions is essential. The costs should be limited and clearly identified in the district budget. Participation in any specific activity should also take into consideration whether the goal is simply fundraising or if there is a broader purpose such as recognizing community leaders, honoring students, or celebrating important accomplishments.

For those events that are selected, it may be appropriate to offer seats to a diverse group that includes teachers, support staff, students or parents who are involved in the partnership or the programs that the organization supports, thereby benefitting a diversity of staff and constituents rather than just district leaders.

Having a consistent and open process not only helps the district make better decisions, but also provides clarity for all those who seek the participation of the board and district leaders at their events. In the end, how a district responds to this ethical question is in large part a reflection of the circumstances peculiar to that community at that point in time.

Each district's leadership and board should determine whether the end result (inter-organizational support) is both consistent and coherent with the means (use of public dollars) and, above all, should ensure that any public review of the practice of purchasing tables would not distract from or become a detriment to the district's primary mission of educating students.

Chapter Twelve

Taking a Stand on Community Issues

When the Los Angeles school board adopted a resolution in 2019 opposing anti-abortion legislation, it prompted much discussion in education circles about whether school leaders should take stands on controversial issues seemingly beyond the scope of their school district responsibilities. Some defended the action as a proper exercise of community leaders' duty to take positions on the important social issues of the day. Others condemned it as partisan politicking.

The debate itself begged the question: What is the school district's role as a "player" in controversies unfolding on the local or national stage? Is it appropriate for school leaders to take stands on issues of social justice, the environment, foreign intervention, economic policies, or other more local issues that are important, but not directly related to the day-to-day operations of your school district?

In this chapter, our contributors explore how school administrators should react when social issues divide the community, or when the community is united in a position an administrator believes is morally or ethically misguided.

Generally speaking, there's nothing in the law forbidding school officials from expressing their positions on pretty much anything they please, so long as they don't purport to speak for the district without due authority, reveal confidential information, or in some way demonstrate unfitness to hold public office. As we explained in our discussion of First Amendment rights, school administrators, when acting as private citizens, also have a constitutionally protected freedom to express their personal views on matters of public concern, within certain limits discussed there.

Having the right to speak out doesn't necessarily mean it's the responsible thing to do. We must start by asking the fundamental question: What is your school district's job? It certainly includes teaching the critical thinking skills necessary for students to function as adults in a democracy, and to decide for themselves where they stand on the hot-button issues of the day.

But is it the district's job to function as a community "thought leader" on these matters? Is it proper for superintendents, as the educational leaders of their districts, to use the authority and prestige of their position to shape public opinion regarding them? And if so, under what circumstances would it be appropriate?

The answer may lie in how your school board views your district's "job description." Lay school board members serve in an oversight capacity, formulating the mission of the district and developing the strategic plan to accomplish it. That mission may or may not include taking stands on important matters affecting life in the community.

School administrators must provide the leadership and expertise board members need to make well-informed judgments on how much to involve themselves in issues not directly germane to the district's day-to-day operations. Once the board makes up its mind, however, the superintendent should not get out in front of the board—at least not when acting in an official capacity.

You may find that your district's own course offerings, approach to teaching, or the books you feature in your school libraries may themselves be viewed as "taking a stand" on issues that some may say are none of your district's business. For example, some states mandate instruction regarding sexual orientation or gender identity as a component of the human sexuality curriculum. Proponents argue it's essential to foster awareness and tolerance of others' sexuality. Critics claim it's normalizing biblically proscribed sin and, even worse, encouraging otherwise well-adjusted students to question their own sexuality. How do you mediate this debate?

Here we can draw a sharp distinction between what students are taught to believe, and how they're taught to behave, at least while they're at school. School administrators have a legal and ethical duty to maintain a welcoming, bias-free environment for all students. It's well-documented that bullying and harassment are often borne of ignorance and fear of unfamiliar cultures and backgrounds. Heightening awareness, and dispelling myths and inaccurate stereotypes, can be accomplished without infringing on the prerogative of students—and where appropriate, their parents—to determine what's normal and acceptable for themselves.

How districts tackle race relations (or don't) is another ongoing battle in the "culture wars." It's difficult to imagine how to teach American history without in some way addressing the experience of African Americans in the era of slavery. Yet some people contend that teaching the Civil War was fought over slavery, instead of merely states' rights, reflects a political stance that districts should shy away from.

Some states have adopted legislation forbidding public schools from teaching politically charged topics that may make some students feel "uncomfortable." The premise of those laws is that public schools should not function as a soapbox to advance the viewpoint of an individual teacher or administrator on matters that are reasonably debatable. The distinction between fact and opinion is key. As education leaders, it is our responsibility to ensure that historical accuracy is not sacrificed on the altar of political expediency.

Are there some issues that are so well-settled there is no "other side" to even acknowledge? Surely, we are on firm ground teaching that slavery happened and was a moral stain on our nation's history, and that the Holocaust actually occurred, without according deniers any credibility. We can probably say the same for the first moon landing as well.

But how about climate change? Though it took a while, there's now broad consensus it's a fact; still, there remains considerable debate over who or what's to blame and how to address it. Be mindful that where you draw the line between debatable issues and those beyond question may be viewed by some in your school community as taking a political stand on the issue itself.

Local issues are often more contentious than those playing out on the national stage. Perhaps your local land use board has been approving warehouses and other industrial development in your district at a rapid clip. Some in town applaud this increase in tax ratables, while others complain it's a sell-out to powerful real estate developers. Ask yourself: Does the school district have a dog in this fight?

Of course, there may be a direct impact on district operations if this development is in close proximity to your schools. The district certainly has standing to request appropriate measures to control truck traffic during school pick-up and drop-off times, or erection of buffers to insulate a school playground from a dangerous or noisy industrial site nearby.

When your school board is uncertain of the impact or fearful of the political ramifications of butting heads with other branches of government in town, it's certainly your role as a school administrator to share with the board your expertise on the operational needs of the district to help them weigh the pros and cons of taking a stand. Once the board has made its decision, however, any positions you take as an official spokesperson for the district should be in sync with your board's approach to advocacy on such matters.

Perhaps this chapter, more than any other in the book, presents more questions than answers as there is no broad national consensus on the topics we address. Nevertheless, the lively discussion of the scenarios in this chapter should help you think your way through to the right answers for your district.

RACIAL TABOOS

Scenario: In a community in the Deep South that considers interracial relationships taboo, the high school principal would quietly address black/white relationships by talking to parents to keep the relationships from advancing. A teacher at the high school tells the wife of the superintendent that she thinks the superintendent's daughter is dating an African American male. "Personally, I wouldn't have cared," the superintendent said. "He was a pretty good kid, but I knew what my community thought." Advice for the superintendent?

Responses

Sarah Jerome

The principal and the superintendent must adopt a twenty-first-century recognition that the world is a diverse community. Continuing to encourage racist attitudes among students and their parents is not the role of enlightened educators. Nor is dodging difficult conversations.

The Southern Poverty Law Center has excellent teaching materials to help both the principal and the superintendent address these important community issues with students, staff, and parents. Modeling acceptance and embracing diversity is one of an educator's most important roles.

Entrenched habits are time-honored in some communities, and courageous acts to reshape community norms toward tolerance and embracing diversity can get a principal and superintendent fired. Some stances are worth getting fired—this is one of them.

Maggie Lopez

The superintendent should not be condoning this principal's practice of telling parents their students cannot date because of their race or color. It is ethically and morally wrong for the high school principal to engage in discriminatory practices of this nature. This behavior could result in a potential lawsuit for the district. Most disheartening is the fact that the superintendent, as the district leader, did not immediately put a stop to the principal's practice but instead supported it, by enforcing it with his own child. The superintendent, like all educators, has a responsibility to maintain a standard that does not tolerate bias.

The superintendent must ensure immediately that the principal does not continue this practice. As school district leaders, the superintendent and principal represent and are the voice for all students, to include all races, nationalities, economic status, abilities, and backgrounds. The superintendent must assure he and all staff are engaging in behaviors that are moral, ethical, and legal, regardless of what the community perceives as taboo. He has an opportunity to show the community that the district's leadership supports the diversity and individual rights of all students.

SITING THE HOMELESS

Scenario: The city has been attempting to find compassionate ways to address homelessness. Most shelters are at capacity. The city council decides to locate camping areas in a few public spaces where small groups of homeless individuals or families can stay temporarily, monitored by nonprofit social service organizations. The city manager has identified a camping area one block from a neighborhood elementary school and asks the superintendent if he can proceed with the plan. What should the superintendent do?

Responses

Sheldon Berman

Finding sites that can support homeless individuals and families is both a courageous and productive act on the part of the city. The lack of effective public attention to homelessness is one of our greatest lapses in public policy.

Although many people hold negative perceptions of homeless individuals, this population includes everyday individuals who have experienced a sudden loss of employment, costly medical issues, death of a family breadwinner, or other circumstances that could be overcome if appropriate assistance were extended. It also includes individuals who suffer from mental illness, struggle with addictions, or otherwise live on the margins of society. There is no one simple characterization of a homeless person.

Given the complexity of homelessness, the often-negative perceptions that people hold of the homeless, and the reality of some homeless individuals behaving in ways that may not be a positive influence on children, it is likely that some parents and community members will be resistant to locating an encampment so close to a school.

It may cause some parents to withdraw their children from the school or to insist that the district provide additional security when children are on the playground or walking to and from school. If it is not handled well, instead of being a positive expression of compassion and support, the camp may escalate tensions around addressing the homeless issue.

The superintendent's first step should be to recommend that the city hold a series of forums and community dialogues at the school and in other areas of the neighborhood to hear community feedback, discuss options, and potentially defuse an issue that could undermine the city's efforts to support the homeless population. For example, such a camp may be more acceptable if the individuals in the encampment are limited to families with children, particularly children who might attend the school and be supported by staff and neighborhood families.

In addition, if the city hasn't already done so, it may be helpful for the community to develop site-location criteria for homeless camps and to develop mutually agreed-upon parameters, thus clarifying expectations and establishing a way to judge current and future siting efforts. The school district could then offer suggestions for these criteria, such as designating sites within a certain distance from schools for families with children only and establishing firm policies around weapons, drug and alcohol use, etc.

Whether the camp is ever located near the school or not, it is likely that many students in the district are encountering homeless individuals in the course of their daily lives. With appropriate planning and adult oversight, such a situation may present an opportunity for meaningful learning at the secondary level.

Going beyond the typical service project of collecting food, bottled water, blankets, and clothing to be donated to persons living on the streets, arrangements could be made for students to research the issue in more depth through interviews with homeless persons and the organizations that provide support to the homeless, and thereby develop greater understanding and empathy for their situation. Shaping such viewpoints among our nation's youth is a key step toward the adoption of public policies aimed at assisting rather than stigmatizing the homeless population.

Mark Hyatt

Homelessness is a vexing and chronic problem that continues to trouble both urban and suburban communities across America. And try as we might to keep the homeless away from our schools, the reality is that they are already in our classrooms. According to the National Association for the Education of Homeless Children and Youth, more than 1.1 million homeless students were enrolled in U.S. public schools in 2012. Today, more and more, we're talking about struggling families, with parents working multiple, minimum-wage jobs and their children doing homework in a different shelter every night.

Unfortunately, the homeless population today also includes many mentally ill men and women who have fallen between the cracks of our public health system and now live among us, unmedicated and unpredictable. Mainly for this reason, and how it bears directly on the safety of our schoolchildren, the superintendent should ask the city manager not to locate the proposed homeless camp so close to the elementary school. Our primary job as administrators is student safety, first and foremost—even before academic achievement and whole child development.

The superintendent could speak privately with the city manager to help her understand that, while sympathetic to the cause, there is just more sympathy for the valid concerns of the students' parents and staff. Explain that locating the camp so close to the school would likely lead to public protests and contentious news coverage. At a minimum, suggest the city hold a preliminary series of public meetings or town halls to get input from those affected by this matter.

On the issue of security, express grave concern about relying only on nonprofit volunteers to monitor the camps. Due to the wide variety of serious problems often present in any homeless population, insist on at least some law enforcement involvement, as well as additional social services assistance from those skilled specifically in working with the homeless.

Bottom line: Certainly sympathize with the problem, donate to the cause, and even volunteer to host fundraisers at the school. But at the end of the day, strongly object to the proposed location of this shelter/camp. Our children need to be set up for safe, secure learning environments. If we are truly to succeed, parents, teachers, and administrators all need this peace of mind, as well.

Roy Dexheimer

Public schools are ethically and legally obliged to educate the youngsters who come to them. And homeless does not mean lawless. The superintendent should welcome the kids and support the parents.

Make sure the new youngsters get breakfast and lunch at school. Make sure they have supplies. Ask the PTA to help with clothing. Alert the school nurse to the new challenges and ensure the kids have their shots. And be certain the board of education is especially well-informed. Ask the social services agency to put families at this encampment, not unattached adults. If there are worries about young children walking to and from the school, ask social services to supply a monitor for those portions of the day.

Our craft requires us to run closer to challenges, not away from them.

SCENERY OR SAFETY

Scenario: A stretch of highway in front of a school was the scene of a school bus accident with minor injuries. The same section has seen numerous other accidents. The county highway department recommends straightening the road for a safer route—an action requiring removal of several trees. This option has drawn public opposition because the trees are the last of a group planted by a famous former citizen on a piece of land considered a historic community treasure. Both sides take up the case in front of the school board. What action should the superintendent recommend?

Responses

Sarah Mackenzie

The superintendent is most concerned about the safety of students. He or she might be well advised to emphasize that stance and avoid weighing in on the question of taking down treasured trees.

If the superintendent were consulted on the issue by the county highway department, he or she might suggest ways that safety could be monitored and ensured through traffic-calming humps or safety officers overseeing traffic at especially heavy times and/or locations without taking down trees. But if the highway department insists on the solution involving the trees, the superintendent may well have to acquiesce to calm nerves and ensure student safety.

Sheldon Berman

Given that this decision is most likely up to the county government, the superintendent first should indicate that a school board meeting is not the most appropriate forum for this dialogue. If the school board wishes to take a position, the superintendent should ask the highway department what alternatives have been considered, such as a traffic signal, lower speed limits, or other road modifications.

Clearly, the historic nature of the property and the trees is important to the community. The superintendent should acknowledge the interests of those who advocate for history and conservation and seek a way to address those interests while still ensuring the safety of students. For example, perhaps a commemorative plaque depicting the historic area could be erected near the school. However, because the children's safety is the paramount concern of the school district, the superintendent must come down on the side that best protects students' safety.

Roy Dexheimer

The superintendent's only position is that of guardian of the safety of the children in his or her charge. Go on record as favoring that option. Then it is a squabble between the highway folks and the historical trust. Help them negotiate a solution that improves safety and somehow preserves the trees, but stay clearly on record as endorsing safety as the priority.

NON-MAGNETIC APPEAL

> Scenario: A new superintendent in an urban district almost immediately receives complaints from parents and community members that the district's magnet schools are drawing the brightest students out of neighborhood schools. Upon investigation, the superintendent finds these schools have far fewer economically disadvantaged, minority, and special education students than the neighborhood schools. Yet these schools have been highly successful in keeping middle-class families committed to the public schools rather than placing children in private education. How should the superintendent respond?

Responses

Sheldon Berman

Magnet schools that are intended to promote integration are often located in less-advantaged neighborhoods. To foster an environment that is attractive to parents, these schools typically establish academic criteria for admission, thereby ensuring a student body that is academically proficient.

In launching magnet schools, the primary objective is generally to balance magnets and neighborhood schools in such a way that the district provides options for parents and maintains strong support for public education. However, over time magnet schools can have an unintended and negative impact on neighborhood schools and on the district as a whole.

Because they are more readily accessed by students and families who have had prior academic success, specialized talents or social capital, magnets tend to enroll fewer economically disadvantaged, minority, and special education students, thereby exacerbating the achievement gap. They can, in effect, achieve unofficial status as elite schools within a system, leaving the impression—and potentially the reality—that neighborhood schools are lower performing and less rigorous. Therefore, magnet schools can accentuate the disparity in performance among schools and concentrate historically underserved students in neighborhood schools.

The overall impact of a magnet policy depends on the percentage of students in a district, or from specific neighborhoods, who attend these schools. If there are only a few magnets with limited enrollment or if the magnets offer specialized programs that are not strictly for high-achieving students, they may not have a significant impact.

However, if the magnets siphon from neighborhood schools the top five to ten percent of higher performing or economically advantaged students, they can undermine confidence in and support for neighborhood schools and contribute to serious inequities, as asserted by the parents in this case. In districtwide choice programs, they can also create a cascading impact or domino effect by drawing from certain neighborhoods, which then draw from the next tier of popular schools, until some schools are left with the most marginalized or disadvantaged population of students.

Alternatively, inequities between magnets and neighborhood schools can result in parents withdrawing those children who are not selected for the magnet schools and sending them to private or charter schools instead.

This is one of the most politically volatile issues district leaders can confront. Dismantling the magnets is not politically viable, nor would it support equity and diversity because returning students to neighborhood schools can perpetuate the socioeconomic and racial segregation stemming from residential housing patterns. At this time, there is little federal or community support for desegregation plans that would provide socioeconomic or racial balance across schools, leaving few alternatives for a district interested in equity to pursue, other than magnet schools.

Well-crafted magnet policies can be effective in retaining middle-class and even upper-middle-class investment in a district. The key challenge is to ensure equitable representation of the district's diversity within the magnet schools, as well as attractive and effective programs in all schools. Successfully meeting this challenge demands a shift from thinking about diversity as exclusively a benefit for the traditionally underserved to recognizing diversity as an asset for the academic and social development of all students.

A superintendent can pursue several strategic initiatives that, taken together, will address to some degree the issue raised by these parents. None are quick fixes, and all require board as well as administrative action.

The first strategy is to require the magnet schools to prepare student recruitment plans that ensure enrollment of a more diverse student body, as well as a sufficiently strong support system so that these students have equitable opportunities for success, and then to hold the schools accountable for meeting those expectations. The district would need to monitor the diversity of the student body as well as the degree to which achievement gaps are closing, not only in grades, attendance, and discipline, but also in access to such advanced programs as Advanced Placement and International Baccalaureate courses.

The second important strategy is to identify attractive programs that can be placed in neighborhood schools to build confidence in and support of these schools. At the elementary and middle school levels, these options might involve special music, art, science, or math programs. At the high school level, these programs might be IB, AVID, or professional career themes. With some additional differentiation among the neighborhood schools, the district might design choice more broadly so that parents could have a choice among multiple neighborhood schools as well as magnet schools.

The above approach necessitates a third strategy, which is additional financial support to strengthen and maintain these programs over time, particularly the ones in disadvantaged communities. To accomplish this long-term support, the district needs to implement an equitable school-funding formula based on a school needs index. This index should include such factors as the percentage of highly mobile, economically disadvantaged, historically underserved, and special education students, as well as other demographic factors that influence student performance.

Because many of these magnet programs are placed in inner-city schools in order to support integration and the reclamation of neighborhoods, a fourth strategy is to identify a neighborhood catchment area for each magnet that enables neighborhood students a choice between the magnet and another neighborhood school. This approach provides balance between selective and neighborhood enrollment, as long as students aren't tracked into separate programs.

Cumulatively, these strategies can help guide a district in establishing a balanced approach to magnets, but it is essential to continually monitor the degree to which the district is achieving equity, as well as retaining its market share. It can be beneficial for the district to produce an "equity score card" as a way to examine and reflect on how district policies are impacting diverse groups of students.

Magnet schools can strengthen a system if designed through an equity lens that views diversity as an asset to the success of all students. Magnet schools can provide programs for which there may not be a sufficient critical mass in a neighborhood, such as a Montessori or language immersion elementary magnet or a performing arts or career technical high school.

They can support the goals of integration and diversity by bringing together from various parts of a city students who would otherwise be more isolated in neighborhood schools. School location, admissions policies, funding priorities, and the parameters of choice are keys to addressing the equity issue.

There will never be a perfect solution that meets all needs and satisfies all stakeholders. The only viable response is one that brings together diverse constituencies within the community to consider the issue and develop effective magnet policy recommendations. Principals play a particularly critical role in the development and implementation of magnet policies because of the inherent competitiveness among schools that choice policies create. Their commitment to promoting the district's overarching goal of equity and their participation in the development of a policy that equitably balances competing policy goals are key to its success.

In this scenario, the superintendent needs to involve the board, staff, community members, and parent representatives in developing a dynamic and productive magnet school policy that strikes a balance among offering desirable programs; ensuring equitable access and success in those programs; and promoting the strength, effectiveness, and attractiveness of all schools in the system.

Sarah Mackenzie

One might argue there is no ethical issue here. Students have applied to magnet schools, met the qualifications, and been accepted. Furthermore, the school system has greater political capital because parents who might have abandoned the town's schools have remained committed. All the students are in the same public school system that offers a variety of schooling configurations to ensure students' various learning needs are met.

So, what's the harm? Even if equitable opportunities are available to all students and certain schools seem more appropriate for particular students, the ethic of critique means that an examination of a process or a structure in the realm of public education that seems to advantage some while disadvantaging others is in order.

It's important for an education leader to use several lenses to examine situations; so it is very appropriate for the superintendent to consider the ethics of justice, care, and critique, as explored in length by Lawrence Kohlberg, Carol Gilligan, and Robert Starratt, respectively. The ethic of critique summons educational administrators to view issues through a lens of social responsibility to operate schools for the common good and to prepare youth to be responsible citizens.

Applying these lenses yields some questions for this situation: Are students getting what they need in the separate schools? Is it fair to have students separated in this way? Are certain students more advantaged in this situation than others? What is fair to all students? It's not easy to rock the boat and to question how things have been done and/or when things seem to be moving smoothly and parents—especially influential ones—are pleased with the system.

The superintendent should consult with leaders (administrators and teacher leaders) in the district to learn as much as he or she can about how the situation evolved and then explore with them the extent to which the situation, the structures and hidden assumptions may be privileging some students over others. These conversations will most likely extend into the school community as parents and other citizens contemplate the issues of how to be just as well as benevolent.

The decision about what to do in any situation like this depends on what the leaders uncover about values and beliefs, coupled with how they push and probe others to delve into values such as justice and equity. Exposing the inequities, though, should lead to more equitable opportunities for all students.

Granted, people have varying views of the purpose of schooling, of education. The superintendent will undoubtedly uncover tensions engendered by disparate views if he or she asks some hard questions like those suggested above. A system leader's responsibility is to conduct pragmatic activities that keep a system functioning efficiently; however, he or she also has a responsibility to investigate practices, work to ensure equity of opportunity, and provide for the needs of all students.

Chapter Thirteen

Board Relations

Throughout this book, we've alluded to your relationship with your school board in general terms. In our final chapter, we squarely confront that relationship and unpack it. What is the allocation of decision-making authority between you and the board? How do you manage disagreements with your board over issues you feel strongly about? What can be done about individual board members who undermine you and the board by engaging in unethical or illegal actions?

The American model of school governance is similar in some respects to a business corporation. After all, what is a school district but a corporate-style entity delivering a vital service to the public in a highly regulated and litigious environment? You buy and sell property, build buildings, hire and fire employees, manage intellectual property rights, negotiate with labor unions, and engage in many of the activities that other large corporations do daily.

Like a corporate board of directors, a school board exercises fiduciary oversight of the district's operations. Your board members may come from all walks of life with no particular expertise in the "business" of education, but they represent the community—your shareholders. The board's job is not to run the schools but to make sure they're well run. The superintendent is the CEO, responsible for the day-to-day operations of the district within the framework of the mission and strategic plan envisioned by the board, which is ultimately accountable to the shareholders: the citizens and taxpayers of the community.

The board may have the final say on matters of policy, and even on more mundane decisions requiring their affirmative vote under your state's education laws, but as the educational leader of the district you're expected to share your expertise and use the platform of your office to inspire and influence the board and the school community.

Of course, there are some significant differences between corporate boards and school boards. The boards of large corporations are often hand-picked by management, meet only a few times a year, and are accountable to the shareholders more in theory than reality. It is within the more political and involved governance role of school boards that tensions are likely to emerge in the relationship between the board and the superintendent.

The key to cohesive relations with your board lies in developing and nurturing common expectations for what success looks like and how to achieve it. Ideally, that begins during the hiring process, which should be a two-way street. It's not just the board interviewing you. You're also interviewing them, and that's your opportunity to seek answers to the questions most important to you: Do these board members share my vision of where I'd like to take this district? Will I have strong majority support or start my honeymoon with a board that's sharply divided? Do I have confidence they are ethical and trustworthy partners committed to my success?

Once you've accepted the position and are settling in, what are your ethical obligations in dealing with your board? First and foremost is to respect their role as the lay representatives of the community. That includes adhering to their internal governance structure, working through the prescribed chain of command within the board, and avoiding the appearance of favoritism toward some board members. Naturally, you have more contact with the board's officers than with the rest of the board, but all board members must feel confident they are in the loop to avoid the sort of suspicion that can lead to fraught relations with them later.

Your board should not be expected to function as a rubber stamp for your recommendations. Inevitably, there will be disagreements, and how you manage them will be key to maintaining a healthy relationship. As with any relationship in life, if you value it, you'll need to pick your battles, clearly communicating what's important to you in a manner that respects the board's sensibilities. Be ever mindful, however, that you work for the board and, in the end, must yield to their position on all matters within their purview—even if you disagree.

How do you deal with that one board member who routinely undermines you and the board by disclosing confidential information to outsiders, making commitments on behalf of the board without any authority, posting inflammatory messages on social media that reflect poorly on the district, or engaging in other inappropriate behavior?

We first must recognize that democracy can be messy at times. Board members are free to be oppositional and unpleasant to deal with, if that suits their style and the electorate will tolerate it. What they may not do is violate their oaths of office by leaking sensitive information they have access to solely in their capacity as board members or otherwise use the power of their office to circumvent the district's established governance structure.

There are several tools available to deal with board members who refuse to honor their sworn obligations. At a minimum, their misconduct should be reported to the board's officers, who may be able to deal with the matter discreetly and internally. If you're concerned about sparking an adversarial relationship if you call those board members out by name, you may wish to consider a full-board ethics training that focuses on the misconduct at hand without specifically targeting any particular board member. In extreme cases, districts have even gone so far as to seek a civil court injunction, enforceable with contempt-of-court sanctions.

What if your entire board has gone rogue? Say a federal court has ordered the board to take certain steps to desegregate your schools—steps requiring adoption of resolutions by the board in order to implement them—but the board members refuse for political reasons. Or they take other stands that are wholly repugnant to your core principles. As the educational leader of the district, it's your duty to inform them of the legal and educational consequences of their actions and attempt to sway them to your viewpoint.

However, if you're unsuccessful, you may need to consider severing your relationship and moving on to another district where you and the board are rowing in the same direction. You've worked too hard, for too long, to tarnish your reputation by association with a board that rejects your values and your vision.

Our contributors address these issues and more in their discussion of the case scenarios that follow. Consider their perspectives and chart your own course to a healthy and productive relationship with your board.

This chapter begins with three cases in which the superintendent believes that the board as a whole has adopted a direction that is either inappropriate or problematic.

A NEW BOARD'S HARD RIGHT TURN

> Scenario: A school board election brings onto the board a majority of members who are hard-line on employee issues. The majority pushes district leadership, which has tried to create a supportive and compassionate culture contributing to quality staff performance, to address discipline, attendance, and other issues with the strongest consequences and exert strict limits on discretionary benefits. The new board members view the culture as not sufficiently demanding or accountable. Should the superintendent adopt their hard-line approach?

Responses

Sheldon Berman

Some school board members are elected thinking that educators are a privileged group who receive unwarranted salaries and benefits for a job requiring only about 180 workdays a year. Others, accustomed to a reward-and-punishment management philosophy from some competitive business environments, bring with them an attitude that strong discipline and dismissals are necessary to make people work harder and to get rid of the slackers who aren't generating sufficient academic gains among students.

The public messaging of these views is often articulated as the need for organizational accountability, but the policies these board members pursue point to a desire for administration to take a hard line on salary, benefits, evaluation, and discipline, and an even harder line on union issues and negotiations.

Although organizational accountability issues are important, these individuals fail to understand that, whether in business or in education, a positive organizational culture is the most effective vehicle for producing beneficial results for the organization and job satisfaction for employees. They also fail to realize that an organization can't punish or fire its way to greatness, but that greatness instead emerges when employees feel supported to collaborate, take risks, grow, and learn.

Leadership that incorporates understanding, compassion and approachability in turn inspires employee effort, commitment, and dedication. When people are valued and appreciated by their leaders, they respond with a level of unity and trust that enables the organization to tackle difficult issues and meet or even surpass its goals.

A shift to hard-line attitudes and policies can have an incredibly destructive impact on a school district. Employees respond by protecting themselves through isolation, narrowing their performance to what is acceptable, resorting to organizing union opposition, or leaving the district for one with more positive support for staff. A hard-line approach from the board and/or administration throws the district into internal turmoil and distracts from achieving strategic goals and addressing problems. Although it may take a very short time to create a negative, antagonistic, or dysfunctional environment, it can take years to rectify and recover from it.

In schools and districts that are implementing or sustaining strong social-emotional learning programs and are creating caring classroom communities, the hard-line ethos can be debilitating. It can cause staff to take a hard line with students, thereby undermining the responsiveness that is core to these programs. Teachers, in particular, can find themselves bewildered if administrators model a form of discipline that is antithetical to the developmental form of discipline recommended for students.

In this case, the superintendent faces the need to educate the new board members—either through his or her own counsel and advice or by bringing in a consultant to work with the board—on their role in shaping and delivering organizational culture. The superintendent can also highlight the accomplishments of staff at board meetings and in board memos and district communications to help board members recognize the prevalence of positive results and the value of staff efforts.

If these efforts are not successful in changing the board's approach, the superintendent can serve initially as a buffer against board attitudes and decisions, remaining responsive to staff while addressing the needs of the board for accountability. However, such actions can only go so far without significant tensions emerging between the board and the superintendent. If the board's hard-line attitude remains, the superintendent may be better off seeking to lead a different district where there is an appreciation of the impact of a positive organizational culture.

Glenn "Max" McGee

Updating the résumé should be the superintendent's first order of business. If his core values regarding employee relationships are not aligned with those of the board majority, he will not succeed and should keep options open for future employment in districts that are more aligned with his core values and beliefs.

His second action should be to meet with each newly elected board member individually to learn why each wants a hard-line culture and to share quantitative and qualitative data that show the value of the current culture. Then he should schedule a facilitated governance retreat to determine the philosophical direction the board will pursue. Ideally, he would be able to make a compelling case for either sustaining the current direction or achieving a compromise on a new vision that balances compassion with some aspects of the new board members' desires for more accountability.

SALARY SHORTCHANGE

Scenario: A district's chief financial officer is retiring. Given the position's competitiveness and the difficulty of filling it, the school board increases the projected salary by $25,000, attracting several strong candidates. As the superintendent prepares to recommend the finalist, an economic downturn leaves the district facing budget cutbacks that may affect staff. The board, believing the position's increased salary now will be viewed negatively by staff and community, requests the superintendent to reduce the offer substantially. Should the superintendent do so?

Responses

Chris Lee Nicastro

This situation illustrates the importance of having salary structures and policies in place. The board of education has a role in determining salary structures and ranges and then approving a budget to fund them. Individual salaries within these ranges are generally at the discretion of the superintendent and are determined based on policy criteria.

While a published salary or range is not necessarily a guarantee of salary, it does communicate the intended terms of employment to prospective candidates. This determines to some extent the pool of candidates from which the superintendent can choose.

The superintendent should alert the candidate to the board's request and, if prepared to make a final recommendation, move forward under the published salary terms. The superintendent should explain to the board that applications had been received, interviews conducted, and a finalist selected prior to their request. If they refuse to honor the published salary, then the process would have to start over.

The superintendent might want to review hiring and compensation policies with the board. The reputation of the district and its ability to attract and retain quality candidates depends to some extent on how this process is conducted.

Sheldon Berman

Although it may seem reasonable to reduce the offer to allay anticipated ire from the staff and community, such action could undermine the search and the potential for securing the strongest candidate. The CFO position is one of the most critical positions in a school district and one of the hardest to fill. Offering a highly competitive salary doesn't always guarantee that a district will secure well-qualified applicants, but it is a strong inducement for someone with skill and experience, especially one who may incur moving expenses.

Reneging on the advertised salary could cause candidates to withdraw, resulting in a failed search. It may also appear to be a "bait and switch" strategy, which could undermine candidates' trust in the board and leadership and deter some from either accepting the offer or applying for a re-advertised position.

While economic downturns are temporary, one's starting salary tends to remain a permanent base for more modest yearly increases. The superintendent should advise the board to have the fortitude to defend the salary it committed to, given that the position is even more critical in difficult economic times—both to avoid errors that could cost more than the projected increase in salary as well as to make informed financial recommendations that may prevent layoffs of existing staff.

If the board is insistent about some accommodation in salary, the superintendent could offer to discuss the situation with the finalist and ask if there is a more modest salary that the individual could accept at this time. The superintendent could work with the board on a contract offer that builds the salary back to the original offer over a period of years plus the cost-of-living increases provided to other administrators. Demonstrating an overall commitment to the advertised salary and giving the finalist the respect and opportunity to discuss what may be an appropriate course could build confidence and secure a more dedicated and positive employee.

THE END-AROUND FACULTY PLAY

Scenario: The teachers' union president sets up a meeting involving several school board members, including the board chair, and a group of faculty members from one school, ostensibly to hear about changes unfolding at the school. The board members are confronted at the meeting by a small group of disgruntled teachers complaining about recent actions of the principal. By statute and board policy, the board is not to engage in personnel matters, so when the principal learns of the meeting, he complains to the superintendent about board interference and inappropriate actions of the union. What should the superintendent do?

Responses

Mark Hyatt

Superintendents and teachers' unions have the mutual interests of teachers as one of their top priorities. The principal involved here has the right to deal with his personnel issues in accordance with agreed-upon processes described in the member-ratified union agreement.

There should be an immediate meeting between the superintendent and the union president to appeal for proper handling of this issue in accordance with statute and policy. The board president should also be asked to review her rules of engagement for school boards and the best practices and norms that all board members agree to when they assume their duties.

It seems the union and board president let this situation get out in front of them. It's time to dial back and adhere to the agreed-upon practices for healthy conflict resolution following personnel policies and procedures.

Sheldon Berman

This incident represents a serious breach of trust and operating guidelines with far-reaching consequences. It was inappropriate for the union president to misrepresent the purpose of the meeting and to put board members in a position that violated their role and responsibility. It was also inappropriate for the board members to attend a meeting without notice to the principal and superintendent, even if it was initially perceived as innocuous. The principal has a right to be professionally and personally concerned.

The entire incident places the superintendent in the very challenging position of admonishing a significant group on the board and the union president while addressing a potential personnel situation between teachers and the principal.

Underlying this incident is an even deeper issue of the concern expressed by the faculty and why that concern was not presented first to the principal and to the superintendent. There is an implied lack of confidence that either the principal or the superintendent will deal effectively with the concerns of these faculty members. Staging the meeting could have been an effort to call attention to a problem that was not being adequately addressed. The superintendent has a lot of listening to do, along with clarifying operating procedures.

First, the superintendent needs to talk with the board members to better understand why they engaged in the meeting, what they did when they realized it was a personnel issue, and how they perceived what happened at the meeting. In the end, the superintendent and board members need to clarify and reaffirm their operating guidelines regarding communication between the board and administration and the board's discretion to meet with staff so that something like this doesn't happen again.

Second, the superintendent should talk with the union president to understand how this meeting took place without the superintendent's first being notified, what the teachers' concerns are, and why they surfaced in such an inappropriate way. Clarifying that this meeting has complicated the ability to address the concerns, the superintendent should discuss with the union president possible steps for addressing them.

The superintendent also needs to hear the teachers' or union's perception that matters related to the principal won't be addressed fairly and to set up a separate process for investigating and resolving trust-related issues.

Third, the superintendent must listen to the principal, who is rightfully concerned about the incident. The principal may believe that he was slandered in front of board members and that his reputation has been seriously damaged in their eyes. While affirming that the meeting was inappropriate and that the board will not be involved in any personnel considerations, the superintendent has to make it clear that the meeting may have arisen because of unaddressed concerns and then listen to the principal's perspective about those concerns and set in motion a process for resolving them.

Trust is hard to reestablish in situations like this because all parties to the incident feel hurt and diminished by it. However, it is the responsibility of the superintendent to believe in the best of intentions among all the participants and to find a way to rebuild communication while simultaneously addressing the real concerns that surfaced.

The cases in the next section represent an all-too-frequent situation faced by superintendents—instances in which either the board as a whole or an individual board member tries to influence an outcome related to personnel.

THE LATE-NIGHT RECONSIDERATION

Scenario: At a school board meeting where only three of the five members are present, a teacher is recommended during executive session for an instructional coach position. Returning to open session, the board approves the appointment 2-1. Later that night, a participating board member calls the superintendent and asks to rescind her vote in favor, saying she did not realize a local candidate had applied for the position. She asks the superintendent not to extend the contract to the teacher appointed at the board meeting. What should the superintendent do?

Responses

Kelly C. Henson

The superintendent should explain to the board member that official action can only be taken at a board meeting, and the superintendent has no authority to change any action of the board. If the superintendent believes there is a lack of support on the board for the candidate, the superintendent can bring this recommendation back to the board at the next meeting, or a called meeting, to determine the will of the full board.

Sheldon Berman

This case illustrates one reason school boards should not be involved in personnel decisions. Hiring, dismissal, and promotion decisions should be made in a fair and independent manner by those who are best able to assess an individual's capabilities to perform well in a position, not by board members who are elected to serve as policy leaders for the district.

Personnel decisions should be based on the competence of an individual to perform well in a position, not on the residency of the candidates. In addition, in order to move a district forward, administrators need discretion to assemble a leadership team that can best achieve the district's goals.

The board's role should be to enable the superintendent to build a leadership team that delivers results for children and parents, rather than a staff that reflects the political favoritism of board members. In this case, a board member is seeking to override the district's standard hiring procedure and the superintendent's recommendation based on an inappropriate preference for a candidate's residence rather than on the individual's competence.

Initially, the superintendent should talk with the board member about the role of the board in personnel decisions. The superintendent should also explain that taking an action to potentially reverse this decision is likely to create resentment and ill will on the part of the teacher and other employees and put the district at risk of losing a valuable and talented employee. It is also likely to put the other candidate in an awkward position in relation to his or her peers, thereby compromising his or her effectiveness.

In addition to the issue of the appropriate role of the board in personnel, this case raises a process issue. By standard rules of order for meetings, the vote of the board stands until a public meeting at which the individual board member can ask to reconsider or rescind that vote. However, under Robert's Rules of Order, if a vote results in a contract and the party has been informed of the vote, the motion cannot be rescinded. Because this vote occurred at a public meeting and resulted in an appointment that could be considered an oral contract, the board may not be able to reconsider or rescind its vote.

Depending upon how the superintendent presented the proposed promotion to the individual and how the motion before the board was framed, the teacher may have legal recourse for a breach of contract. To ensure that the board does not violate a contract or its own rules of order, the superintendent should have a legal counsel review the implications of the board member's request.

It is appropriate for the board member to forewarn the superintendent of her intention to propose reconsideration of the appointment at the next meeting. Likewise, it is appropriate for the superintendent to indicate to the board member that such action would require a review by legal counsel of the rules of order for the meeting and that it could have a significant and negative impact on staff involved in the hiring process.

It may be politically expedient for the superintendent, in consultation with the board chair and legal counsel, to delay offering a written contract until after the next board meeting where the role of the board in personnel matters, the board's decision in this particular case, and the procedural rules governing such decisions can be discussed. In the meantime, the superintendent should inform the teacher of the board member's request and should hold off on confirming the appointment until the legality of reconsideration is determined.

This case may be an exceptional situation reflecting the behavior of one board member. However, if this member's approach reflects the past behavior of board members, the superintendent should recommend a facilitated retreat for the board to consider its roles and responsibilities in relation to personnel. If the board persists in similar intrusions in personnel decisions, it will compromise the superintendent's ability to lead and the district's ability to hire and promote the best individuals for positions. In that case, the superintendent should find another district to lead.

CLEANING OUT A "RATS' NEST"

Scenario: A superintendent, newly hired, is presented evidence of employee malfeasance among central-office staffers. He takes the matter to his board, which collectively says: "Fire those dumb sh*ts. Fire 'em. We've never had a superintendent who could stand up and do it. We've known these were problem people for a lot of reasons. Everybody knows they're a problem. We'll stand with you."

The superintendent agrees to tell all four the next morning, "I'm going to fire you, or you're quitting," but only after asking the board, "I expect your support no matter who calls you or what the circumstances are. Everybody agree to that?" Should the superintendent proceed?

Responses

Sarah Jerome

When a superintendent discovers wrongdoing among employees, it is appropriate to investigate thoroughly. It is also important to provide an opportunity for the accused to have due process.

If the superintendent determines the wrongdoing is deliberate and warrants appropriate consequences, the next step is to determine what those appropriate consequences are. Depending on the severity of the offenses, dismissal may be the appropriate consequence. In fact, referral to the police also may be appropriate.

Having board support in this action is comforting and perhaps reassuring to the newly hired superintendent, but if the investigation reveals laws being broken by the offenders, the superintendent should proceed no matter whether he has board support. The superintendent must uphold the law and set an example by his action of courageous and ethical behavior—an example that will be noticed by all employees.

Sheldon Berman

This is not the way a superintendent should handle personnel matters. The first step, after being presented with evidence, is to pursue a thorough and fair investigation, preferably consulting with the district's attorney to ensure the process and the investigative findings will enable the superintendent to take disciplinary action. The superintendent needs to verify the involvement of each of the four individuals and any others who may be implicated. He needs solid evidence that, if challenged in a hearing or in court, will substantiate the personnel decisions made.

He also needs to give each individual an opportunity to present his or her case in their own defense. In a district with a human resources department, the investigation should be primarily handled by the human resources director so the superintendent can remain neutral and hear the case if there is an appeal of the HR director's decision.

In general, school boards should not be involved in personnel matters. However, in situations that will be politically charged or publicly controversial and may have serious consequences for the district, boards need to be informed of actions being taken.

Only after the superintendent has made a determination based on the investigation should he inform the board of the actions he plans to take. It is helpful if the board supports him, but if the malfeasance was serious, the superintendent bears a legal and ethical responsibility to take the necessary personnel actions with or without the support of the board. To do otherwise is to compromise his standing and potentially his employment.

A SWERVE OUTSIDE THE LINES

Scenario: A board of education member contacts the superintendent over a weekend with a request. She wants a letter of reprimand placed in a teacher's personnel file based on his comments to a student over an episode in school involving a second student. The superintendent responds immediately, telling the board member she is "out of your role." At the subsequent school board meeting, the superintendent, with thirty-two years of administrative experience in four school districts, reminds all members their role is not to be involved in personnel matters. Did the superintendent respond appropriately?

Responses

Sheldon Berman

Right message but wrong way to communicate it. The superintendent is correct. Board members are policy makers, not administrators, and should refrain from involvement in personnel matters. Personnel matters, including the investigation into an incident and the consequences for any violation, are private and protected from public intervention. Undue influence by a board member violates the individual's rights and opens the district to liability.

If a board member is concerned about a teacher's behavior or learns of something that warrants investigation, he or she should report it to the superintendent. From that point on, it is up to administration to handle it. A better approach in this case would have been to thank the board member for bringing the problem forward, to explain that any action is dependent on an investigation, and to diplomatically affirm that the matter will be handled appropriately—even though rights to privacy prevent the outcome from being shared with the board member.

By issuing a public reminder to all board members, the superintendent risks damaging the relationship with all of them—both the individual board member who may feel she was being admonished in front of her peers and the other members who may feel they were unfairly tarred with the same brush in the eyes of their constituents. It is far better to hold an annual work session where the board reviews and affirms its operating norms and guidelines. In that way, it isn't the superintendent who holds responsibility for ensuring compliance with these norms, but the board as a whole.

This case may be an exceptional situation reflecting the behavior of one board member. However, if this member's approach reflects the past behavior of board members, the superintendent should recommend a facilitated retreat for the board to consider its roles and responsibilities in relation to personnel. If the board persists in similar intrusions in personnel decisions, it will compromise the superintendent's ability to lead and the district's ability to hire and promote the best individuals for positions. In that case, the superintendent should find another district to lead.

Mario Ventura

The relationship between the superintendent and the governing board is influenced by political, social, cultural, and institutional factors unique to each school community. The push and pull of these influences can impact how the superintendent and governing board behave toward one another. In some school districts, the superintendent's response may be appropriate and within the norm of communication. In other districts, this type of communication could have a negative impact on the relationship between the superintendent and board.

In this scenario, the superintendent needed to be direct and set boundaries for the board members. The publicly stated reminder to the entire board could lead the community to perceive conflict exists between the board members and the superintendent. This could have a negative impact by creating tension within the district.

To promote a strong collaborative relationship, the superintendent should ask clarifying questions to better understand the board member's need to get involved in this issue. Steps can be taken to reassure the member that policies and procedures are followed to investigate situations and, if necessary, reprimand employees for inappropriate behavior.

Another consideration is to conduct a yearly retreat to review the district strategic plan, values and the roles of the governing board and superintendent. Clarity of each party's role and respectful communication help promote an effective relationship between the superintendent and the governing board that will serve to mediate conflict when it arises.

RECONSIDERATION OF A HIRE

Scenario: After a recent board meeting where several hires were approved in the consent agenda, a board member followed up with the superintendent about a groundskeeper appointment. This hire was a boyfriend of the HR director's daughter and had a felony conviction while a minor. The superintendent was aware of his background, but the board member was not and felt it was a breach of trust. He wanted the boyfriend fired and called for dismissal of the HR director, saying he had lost all trust.

Responses

Meira Levinson

The HR director should have been upfront with the school board about potential conflicts of interest in any hiring recommendation. Because it is the board rather than the superintendent that must sign off on all hires, the board has a right to know about even the appearance of an ethics violation. Transparency helps to stave off loss of trust, not only by the board but also by parents, students, and citizens in the district. The HR director also should have consulted the district's or city's ethics board, which could have issued a ruling about whether the hiring recommendation violated conflict of interest standards or not.

It is less clear how the groundskeeper's prior conviction is known to the participants, or relevant to the case. Because he was convicted as a minor, his record would presumably have been sealed and in many jurisdictions eventually expunged. Under these circumstances, it would be irresponsible (and perhaps illegal?) to reveal the job candidate's juvenile record to the school board.

Furthermore, it is often ethically inappropriate to hold a person's actions—even felony convictions—against them once they have paid their debt to society. School districts, in particular, should take a developmental stance toward the adults in their employ, not just toward students.

However, if the felony conviction were relatively recent and of a nature that would lead one to be concerned about the man being around children, then one could understand the board member's concern. But if this were the case (for example, if the groundskeeper is now nineteen years old, and had been convicted of statutory rape or assault and battery at age 17), then neither the HR director nor the superintendent would have gone forward with the hiring recommendation in the first place.

Sheldon Berman

At times, school district personnel as well as board of education members can have an inappropriate and undue influence on hiring decisions that are made based on personal advantage, personal relationships, or direct nepotism. Such behavior is not only ethically problematic; it compromises the organization's capabilities and undermines public trust.

However, there are significant factors to consider in this case. The superintendent was aware of the candidate's background and his connection to the HR director, yet believed it was still appropriate to hire the individual as a groundskeeper. The board member should respect the superintendent's judgment and not jump to conclusions, but rather ask questions to clarify the individual's qualifications as well as the hiring process used.

In terms of the felony conviction, the individual was a minor at the time; those records are generally sealed and subject to a statutory time limit for job consideration. The felony could have been relatively minor, such as property damage or disorderly conduct that reflected juvenile behavior and should not be considered now that the individual has met the legal consequences for his offense. The important question is whether the conviction in any way diminishes his ability as an adult to handle the responsibilities of the position.

As for the appointee's relationship to the HR director, the district's hiring process should have been designed to eliminate any personal bias on the part of the director. Typically, the hiring for a position such as groundskeeper would at a minimum involve interviews by a grounds supervisor as well as a facilities and grounds director. If the individual emerged as the best candidate based on an independent and unbiased process, then the HR director is accepting the recommendation of administrators in the field rather than imposing his or her own judgment.

In this case, it appears that the HR director was sufficiently concerned about both the individual's background and the relationship to the director to make the superintendent aware of the hiring circumstances and to receive the superintendent's support and recommendation to the board. Although the individual hired was not technically immediate family, it may have been better if the HR director had assigned an assistant or another individual to oversee this hiring process to avoid even the appearance of a conflict of interest.

Given the confidentiality around juvenile convictions, it isn't clear if the board member's knowledge of the conviction reflects some personal involvement or connection, which would make it even more important that the board member refrain from rash judgments or actions. The superintendent should meet with the board member to clarify the standards regarding both juvenile convictions and the hiring process. The superintendent should further meet with the HR director to verify that hiring processes in the district meet both functional and ethical standards and then ensure that all board members are knowledgeable about these processes.

The preceding cases dealt with situations in which board members interjected themselves into matters related to personnel. However, as the next several cases illustrate, an individual board member's actions—or sincere advocacy—around even non-personnel matters still may not be in the best interest of the district, the superintendent, or the board as a whole and so become problematic.

FOOTBALL FIREWORKS

Scenario: It's been a longtime tradition for a member of the school board to shoot off fireworks as the varsity football team in a small, rural community rushes down a hill toward the playing field before its home opener each fall. The practice violates state law, and the superintendent, who is new to the area, has brought the matter to the board's attention. The board member's response: "If there's a fine, I'll pay it." The rest of the board takes no action. The superintendent allows the practice to continue. Should he?

Responses

Glenn "Max" McGee

The superintendent cannot stand by ethically or legally and let the opening game fireworks continue. As the district's leader, he has the responsibility to demonstrate respect for state law, and he knows that local policy or practice cannot override it. It is his job to provide a firm decision and clearly and widely communicate the legal rationale for doing so. This communication requires more than an e-mail. It means engaging the local traditional and social media, meeting with boosters and players, responding promptly to critics and complaints, preparing talking points for his leadership team, and ideally engaging others to carry his message.

In addition, it is not up to either the superintendent or the board as to whether an individual board member chooses to pay the fine. In fact, the board was right to take no action, because unless there is a written policy about the tradition, it is not their decision to make. The individual board member can choose to do what he or she desires but cannot act on behalf of the board or administration without their approval, and so the superintendent can and should end the display.

It is also an ethical imperative for the superintendent not only to communicate the decision widely through multiple media and ideally other messengers, but also to seek to understand the "why" behind the tradition. While it will take many conversations—and probably more than a few unpleasant ones—as well as document research, once the superintendent understands what drove this tradition, he will be able to propose acceptable alternatives, one of which might even be advocating to change the existing state law or striving to obtain an annual waiver from it.

Regardless, acting ethically, communicating clearly, listening carefully, and understanding deeply will demonstrate courageous leadership that will enable him to survive the fireworks and ideally give him a home team victory!

Sheldon Berman

Two issues are raised by this practice—knowingly violating state law and opening the district to liability if the fireworks injure someone or start a fire. If the new superintendent takes action to end the practice, he risks alienating the board, being viewed as undermining long-held traditions, and perhaps putting his position on the line. On the other hand, continuing the practice in the face of clear legal limits could cost the superintendent his administrative license. As the district's leader, he was correct to inform the board of his concern. For his own protection, he should have done so in a way that was documented for public record.

In this small, rural community, it is likely that local police and fire officials have or have had children in the school or have attended home openers themselves. They probably are aware of the practice and chose to turn a blind eye. If this is the case, the superintendent's position is even more difficult.

He should begin by seeking ways to retain the fireworks display while protecting students and attendees from harm. The first step is to consult with the fire and police chiefs about how best to ensure a safe and authorized display. Because police and fire departments share responsibility for safety, their participation is critical in finding a solution. In this way, the superintendent can actively support the tradition and the board, while serving to protect people and property from harm and injury. Alternatively, if there is no way to pursue this practice legally, the responsibility for stopping it is shared among community leaders.

If the practice needs to be discontinued, the superintendent must work with the high school principal and the community to find alternative ways to show enthusiasm and support for the football team at its opening game. Together, they can propose activities that will make this school and community event even more significant, retaining the spirit of the fireworks while avoiding the danger. This approach may not allay the resentment of the one board member who is personally invested in the practice, but it could offset some of the community's sense of loss of an important tradition.

THE PERSISTENT BIGOT

Scenario: The vice president of a suburban school board is under fire for posting images on his personal Facebook page that critics claim are racist, homophobic, and bigoted. Protests before the start of a board meeting include demands for the board president and superintendent to insist the offender resign. The board president has asked him privately to stop posting such images, yet they continue. The superintendent says he doesn't agree with the posts but sides with the First Amendment. The district does not have a code of conduct. Do the board and superintendent have options?

Responses

Sarah Jerome

The school board must adopt an ethical code of conduct policy. Almost every state school boards association has model policies to share with local school boards. These can be helpful especially when a policy needs to be put into place right away. The dialogue about these policies can be highly instructive and healthy for all members of the board.

Each board member represents all constituents. If images are posted by one member that are disrespectful, a breach is created with the public trust that is difficult to repair. The disrespectful postings also serve as an extremely poor example to the students in the district.

Certainly, the board president and the superintendent along with the district's legal adviser should speak with the errant board member about his role and responsibilities as a board member. He should be asked to resign if he can't or won't fulfill those responsibilities in a productive manner. He may choose not to resign. State laws vary regarding the recall or dismissal of an elected board member. Legal advice will be important in this arena.

Sheldon Berman

School board members are elected. The critics' ultimate resolution is to ensure this one isn't reelected. Removal from office by the board is not a realistic option. It is unlikely that state law has provisions sufficient to recall him from office and neither the board nor the superintendent has the authority to remove him. When it comes to free speech rights, even speech that some deem unpopular or offensive, the courts have historically given elected officials a good deal of latitude.

Any board action depends on the nature of the postings. The board must be exceedingly careful not to violate the member's First Amendment rights and would have to show a compelling governmental interest in limiting an individual's speech. If the postings rise to the level of hate speech, they could be reported to the police who have legal recourse to intervene.

Absent hate speech, there still are alternatives. The board president could request in a public meeting that the individual stop posting the images. If that is not sufficient, it could be argued that the postings compromise the member's willingness and ability to enforce the district's non-discrimination and harassment policies and thus create a significant disruption to the school district's operations.

The board could then pass a censure resolution stating the postings do not represent the views of the board or the district and calling on the member to stop posting such images. However, censure is only a public slap on the wrist unless there is specific board policy or state law that provides additional consequences. Even with a censure vote, the board cannot stop the individual from posting.

The superintendent's role is even more constrained. Although he can publicize his concern about the posts and his support for inclusiveness, tolerance and respectfulness, the board member is his supervisor, and the superintendent has no authority to intervene.

He can personally meet with the individual and respectfully discuss how these actions may erode the community's confidence in the member's willingness to uphold district policy that prohibits racial and other discrimination and harassment. He can point out that the postings distract from the district's work and the superintendent's ability to move the district forward and may also undermine community support for the schools.

However, the superintendent has few alternatives to personal persuasiveness. His best course of action is to help the member understand the implications of his postings and let the board and electorate deal directly with the member.

A BULLISH BOARD DEMAND

> Scenario: A board member has a twelve-year-old nephew in another state who commits suicide in response to persistent bullying. The board member insists the district should require every student in grades K–8 to participate in an anti-bullying curriculum for thirty minutes a week. He contends student safety is the one priority that trumps academic achievement. At a public meeting, he says the superintendent would be "ethically remiss" for not tackling this problem—even if it means cutting out time from academics. How should the superintendent respond?

Responses

Paula Mirk

The school board member is right: it would be "ethically remiss" to provide only academics in any of our schools, given that the broadest purpose of our public education system is to contribute to a better society through our students as future leaders and participants.

But the superintendent knows this is not an either/or issue. It's possible, and preferable, to integrate an ethical lens into all activity of a school by building a culture based on integrity. Schools that use questions about "what's right" to undergird programming, discipline approaches, and communication, and as a vital dimension to curriculum, create meaningful learning environments with a better chance of meeting the needs of all students on a variety of levels—not just academic.

Also, there is no reason to limit this focus to K–8. Adolescence is a formative, impactful opportunity for ethical development. Infusing the life of high schools with substantive, relevant questions about "who we are" stimulates learning while contributing to emotional and societal well-being.

Sheldon Berman

The board member's emotional response to his nephew's suicide is understandable, as is his desire to take whatever measures are necessary to prevent bullying. Suicide produces significant trauma in families, and its causes are complex. As in this case, bullying can be a contributing factor, often in conjunction with other circumstances.

Schools can and should take an active role in helping to prevent bullying. It is important for all students to understand the dynamics of bullying and how to best intervene and seek adult assistance. However, an anti-bullying curriculum offered thirty minutes each week is likely to have limited impact because it does not deeply penetrate the students' environments—the environments where bullying takes place.

The most powerful preventive program for bullying is a strong, school-wide, social-emotional learning program that teaches students positive social skills, creates a caring community in the classroom and school, and supports the development of social responsibility. Classrooms where respect, tolerance and social support are the norm create a foundation of social-emotional safety that both prevents bullying and supports academic progress. Integrated into this larger context, curricular discussions of bullying can present helpful case studies of how to identify and address demeaning verbal, physical and cyber acts of aggression.

In response to this grieving board member, and to help him understand how a comprehensive approach can be more effective than a narrow curriculum, the superintendent should share the research on social-emotional learning programs. The superintendent should also ask him to attend conferences and seminars on the subject so that he could help provide the necessary leadership to encourage the board to take a more comprehensive approach. His passion and understanding could help the district create a more positive social and academic climate, while addressing his desire to prevent bullying that may contribute to youth suicide.

With this approach, curricular time constraints do not need to pit anti-bullying against instruction in core subject areas. Social-emotional learning enables an anti-bullying climate to permeate the students' entire academic and extracurricular day—an approach more likely to have a significant impact on the lifelong interactions of impressionable youth.

A PARENT'S SMEAR CAMPAIGN

> Scenario: A school board member is furious that a principal will not transfer his son out of a class in which he is getting a D due to "a personality conflict" with the teacher. The board member is a friend of the local newspaper editor and begins a smear campaign, including letters to the editor claiming the principal protects bad teachers and shows favoritism to certain students. He asks acquaintances to speak out against the principal at board meetings and tells the superintendent to recommend dismissal—or else. The principal has been impacted mentally by the attacks. How should the superintendent proceed?

Responses

Sheldon Berman

It appears that the board member is attempting to use his standing in the community and his political office to influence the grading and placement decisions of educators, as well as their employment. While finding this behavior objectionable, the superintendent needs to investigate and determine whether the board member has a legitimate complaint about the teacher and the principal's decision.

The superintendent should request that the board member refrain from any further comment or action until the investigation is completed. If the investigation reveals the board member's complaint to be valid, the superintendent should work with the principal to resolve the issue.

On the other hand, if the investigation supports both the teacher and the principal in this matter, those individuals need to be reassured of that fact so they can focus on their professional responsibilities. In either case, the superintendent should relay the findings from the investigation to the board member.

If the superintendent supports the principal's decision and the board member persists in his egregious smear campaign and his threat of retaliation against the superintendent, the superintendent should discuss the issue with the board chair and ask for the chair's intervention. In many states, it is a violation of state law and ethics regulations for board members to become involved in personnel issues.

The board chair could remind the member of his role in relation to personnel and ask him to desist from his campaign. The chair could also indicate to those who have been enlisted to speak about the principal at board meetings that personnel matters are not an appropriate topic for board discussion. The superintendent also should advise the teacher and principal to contact their state association or an attorney to ensure they are protected.

The board member has a right to his opinion and to free speech, which limits the superintendent's options for changing his behavior. However, his actions appear unethical and could have legal consequences for him and the board.

If the campaign continues, the board and superintendent may have an obligation to file a complaint with the state ethics commission to determine whether the board member's using his position to improperly procure a personal benefit for his family and to influence personnel decisions are violations of state ethics rules for elected officials. If other members of the board are concerned about this behavior, the board can move to publicly censure him.

The smear campaign against the principal and the attempt to force the superintendent to breach the contract with the principal are efforts to interfere with the principal's contractual rights. As a result, the board member and the district could be liable for a claim of tortious interference with contractual relations, that is, when one party interferes to breach an existing contract between other parties—in this case, the district and the principal. If the information relayed in the smear campaign is blatantly false and damaging to the individual, the principal could sue for defamation of character.

As this conflict spills into the court of public opinion, it undermines the community's confidence in the school district and the board. Although perhaps unable to control or even influence the actions of the board member, the superintendent should convey with great clarity to the other board members the reasons for deep concern about what this one member has done. One or more of these peers may be able to help the board member understand that personal conflicts are best resolved through dialogue rather than vengeful smear campaigns.

Depending upon the age of the student at the center of this matter, the board member may also want to consider what life lessons his son is learning about how to handle disagreements.

Glenn "Max" McGee

This calls for courageous action because the ramifications of giving into the board member's demands will set precedents that will disrupt the system and soon pit teachers against board members and administrators, to the detriment of students. Even a compromise will embolden the board member—and other members—to use similar unethical tactics to get what they want regardless of board protocols and policies.

The superintendent should meet with the board president and board member immediately to review any hard evidence of the board member's claim, to share any counterevidence, and to illustrate how the member violated protocols and policies. If there is evidence to support the member's anger with the teacher and principal, the superintendent will need to follow up with some corrective action, short of dismissal.

Whether or not evidence of a personality conflict exists, the superintendent must request strong support from the president and the rest of the board to curb the member's tactics and personal attacks. Finally, the superintendent needs to leap to the aid of the principal by tangibly showing personal concern for his health, by having the human resources director share options for mental health supports, by ensuring the principal has 24/7, front-of-the-line access to the superintendent and HR director as needed, and by recognizing and reviewing the positive contributions of the principal.

Sadly, cases like this seldom end well for either the principal or the superintendent and ultimately both may need to decide if they really want to continue to work in a system where an elected member's actions are inappropriate and unethical.

The final cases in this chapter address one of the thorniest issues of school district leadership: direct conflict with the board over the superintendent's contract.

DECLINING A PAY INCREASE

> Scenario: A school district that has just endured significant budget reductions settles a difficult contract negotiation with the teachers' union by agreeing to a small salary increase that results in a further reduction of teaching positions. The superintendent's contract indicates that she will receive no less than what is negotiated with the teachers. Several board members ask the superintendent to refuse to take any increase as a statement to the community. Should the superintendent reject her expected salary increase?

Responses

Sheldon Berman

Unlike teachers, who frequently have job stability thanks to tenure and a union that negotiates on their behalf, a superintendent's employment, and often salary, depends on performance. Therefore, the superintendent's contractual benefits should be considered independent of negotiations with bargaining units.

However, because the superintendent is a community leader, his or her actions have political and symbolic import. When a district is under significant economic stress, it may be a beneficial statement to the staff and the community for the superintendent to demonstrate that he or she recognizes and shares the burden of these reductions.

This statement could consist of accepting only the same increase given teachers, refusing to take any increase at all, forgoing a performance bonus or making other sacrifices in salary or benefits. In this situation, it appears reasonable for the superintendent to accept the suggestion of her board and decline a salary increase this year.

Mark Hyatt

The superintendent, in many cases, is the sole employee of the school board. As such, she should seriously consider their request. There is a big difference between what is legal and what is the right decision for the district.

Legally, the superintendent can adhere to her contract and take the same small increase in compensation as the teachers. But the superintendent is in a position that is very visible in her community. What she does and what she doesn't do sends messages to all stakeholders. She would be wise in not taking the raise to show solidarity and empathy toward the teachers and respect for the district's financial state.

A NEWS LEAKER

Scenario: The school board president, who is not a supporter of the superintendent, at the request of the full board invites the superintendent to submit a laundry list of proposals relating to his compensation and benefits package for next year's expected renewal of a multiyear contract for consideration by the board during its executive session. The board president, however, then gives the discussion list to the editor of the local newspaper, describing them as demands by the superintendent. What does the superintendent do next?

Responses

Mario Ventura

Strong communication and trust are two important variables in superintendent–governing board relationships. A positive working relationship is vital to ensure students, staff and the community have confidence in both the governing board and the superintendent. This incident and the knowledge that the board president does not support the superintendent may have caused serious damage to their relationship. It also will have a negative impact on the negotiation process for the contract extension.

The superintendent should obtain the guidance of an attorney as the negotiation process continues. Although it will bring an expense to both the superintendent and the school district, each party's attorney can negotiate in the best interest of their client. Any conflict that arises during negotiations can be handled between the attorneys.

Sheldon Berman

The board president's action appears to be an intentional effort to undermine the public's perception of the superintendent. Or, since the board president does not support the superintendent, the president may regard the list as excessive compensation for a job not performed to her or his satisfaction. In either case, the board president acted hostilely and without the knowledge or authority of the full board.

The worst thing the superintendent could do is to confront the board president publicly—whether in person or in the media. Such action would appear defensive and might escalate the conflict with the board president. Hopefully, the superintendent's document explicitly framed the written list as options for discussion. If not, he may wish to privately clarify that intent with the board.

Given that he was responding to a request from the full board and that other board members are supporters, his best course of action is to allow this matter to be an internal issue when the board convenes in executive session. Other board members may very well be concerned by the president's action and come to the defense of the superintendent.

He may also wish to meet with the board president to hear the rationale for releasing the document and to clarify that the items were options, not demands. The superintendent will need to continue working with the board president. Striving to understand this particular action from the board president's perspective may help build a more positive relationship over the long term.

THE RETRIBUTIVE BOARD MEMBER

Scenario: An administrator is moved from a principal position to a less critical administrative role in the central office after several years of poor performance on the job. The new superintendent, as part of an administrative reorganization, transfers him to a department led by an individual with high expectations of all staff.

The transferred administrator, seeing what is likely to happen, retires but then runs for the school board. Once elected, he makes it clear he intends to press for non-renewal of the superintendent and the resignation of the supervising administrator. The superintendent assumes the other board members are unaware of the circumstances surrounding their colleague's underperformance. With his contract up for renewal, what should the superintendent do?

Responses

Mark Hyatt

The superintendent is on the high moral ground. Moving his newly elected board member to a new position was the right thing to do for the children, teachers, and other administrators, too.

As for pressing non-renewal, the new board member might have some challenges. Most superintendents and intermediate supervisors who are known for maintaining high standards will have the support of a majority of stakeholders. The superintendent should talk with the board chair to explain his concerns and solicit advice from the chair in private.

Good board governance doesn't include micromanaging hires and terminations unless the superintendent isn't doing his job. The superintendent here is proactive and making decisions in the best interests of students.

Sheldon Berman

This case is troubling, not only because of the ethical dilemmas and personal conflict that it poses, but also because such circumstances arise all too frequently. Similar to the ethics provision that legislators not become lobbyists for a period of time after leaving office, states should establish provisions that restrain staff membership on school boards for a comparable period of time.

In this case, the confidentiality provided by personnel policies prohibits the superintendent from sharing past performance information with the board. The superintendent should seek to strengthen relationships with the other members, while meeting with this new member to develop a different and more constructive relationship. If the new member continues to pursue an antagonistic or duplicitous role, he may undermine his own alliances on the board.

The superintendent should be careful not to compromise his own integrity and should avoid entering into a public sparring match with the new board member. However, the entire situation places the superintendent in a difficult position and may eventually diminish his ability to lead. Given the typical controversies a superintendent must manage and the often-divided sentiment of boards surrounding these controversies, it may be wise for the superintendent to begin preparing a résumé for a potential move to another district.

Conclusion

Ethical Choices Are Not an Afterthought

If you are reading this page, we hope that means you have read all or most of the pages that preceded it. And if you did that, we hope you found those pages helpful and thought-provoking.

We don't need to tell you that being a school administrator is a challenging role—one that requires the wisdom of Solomon, the patience of Job, and the luck of the Irish. But sometimes, even all those qualities combined can seem insufficient to the task.

Whether you have two years of experience in your job or forty-two, the world keeps changing, and there will always be new problems that keep you awake at night as you ponder your next steps. We are confident you will sleep better if your decisions are firmly grounded in figuring out, as Mary Gentile put it, "how we can get the right thing done"—a task that entails a nuanced blend of principled action, informed respect for laws and policies, and a dose of empathy for those who seek your guidance.

The one hundred scenarios in this book only scratch the surface of the multiple and complex issues that land on school administrators' desks over the course of a school year. However, many of these cases can function as exemplars that shed light on other situations involving differences of opinion with district employees, parents, community members, board members, and others. They can also serve as a way to expand your repertoire of possible responses and to mentally practice in advance how you might address similar cases.

As evidenced by the different perspectives voiced by our contributors, there usually is no cookie-cutter solution to the ethical dilemmas you will face throughout your career, no answer you can just "look up." What we have proposed, instead, is a way of thinking—of recognizing when you're in an ethical quandary to begin with, asking the right questions, properly framing the issue, and ultimately achieving an ethical outcome by applying the principles we have presented in the preceding chapters.

Several themes have permeated this work: adherence to legal requirements, fundamental fairness in all things, treating equally situated individuals equally and unequals equitably, respecting confidentiality, avoiding conflicts of interest, working within the established governance structure, making sensible compromises without compromising your core values, and always pursuing the greater good for your district. These are the attributes of the ethical school administrator.

If you perused this book and tomorrow you relegate it to a shelf where it will gather dust, then we have failed you. Passive reading does not prepare you to grapple with the controversies and conundrums of school leadership.

Instead, our goal in presenting these cases and responses was to engage you in agreeing or disagreeing with the contributors' responses and perhaps formulating what steps you would have taken in similar circumstances. While we never intended for these pages to supply you with all the answers, we hope you find this book continues to be a good reference tool in the coming months and years—one that helps you look ahead and avoid pitfalls to the extent possible and that offers you some pointers when problems do arise.

Mostly, we hope it provides you with some of the questions you should routinely ask yourself when confronted with an ethical quandary—questions such as: How do I uncover what I don't know about this situation? Who will be affected by my decision, either positively or adversely? What is the right action to take as opposed to one that is simply expedient or popular? And how do I best prepare to deal with the ramifications of my decision, especially from people who don't agree with it?

Once you have arrived at a potential decision, before acting, take a moment to evaluate it on ethical grounds. Ask yourself: Am I treating others the way I would want to be treated? Should everyone be treated this way? Will this decision provide either the greatest good for the greatest number of people or the least harm to the greatest number? Does this situation justify preferential treatment of those who are in some way less advantaged? What will be the reaction when everyone discovers this decision has been made?

Although the answers to these questions can point you in different directions, asking such questions may guide your thinking toward a decision that is both ethically justifiable and publicly defensible.

Another suggestion, borne of experience—don't feel you have to climb every mountain all alone. When utterly confounded by a thorny problem, reach out to a more experienced colleague who may have encountered a similar situation and found an effective way to address it. Through AASA, your state administrator organization, and your district's legal counsel, establish relationships with mentors and colleagues you can consult, in confidence, for guidance and perspective.

It is worth taking the time to think through the problem carefully and consult with others whose perspectives you trust. Recognize that ethically challenging situations give us an opportunity to better define who we are as leaders and to educate others in the process.

On a broader scale, we hope you find ways to share this book or its contents with others. Whether you're planning a meeting with your board members or a retreat with your faculty, there are cases in this book that will resonate with each audience. Examining selected scenarios and discussing them in a group setting will help others gain a better understanding of how you go about making difficult choices. Of even greater importance, it will encourage them to hone their own expectations and powers of ethical decision making—and to go forth and "get the right thing done."

We end this book with perhaps the most critical question of all: When faced with an ethical quandary, ask yourself: Am I the sort of leader who demonstrates the courage of my convictions? That is a question only you can answer.

Appendix

The Code of Ethics of AASA, The School Superintendents Association

CODE OF ETHICS: AASA'S STATEMENT OF ETHICS FOR EDUCATIONAL LEADERS

An educational leader's professional conduct must conform to an ethical code of behavior, and the code must set high standards for all educational leaders. The educational leader provides professional leadership across the district and also across the community. This responsibility requires the leader to maintain standards of exemplary professional conduct while recognizing that his or her actions will be viewed and appraised by the community, professional associates and students.

The educational leader acknowledges that he or she serves the schools and community by providing equal educational opportunities to each and every child. The work of the leader must emphasize accountability and results, increased student achievement, and high expectations for each and every student.

To these ends, the educational leader subscribes to the following statements of standards.

The educational leader:

1. Makes the education and well-being of students the fundamental value of all decision making.
2. Fulfills all professional duties with honesty and integrity and always acts in a trustworthy and responsible manner.
3. Supports the principle of due process and protects the civil and human rights of all individuals.
4. Implements local, state, and national laws.

5. Advises the school board and implements the board's policies and administrative rules and regulations.
6. Pursues appropriate measures to correct those laws, policies, and regulations that are not consistent with sound educational goals or that are not in the best interest of children.
7. Avoids using his/her position for personal gain through political, social, religious, economic, or other influences.
8. Accepts academic degrees or professional certification only from accredited institutions.
9. Maintains the standards and seeks to improve the effectiveness of the profession through research and continuing professional development.
10. Honors all contracts until fulfillment, release, or dissolution mutually agreed upon by all parties.
11. Accepts responsibility and accountability for one's own actions and behaviors.
12. Commits to serving others above self.

About the Authors

Sheldon H. Berman, EdD, served as superintendent of four districts in three states—Hudson, MA; Jefferson County (Louisville), KY; Eugene, OR; and Andover, MA—spanning twenty-eight school years. He provided leadership in state superintendent associations as well as in local and national education organizations. He served as Massachusetts Association of School Superintendents president and received the 2003 Massachusetts Superintendent of the Year Award and AASA's Distinguished Service Award in 2022, in addition to lifetime achievement awards for social-emotional learning and character education. He has made nationally significant contributions by furthering social-emotional learning practice, expanding special education funding and enhancing inclusive instructional strategies, advocating and implementing school integration, contributing guidance on administrative ethics through a decade of *School Administrator* Ethical Educator columns, and launching state-of-the-art virtual learning and instructional innovations. He has authored two books and numerous book chapters, articles, policy reports, and op eds, and presented nationally and internationally on educational issues and innovations. Retired as a district superintendent, he is currently the AASA lead superintendent for social-emotional learning.

David B. Rubin, Esq., is a sole practitioner in Metuchen, New Jersey, and of counsel to the Busch Law Group, LLC. He represents public school districts and private schools throughout New Jersey and is nationally recognized in the field of education law and legal ethics. He has served as president of the New Jersey Association of School Attorneys and chair of the National School Boards Association's Council of School Attorneys, is a frequent speaker and author in the field, and has argued numerous precedent cases in federal and state court, generating over fifty published judicial decisions. Listed in *Super*

Lawyers Magazine and *Best Lawyers in America*, he holds the AV rating from the Martindale Hubbell Legal Directory, the highest rating for competence and character.

Joyce A. Barnes, EdS, is a freelance writer and editor in the field of pre-K–12 education. Her career in public education spans decades as a classroom teacher, special education administrator, program/resource developer, and past president of the Kentucky Council of Administrators of Special Education. In her administrative capacities, she navigated such ethical quandaries as differences between parents on the classroom placement of their child with disabilities, the allocation of resources among special programs serving widely disparate numbers of students, and equity in grading for students with special learning needs. These experiences led to insights that informed her contributions to the development of this book. More recently, she provided editing support for the 2019 report *A Nation at Hope*, written under the auspices of the Aspen Institute National Commission on Social, Emotional, and Academic Development, and for the AASA SEL Impact Project. She currently serves as a writer/editor for the Global Youth and Education division of Special Olympics International.

Note: While all three co-authors contributed to all sections of the book, each one also assumed primary responsibility for a specific section. Sheldon Berman was lead author of the book's introduction and a contributor to cases, David Rubin was lead author of the chapter introductions, and Joyce Barnes was lead author of the book's conclusion.

About the Contributors

The following education leaders brought a wide array of experiences to their responses to the Ethical Educator scenarios. Individually, the contributors were involved with the column anywhere from one to five years, with that difference being reflected in the number of responses selected for inclusion in the book.

Roy Dexheimer retired after forty years as a BOCES superintendent, followed by two years as vice-president at Hobart College in Geneva, New York. He was one of the original contributors to the *Ethical Educator* column—a fitting sequel to his dissertation about superintendents' allegiance to the AASA Code of Ethics.

MaryEllen Elia is the retired superintendent of Hillsborough County School District in Florida and the former New York state commissioner of education. She is currently a senior consultant with AASA's Learning 2025 Initiative.

Kelly C. Henson served as executive secretary of the Georgia Professional Standards Commission from 2007 until his retirement in 2018. Previously, he was the superintendent of schools in Floyd County, Georgia, and received the Georgia Association of Educational Leaders Fulbright Distinguished Service Award.

Karl Hertz is a retired superintendent of the Mequon-Thiensville School District in Wisconsin, past president of AASA, and past village president and county supervisor. He received the Outstanding Education Alumnus Award from Indiana University and the Norman Gill Individual Excellence in Government Award.

Mark Hyatt is an educational entrepreneur who served as an advisor to the U.S. secretary of defense and two White House administrations on school choice, safety, and social climate. He was director of the USAF Academy Center for Character and Leadership Development and president of the Character Education Partnership.

Sarah Jerome is a retired superintendent of twenty-three years at Kettle Moraine School District in Wisconsin and District 25 in Arlington Heights, Illinois. In 2007–2008, she served as the second female president of AASA. Residing in Wisconsin, she is active as a search consultant for Hazard, Young, Attea, and Associates.

Meira Levinson is Juliana W. and William Foss Thompson Professor of Education and Society at Harvard University. She is co-editor with Jacob Fay of *Dilemmas of Educational Ethics* and *Democratic Discord in Schools: Cases and Commentaries in Educational Ethics*.

Maggie Lopez retired as superintendent from Colorado's Pueblo District 60 and then served as interim superintendent for Vail Valley's Eagle County Schools. She was honored with a Milken Educator Award. She resides in Colorado Springs, where she is a hospice volunteer and education consultant.

Sarah Mackenzie is retired from the educational leadership faculty of the University of Maine. She is co-author, with her political scientist husband, of *Now What? Confronting and Resolving Ethical Questions: A Handbook for Teachers*.

Glenn "Max" McGee has held positions from substitute teacher to Illinois state superintendent of schools and has published and presented on leadership, equity, and mental health and wellness. He and his wife currently run the nonprofit Center for Success for High Need Schools.

Joan McRobbie is a consultant on education policy and communication. Formerly senior associate at WestEd and at the Community Training and Assistance Center, she also served as ethics officer and chief of staff in the San Diego Unified School District.

Paula Mirk has taught in a variety of settings in the United States and abroad. From 1996 to 2013, she served as the director of education at the Institute for Global Ethics in Maine. She currently provides financial coaching for low-income families in New Jersey.

Chris Lee Nicastro is a former superintendent and Missouri Superintendent of the Year. She served on several AASA committees and was elected to the governing board and executive committee. She served as Missouri commissioner of education and is now an associate with Hazard, Young, Attea, and Associates.

Mario Ventura has been superintendent since 2012 of Isaac Elementary School District #5 in Phoenix, Arizona. He is on the Minority Student Achievement Network of the Wisconsin Center for Educational Research and formerly served on the National Association of State Directors of Teacher Education and Certification (NASDTEC) Model Code of Educator Ethics Committee.

Louis N. Wool is the superintendent of schools in Harrison, New York. He was named New York State Superintendent of the Year (2010), earned the Distinguished Service Award from the Lower Hudson Council of Superintendents (2012), and received the Carroll F. Johnson Award from Teachers College, Columbia University (2002).

Note: Sheldon Berman has contributed to the column from its inception in 2012. His background is available in the "About the Authors" page.

www.ingramcontent.com/pod-product-compliance
Lightning Source LLC
Chambersburg PA
CBHW021700230426
43668CB00008B/683